COMMUNITY STUDIES

COMMUNITY STUDIES

An introduction
to the sociology of the local community

Colin Bell and Howard Newby

Praeger Publishers
New York • Washington

BOOKS THAT MATTER

Published in the United States of America in 1972
by Praeger Publishers, Inc.
111 Fourth Avenue, New York, N.Y. 10003

© *George Allen & Unwin Ltd 1971*

Library of Congress Catalog Card Number: 71–185773

PRINTED IN THE UNITED STATES OF AMERICA

Who reads Ferdinand Tönnies today?

PREFACE

It is possible to acknowledge most of those who have had a direct influence on this book. None are responsible for what is in it but I value more than they realize various conversations around its subject over the last seven years with Margaret Stacey, David Lockwood, Johan Galtung, Art Stinchcombe, André Béteille and Ray Pahl.

I owe special debts to the first named as I worked with her on the second study of Banbury, and to the last named who invited me to teach his 'urban' course at the University of Kent at Canterbury, 1970-1. The students on that course improved enormously those parts of the book to which they were exposed.

W. M. Williams was more than the perceptive and kindly editor of this series: he was my first teacher in sociology. That he disapproves of some of this book is no doubt inevitable. It would, however, not have been written without him.

C. B.

We would like to express our appreciation to Marion Haberhauer, Luise Gillmore and particularly Assumpta McEvoy, now lamentably returned to Ireland, for both their services and for the toleration they showed whilst they typed the manuscript.

Finally, we wish to thank our wives for their lack of direct help in the production of this book; had it been any different we should have been even slower.

C. B. and H. N.

University of Essex
May Day, 1971

CONTENTS

1

Introduction

'THE poor sociologist's substitute for the novel' – that was Ruth Glass' exasperated verdict on community studies.[1] It is not difficult to see the basis of her accusation. Community studies often exhibit not only a degree of subjectivity, but also downright idiosyncracy and eccentricity. This is partially reflected in the title of this book – 'Community *Studies*' – which echoes the non-cumulative nature of many of the monographs with which we shall deal. We cannot simply concern ourselves with a branch of sociology called 'the community' in the way that we can discuss 'the family', 'stratification', 'organizations' and so on. Indeed, one of the problems we shall encounter in this book is the extent to which 'the community' can be considered a justifiable object of sociological study at all. But Ruth Glass' criticisms went further than this. She also castigated community studies for their innumeracy, a simple lack of figures, even, in some cases, such basic ones as population statistics. Accompanying this has been a penchant for a descriptive, narrative style which, while frequently admirable in its clarity, has meant that community studies can often be read *like* novels and some have, indeed, reached the best-sellers' lists. This has had two detrimental results. Firstly, the highly descriptive nature of many community studies leads to the danger of their being dismissed as mere pieces of documentary social history, contributing little to our knowledge of social processes. One of the best tests of this is time: in encountering the earlier studies, the reader may indeed consider some of them as historical curiosities, glimpses of social life from a bygone age. Secondly, the lack of numerical data means that many community studies are not comparable, and where numerical data have been collected a lack of definitional consistency has had similar results. Nevertheless, many students continue to be introduced to sociology

[1] Ruth Glass, 'Conflict in Cities', p. 148 in *Conflict in Society*, London Churchill, 1966.

through the medium of community studies, for they undoubtedly provide, to use a phrase we shall employ frequently in this book, a means of 'getting to grips with the social and psychological facts in the raw'.[2]

The reader may care to turn Ruth Glass' argument back on her – consider the many novels that are comparable with community studies and decide which contributes the most to our knowledge of society. Many novels provide extremely useful complements to community studies but few, we would maintain, are substitutes for them. We can only give a few examples here. There is far richer material for this exercise in America, as at one time the 'small-town' novel was a thriving *genre* there. Sinclair Lewis on Gopher Prairie and Zenith City in *Babbitt* and *Martin Arrowsmith* can be compared to Lloyd Warner on Yankee City and Jonesville. Indeed, Warner analyses the 'class' structure of Zenith in his *Social Class in America* in such a way that it is difficult to distinguish it from Newburyport, for which Yankee City is a pseudonym. Newburyport also appears under another pseudonym, 'Clyde', in John Marquand's *Point of No Return*. Marquand was a native of Newburyport and, to add to our enjoyment, Warner himself appears in this novel, thinly disguised as 'Malcolm Bryant'. Marquand's account of the 'Confessional Club'[3] is paralleled by Warner's account of 'Lower-Upper' clubs and associations. Early in the novel 'Bryant' is described as 'the one who says, "my God, this is a wonderful town" ', but later is reported as saying, 'God, this is a hell of a town'. This change in attitude will strike a familiar chord with anyone who has ever done fieldwork in a community. One further point: Marquands' hero, Charles Gray, has been socially mobile *out* of the town and, as will be shown, it is precisely this pattern of social and geographical mobility that Warner overlooks in his analysis of Newburyport in the five large volumes of the 'Yankee City' series. Other American Community studies have their fictional counterparts, however. William Faulkner's novels can be put against Davis and Gardners' *Deep South* and Dollard's *Class and Caste in a Southern Town*, which are discussed along with Warner's work in Chapter 4. The situation of the European imigrant in Chicago in the early decades of this century inspired Upton Sinclair's polemical *The Jungle*, and this should be read with the monographs of the Chicago school – for example, Zorbaugh's *The Gold Coast and The Slum*. Suburban communities have also inspired a rush of novels, which frequently lack social perception, but David

[2] C. Arensberg and S. Kimball, *Community and Culture*, New York, Harcourt Brace and World, 1967, p. 30.

[3] J. Marquand, *Point of No Return*, New York, Grosset and Dunlop, 1949, pp. 271–81.

Karp's *Leave Me Alone*, with its description of the conflict between the male world of career, the female world of local and domestic sociability and the role of the estate agent in correctly placing families in the suburban social structure, can be put against Seeley, Sim and Loosley's *Crestwood Heights*, also discussed in Chapter 4.

Britain is less well served with community novels. However, there are a few that can be read along with British community studies. The emphasis on the men's world in mining communities which is to be found in Dennis, Henriques and Slaughter's *Coal Is Our Life*, is also exemplified by, for instance, Clancy Sigal's *Weekend in Dinlock* and David Storey's *This Sporting Life*. Thomas Hinde's *The Village*, set within commuting distance of London, can be put alongside the work of Pahl considered in Chapter 6 as can Margharita Laski's of the same title. Hinde's 'villagers' have precisely the limited view of the village community that would be expected from those who, in Pahl's terms, have 'a village in the mind'. The early part of George Orwell's *Coming Up For Air* describes a native's return to 'Lower Binfield' in terms that could well have been those of a Banburian returning to Banbury in the late 1930s after the aluminium factory had been built. Margaret Stacey's *Tradition and Change: a Study of Banbury* is discussed in Chapter 5. Anthony Burgess was a schoolmaster in Banbury when Stacey was doing her fieldwork and his book, *The Worm and the Ring* is a very thinly disguised portrait of some aspects of the town in 1950 from the point of view of a somewhat alienated outsider – a 'non-traditionalist' in Stacey's terms. It has the shrill tone of a deeply-felt resentment against the oligarchy of builders' and undertakers' resolutely philistinistic running of the town. The novel was the subject of a libel suit. Ronald Blythe's *Akenfield* has been a huge commercial success and is well worth the attention of the sociologist. His portrait of a south Suffolk village brilliantly handles the experiences of individuals in the community, but is less successful in considering the social structure of the community as a whole. Whilst it is deeply perceptive and finely wrought, it remains more art than science, though this should be no reason for totally rejecting it.

But what is community? In Chapter 2 it will be seen that over ninety definitions of community have been analysed and that the one common element in them all was man! In a recent introductory collection of readings the editors point out that 'community tends to be a God word. In many circumstances, when it is mentioned, we are expected to abase ourselves before it rather than attempt to define it.' They do, however, offer the following suggestions when they write that '(community) contains some or all of the following: a territorial area,

a complex of institutions within an area, and a sense of belonging'.[4]
Though these seem to be the key aspects of community as it is normally
used, there is also a certain lack of specificity. The same is true of the
two other recently published readers on community. Minar and Greer,
for example, write the following: 'At the roots of the human community
lie the brute facts of social life: organization[5] . . . organization of a
human aggregate requires . . . shared perspectives . . . culture.[6] By
customary usage community often means place. . . .' They do, however,
consider displacing 'this notion with a broader view of community as a
set of social identifications and interactions'. However, 'most of the
social systems to which we would apply the concept are geographic
entities of one sort or another. . . .' They refer to the 'mere fact that they
live together' and the 'geography of the local living and working
situation'.[7] We are told that 'what finally binds a community together
is a state of mind on the part of its members . . . a sense of interdependence and loyalty'.[8] Similarly Warren wrote in the introduction to
his reader that 'all of these basic approaches, in some way or another
come to grips with the inescapable fact that the clustering of people
for residence and sustenance involves a relationship of social interaction within a geographic locality'.[9] Community usually gains perspective when it is contrasted with non-community. This dichotomous
approach to the concept will be one of the themes of the second
chapter where it will be argued that *Gemeinschaft-Gesellschaft* dichotomies, or continua as they are frequently known, revolve less around
place than around the degree of involvement of the human being.
Below the surface of many community studies lurk value judgements,
of varying degrees of explicitness, about what is the good life.

Community study is also a method. This will be discussed in
Chapter 3. The problem to be faced is, how can the reader of a community monograph check the validity of the data when many leading
practitioners appear to celebrate their subjectivity? Vidich, Bensman
and Stein write for example, that 'it appears that the ear and the
eye are still important instruments for gathering data and that the
brain is not always an inefficient mechanism for analysing them'.[10] As
they observe, the weaknesses of the community study method can be

[4] E. Butterworth and D. Weir, *The Sociology of Modern Britain*, London,
Fontana, 1970, p. 58.

[5] D. W. Minar and S. Greer, *The Concept of Community*, Chicago, Aldine,
1968, p. 3.   [6] *Ibid.*, p. 26.

[7] *Ibid.*, p. 47.   [8] *Ibid.*, p. 60.

[9] Roland L. Warren, *Perspectives on the American Community*, Chicago (and
London), Rand McNally, 1966, p. vi.

[10] A. J. Vidich, J. Bensman and M. Stein, *Reflections on Community Studies*,
New York (and London), Wiley, 1964, p. xi.

easily listed: it all too frequently rests on the observations of a single person, the procedures of observation are not systematized, there is no guarantee that another investigator would produce similar results, and the values of the observer cannot be disentangled from his data. In short, there must be some question about the scientific validity of the community study method. As the authors quoted above say, there is a feeling that whilst the community study is perhaps acceptable as a branch of humanistic studies it certainly cannot be taken seriously as social science. With a distaste that shouts from the page, Vidich and his two colleagues complain that 'the development of abstract concepts, complex indices and statistical devices in the more scientific methodologies and the use of highly "structured" research "instruments" has left the analysists using these instruments in the position of having little direct knowledge of the social world they are supposed to survey'.[11] Instead, they themselves are after 'reality' described and analysed as a 'totality' (i.e. 'interrelationships between the various segments of community life') which usually implies that community researchers are 'functionalists' in the symphonic sense, whether they have bothered to use the rhetoric of functionalism or not. They are stressing a certain style of research, of direct observation and reporting. They are empiricists in this sense, and in the sense that they eschew a 'general, a historical, all-encompassing theory', they refer to 'the press of the data' and they argue that the best community researchers 'capture some segment of elusive reality which would be true to the world of the observed as seen by the particular perspective of the observer'.[12] There is often a *personal* quality to most community studies; as Vidich *et al* say there is an 'intimate connection between the investigator, his method of investigation, his results and his own future intellectual development'.[13] One task for Chapter 3 is to disentangle this 'intimate connection'.

Perhaps the best statement of the aim of a so-called community sociologist with whom Vidich *et al* are in sympathy is that of William Whyte who wrote that: 'Although I could not cover all Cornerville, I was building up the structure and functioning of the community through intensive examination of some of its parts *in action*. I was relating the parts together through observing events between groups and between group leaders and the members of the larger institutional structures (of politics and the rackets). *I was seeking to build a sociology upon observed interpersonal events.*'[14] The implication must be that the

[11] *Ibid.*, p. x.   [12] *Ibid.*, p. ix.
[13] *Ibid.*, p. ix.
[14] 'The Slum: On the Evolution of Street Corner Society' in Vidich *et al*, p. 69.

sociology based upon observed interpersonal events must be a sociology of the small scale. There is a limit to what can be observed. Indeed we shall see most, but not all, community studies are of relatively small places. However, not all of them are as limited as Whyte's *Street Corner Society*, which would seem to have more significance for the sociology of small groups than for the sociology of the community.

Another line of criticism of community studies that is increasingly persuasive is that in 'post-industry society' (or some such cliché) all become so mobile that community has become irrelevant. Marshall McLuhan would have us all living in 'global villages' and now 'that the message can travel faster than the messenger'[15] face-to-face communities are unnecessary. This message has also been picked up by the town-planning *avant-garde*. Melvin Webber's paper 'Order in Diversity' has the cryptic subtitle that sums up his message: 'Community Without Propinquity'. His argument is based on the assumption that we are all 'flooding into the middle class' which characteristically has a wide access to information and ideas and so the community to which we 'belong' is 'no longer the community of place . . . but an interest community which within a freely communicating society need not be spatially concentrated for we are increasingly able to interact with each other wherever we may be located'.[16] Ignoring the sociological naiveté of his assumptions and his gross exaggerations, the basic point that needs to be made is that what he calls an 'interest' community is an essentially single-stranded (simplex) relationship, whereas community is about multi-stranded (multiplex) relationships. Most people do *not* move most of the time. Urbaness or urbaneness may well be, as Webber argues, cultural rather than territorial, but where *do* people live? Where *do* they send their children to school? Do none of them belong to PTAs and other voluntary associations? Do none of them go to church, and work for political parties? Do none of them speak to the neighbours? It is likely that even the most dedicated bachelor professional has some extra-work social relationships. This is not to say that more people (how many and who should be the subject of empirical investigation not assertion) may have networks of social relationships that are not bounded by the locality in which they live, but there is no study which has demonstrated that nobody has any local relationships: indeed, precisely the opposite is the case, especially for wives. While

15 M. McLuhan, *Understanding Media*, London, Sphere books edition, 1967, p. 99.
16 Melvin M. Webber, 'Order in Diversity: Community without propinquity', p. 29 of *Cities and Space* edited by L. Wingo, Baltimore, John Hopkins Press, 1963.

this remains true, and it is not disputed that for some – but only a minority – increasingly fewer social relationships are locality bound, sociologists will find the community of place a productive unit of study and a useful location for investigating sociological problems. Other problems cannot be studied in a locality, but then no one has suggested that *all* sociological problems can be studied in a locality. Even the somewhat extreme habitats of the new suburbia, in which supposedly are living the new mobile and cosmopolitan middle class, have proved to be viable locales for sociological investigation. 'Suburban' community studies, such as those by Gans, Whyte and Pahl discussed below, have in fact shown the community without propinquity to be a myth, more related to certain ideas about the good life than to actual empirical description.

One of the difficulties in writing a book of this nature is the selection of material. There are so many community studies that any author would be forced to be extremely selective, and we have tended to concentrate on studies in Europe and North America. Even within these limits, however, we have been forced to select further. Those chosen are generally considered both to be the most important and, it will be argued, to raise most of the crucial theoretical and methodological problems in the field. We have also been forced to impose a minimum definition of a community study which all those included must meet: a community study must be concerned with the study of the *interrelationships* of social institutions in a locality. This does not mean that *all* social institutions locally present have to be studied but, unless these *interrelations* are considered, they will not be considered community studies for the purposes of this book. Thus, on these grounds, we have omitted, for example, the work of the Institute of Community Studies in Bethnal Green. The study of one social institution in a locality, such as the family in Bethnal Green, does not meet the minimal definition of a community study that will be followed here.[17]

The plan of this book is straightforward. There are two general chapters following this one. Chapter 2 is concerned with the theoretical inheritance of the sociological tradition of community and on more recent conceptualizations and approaches; Chapter 3 is on the community study as a method of empirical investigation. These are followed by two further chapters which consider particular studies in some detail: Chapter 4 is concerned with American studies and Chapter 5 with studies of European communities. The two concluding chapters are more analytic than narrative, taking two central problems that have had to be faced in most community studies – stratification and power.

[17] Also Jenny Platt's forthcoming book on the work of the Institute of Community Studies has lightened our task.

Both of these chapters show that it is indeed extraordinarily difficult to unravel theory from method in community studies. Thus, in some senses, this book can be considered as a somewhat extended footnote to the sociology of knowledge. It asks continually, how do we know what we know?

2

Theories of Community

IN considering the concept of community, the sociologist shares an occupational hazard with the architect and the planner: the more he attempts to define it in his own terms, the more elusively does the essence of it seem to escape him. The concept of community has been the concern of sociologists for more than two hundred years, yet a satisfactory definition of it in sociological terms appears as remote as ever. Most sociologists seem to have weighed in with their own idea of what a community consists of – and in this lies much of the confusion. For sociologists, no more than other individuals, have not always been immune to the emotive overtones that the word community consistently carries with it. Everyone – even sociologists – has wanted to live in a community; feelings have been more equivocal concerning life in collectivities, groups, networks or societies. The subjective feelings that the term community conjures up thus frequently lead to a confusion between what it *is* (empirical description) and what the sociologist feels it *should be* (normative prescription). The reasons for this enduring confusion can be related to the history of sociology itself. What the concept *involves* has not proved too difficult to elaborate; attempts to describe what it *is*, however, have proved impossible without making value judgements.

The Theoretical Inheritance

'Community' was thought to be a good thing, its passing was to be deplored, feared and regretted. The events surrounding the supposed causes of its eclipse – the democratic political revolutions of America and France and the industrial revolutions of Britain and, later, the remainder of Western Europe – were to a remarkable extent the starting point of Tocqueville, Comte, Tönnies, Le Play, Marx and Durkheim, some of the most eminent of sociology's founding fathers. What they understood by community makes an appropriate starting place for a discussion of community studies, for in the nineteenth century 'community' occupied a position in the minds of intellectuals similar to the idea of 'contract' in the Age of Reason. The concept of community, however, was not a cold, analytic construct. On the contrary, the ties of the community, real or imagined, came from these thinkers' images of the good life. Community was thus used as a means of invidious comparison with contemporarily exemplified society, yet community, consisting as it did of what the particular writer believed it *ought* to consist of, was capable of encompassing any number of possibly contradictory values which each saw fit to include. This amorphous quality allowed an endless array of social thinkers to unite in their praise of community, no matter how diverse their interpretations of it might be.[1] Overlying this positive evaluation of community, there was frequently a pervading posture of nostalgia – of praising the past to blame the present – and the two themes combined when present 'society' was criticized with reference to past 'community'. The upheavals of industrialization enabled these feelings to be given full rein. Industrial society – and its ecological derivative, the city – was typified by competition and conflict, utility and contractual relations; the community – and its ecological derivative, the village or, at the the most, the small town – was the antithesis of these. The impersonality and anonymity of industrial society were highlighted by reference to the close personal ties of the community. The trend appeared to be away from the latter and towards the former: thus there is in writers such as Comte an anguished sense of the breakdown of the old.[2] Comte's sociological interest in community was, as Nisbet has pointed out, born of the same circumstances that produced his conservatism: the breakdown or disorganization of the traditional forms of association. The community, in other words, was viewed as man's *natural* habitat.

Sir Henry Maine was not concerned with the community as such, but his work exercised a great influence upon his contemporaries and successors and, most importantly from our point of view, upon Tönnies. Thus, while we should be wary of plundering the corpus of his work looking for antecedents to our present concerns,[3] Maine's

[1] For an interesting account of this theme in relation to the British literary and philosophical tradition see W. Peterson, 'The Ideological Origins of Britain's New Towns', *American Institute of Planners Journal*, XXXIV, 1968, pp. 160–70.

[2] See R. Nisbet, *The Sociological Tradition*, London, Heinemann, 1966, Chapter 3.

[3] See J. Burrows, *Evolution and Society*, London, Cambridge U.P., 1966, for the dangers inherent in the Whiggish interpretation of nineteenth century intellectual history.

work forms an important prelude to later, more narrowly sociologically inclined, thinkers. What Maine wanted to know was how the institutions of his day had evolved from those of antiquity. On the basis of the early writings of the Hebrews, Greeks and Romans, Maine argued that early society was patriarchal, the oldest male having held absolute supremacy over the extended family. Society as a whole was a conglomeration of familial units. In contrast, Maine noted, the basic unit of modern society was not the family in its extended form but the individual. Using the legal system as evidence, he discovered that primitive law was concerned with family groups as corporate entities defined by kinship. Crime was a corporate act, land was held jointly. When societies expanded, however, locality rather than kinship became the basis of organization. The crux of Maine's argument was that the powers, privileges and duties once resident in the family had shifted to the state. And the nature of men's interrelations, instead of being based on his *status*, became based on individually agreed *contracts*.

Another who used law as an index of social change, was of course, Emile Durkheim. While Comte's overriding emotion was anguish, Durkheim's was concern, concern for the 'moral consolidation' of the society in which he lived. If Durkheim's work was 'a memorial to the ability of a gifted man to utilize the work of others in the pursuit of his own designs',[4] it is as well to be aware of what these designs were. What Durkheim feared was the disintegration of social relations into 'anomie' – a state of 'normlessness' where there was complete social breakdown – but what he perceived in contemporary society was not so much the breakdown of community as the transition from community based on one kind of social relations to community based on another, from mechanical solidarity to organic solidarity.[5] According to Durkheim the increased division of labour in more advanced societies leads to organic solidarity – solidarity based upon the interdependence of specialized parts, on diversity rather than similarity. He used legal indicators to show that as one type of solidarity advances, the other regresses; and it was organic solidarity that was increasing. Durkheim was gratified to conclude that, far from community disintegrating, society was becoming one big community.

If there is a founding father of the theory of community, however, the label perhaps suits Ferdinand Tönnies more than any other individual. Tönnies' book *Gemeinschaft and Gesellschaft* (usually trans-

---

[4] H. Stuart Hughes, *Consciousness and Society*, New York (and London), MacGibbon and Kee, 1967, p. 280.
[5] E. Durkheim, *The Division of Labour in Society*, New York, Free Press, 1964 (London, Collier-Macmillan).

lated as *Community and Society*) was first published in 1887. It has provided a constant source of ideas for those who have dealt with the community ever since.[6] In *Gemeinschaft* ('community') human relationships are intimate, enduring and based on a clear understanding of where each person stands in society. A man's 'worth' is estimated according to *who* he is not *what* he has done – in other words, status is ascriptive, rather than achieved. In a community, roles are specific and consonant with one another: a man does not find his duties in one role conflicting with the duties that devolve upon him from another role. Members of a community are relatively immobile in a physical and a social way: individuals neither travel far from their locality of birth nor do they rise up the social hierarchy. In addition, the culture of the community is relatively homogeneous, for it must be so if roles are not to conflict or human relations to lose their intimacy. The moral custodians of a community, the family and the church, are strong, their code clear and their injunctions well internalized. There will be community sentiments involving close and enduring loyalties to the place and people. So community encourages immobility and makes it difficult for men to achieve status and wealth on the basis of their merits. Community makes for traditionalistic ways and at the very core of the community concept is the sentimental attachment to the conventions and mores of a beloved place. Community will reinforce and encapsulate a moral code, raising moral tensions and rendering heterodoxy a serious crime, for in a community everyone is known and can be placed in the social structure. This results in a personalizing of issues, events and explanations, because familiar names and characters inevitably become associated with everything that happens. Tönnies continued the nineteenth-century theme that community makes for solidary relations among men, a theme which over the years has laid stress on one factor for its basis – the territorial factor, the place, the locality. When sociologists now talk about community, they almost always mean a place in which people have some, if not complete, solidary relations. Yet community as originally used, though it included the *local* community, also went beyond it. It encompassed religion, work, family and culture: it referred to social bonds – to use Robert Nisbet's own key term – characterized by emotional cohesion, depth, continuity and fullness.

Opposed to the concept of community was *Gesellschaft* (variously translated as 'society' or 'association') which essentially means every-

[6] See for example, J. C. McKinney and C. P. Loomis, 'The Application of *Gemeinschaft* and *Gesellschaft* as Related to Other Typologies', in the introduction to the American edition of F. Tönnies' *Community and Society*, New York, Harper Torchbook, 1957, pp. 12–29.

thing that community is not. *Gesellschaft* refers to the large scale, impersonal and contractual ties that were seen by the nineteenth century sociologists to be on the increase, at the expense of *Gemeinschaft*. Here is the central idea that runs through so many community studies: social change is conceptualized as a continuum between two polar types: *Gemeinschaft* or community and *Gesellschaft* or society. For Tönnies, there are three central aspects of *Gemeinschaft*: blood, place (land) and mind, with their sociological consequents of kinship, neighbourhood and friendship. Together, they were the home of all virtue and morality. *Gesellschaft*, however, has a singularity about it; in Tönnies' terms, 'all its activities are restricted to a definite end and a definite means of obtaining it'.[7] This rationality is, of course, usually seen as a key aspect in the development of western capitalism. Indeed it might be claimed that in *Gemeinschaft* would be found what Max Weber calls 'traditional' authority where as *Gesellschaft* incorporates what he would call 'rational-legal' authority. Yet it should be understood that whereas the loss of community is something that is treated as a consequence of capitalism by Marx – and others since then, making it a strong tradition today – for Tönnies capitalism was treated as a consequence of the loss of community. Chicken-and-egg arguments are rarely easily soluble and no attempt at a solution is made here. Nevertheless, it is important to realize that the conferring of causal status on the concept of community is at the very essence of Tönnies' typological use of it.

Tönnies' greatest legacy is this typological usage – a typology usually expressed in terms of a dichotomy. The 'community-society' dichotomy along with 'authority-power', 'status-class', 'sacred-secular', 'alienation-progress', have been represented by Nisbet as the unit ideas of the sociological tradition. They are, as he wrote, 'the rich themes in nineteenth-century thought. Considered as linked antitheses, they form the very warp of the sociological tradition. Quite apart from their conceptual significance in sociology, they may be regarded as epitomizations of the conflict between tradition and modernism, between the old order made moribund by the industrial and democratic revolutions, and the new order, its outlines still unclear and as often the cause of anxiety as of elation and hope.'[8] These ideas were not, of course, new to the nineteenth century – Sorokin, for example, takes the basic idea of community back to Confucius and runs through Ibn Khaldun and St Thomas Aquinas.[9] They remain, though, the most relevant theoretical inheritance for modern community studies, and must be the starting place for more recent conceptualizations of the concept.

[7] Tönnies, *op. cit.*, p. 192.
[8] Nisbet, *op. cit.*, p. 6.
[9] See his introduction to Tönnies, *op. cit.*

The *Gemeinschaft-Gesellschaft* dichotomy can be incorporated into the structural-functional theories of Talcott Parsons. What Parsons terms 'pattern variables' form the basis of his system for the analysis of social action. They are seen as continua or 'ranges' between polar opposites, each of which expresses a 'dilemma' of choice between two alternatives that every 'actor' faces in every social situation. As Parsons states, the clusters at the ends of these continua 'very closely characterize what in much sociological literature have been thought of as polar types of institutional structure, the best known version of which perhaps has been the *Gemeinschaft-Gesellschaft* dichotomy of Tönnies'.[10] These pattern variables are:

1. Affectivity versus affective neutrality: which refers to whether immediate self-gratification or its deferment is expected.
2. Specificity versus diffuseness: which refers to whether the scope of a relationship is narrow, like that between a bureaucrat and his client, or broad and inclusive as between a mother and her child or between spouses.
3. Universalism versus particularism: which refers to whether action is governed by generalized standards (equal opportunity) or in terms of a reference scheme peculiar to the actors in the relationship (e.g. nepotism.)
4. Quality versus performance (also called ascription verses achievement): which refers to whether the characterization of each actor by the others is based on who or what the person is or on what he can do, on whether he is the son of a duke (ascription) or a college graduate (achievement).

Community would seem to involve particularism and ascription and diffuseness and affectivity – as a consequence, for example, of kinship being important and of stability and 'knowing' everyone. On the other hand, the emergent pattern in most industrial societies is that of universalism and achievement and specificity and affective neutrality. There is a clear tendency for these pattern-variables to co-vary between the extremes, although all societies show mixtures of the two sets of characteristics. The relative emphasis clearly differs and the pattern-variables can be used as more precise analytic tools to describe the loss or otherwise of community. It should be noted, however, that Parsons is not talking particularly about local social systems but society in general. The pattern-variables can be applied to all forms of social action, having emerged out of the classic dichotomies of the sociological tradi-

[10] T. Parsons and E. Shils, *Toward a General Theory of Action*, New York (and London), Harper Torchbook, 1952, pp. 207-8.

tion, and their application to community represents only a small part of Parsons' much grander theoretical scheme.

Definitions of Community

While the foregoing has described how sociological theory has impinged upon the concept of community, we have yet to examine in detail precisely what the term has been believed to denote. The difficulties involved in this somewhat intricate task have already been alluded to. Every sociologist, it seems, has possessed his own notion of what community consists of, frequently reflecting his ideas of what it *should* consist of. Exhortations to 'define your terms' have been taken to heart in this case – sociologists have frequently launched into defining community with a will bordering on gay abandon. Indeed, the analysis of the various definitions was at one time quite a thriving sociological industry. The *piece de resistance* was George A. Hillery Jr's analysis of no fewer than ninety-four definitions in his paper, 'Definitions of Community: Areas of Agreement'.[11] Needless to say, the very thing that was missing was agreement – indeed Hillery's conclusion hardly seemed to advance the analysis much further. In the convoluted verbiage beloved of many American sociologists he concluded, 'There is one element, however, which can be found in all of the concepts, and (if its mention seems obvious) it is specified merely to facilitate a positive delineation of the degree of heterogeneity: all of the definitions deal with people. Beyond this common basis, there is no agreement.'[12] This hardly seems very encouraging.

Hillery's efforts, however, were not entirely wasted, for from his inspection of the ninety-four definitions he was able to discover, he abstracted sixteen concepts. These concepts were linked by twenty-two different combinations, and though one may regard sixteen elements as an unwieldy classification, at least it is an advance in parsimony compared with ninety-four. The following table is an adaptation of Hillery's. We have followed Hillery in his two major distinguishing categories. *Generic* community refers to the use of the word community as a conceptual term. *Rural* communities refer not to the community but to a particular type of community. The prevalence, which Hillery discovered, of conjoining community with a specifically rural environment, can be seen as the continuing presence of the anti-urban trait in sociology referred to earlier. We have followed Hillery in believing, that, while the division of definitions into 'generic community'

[11] G. A. Hillery Jr, 'Definitions of Community: Areas of Agreement', *Rural Sociology*, 20, 1955.
[12] *Ibid.*, p. 117.

and 'rural community' is not a logical one, the attempt to delimit the characteristics of community contained in the latter should not be discarded.

A Classification of Selected Definitions of Community (after Hillery)

DISTINGUISHING IDEAS OR ELEMENTS MENTIONED IN THE DEFINITIONS	NUMBER OF DEFINITIONS
I. Generic Community	
A. Social Interaction	
I. Geographic Area	
A. Self-sufficiency	8
B. Common Life	9
Kinship	2
C. Consciousness of Kind	7
D. Possession of common ends, norms, means	20
E. Collection of institutions	2
F. Locality Groups	5
G. Individuality	2
2. Presence of some common characteristic, other than area	
A. Self-sufficiency	1
B. Common Life	3
C. Consciousness of Kind	5
D. Possession of common ends, norms, means	5
3. Social System	1
4. Individuality	3
5. Totality of Attitudes	1
6. Process	2
B. Ecological Relationships	3

II. Rural Community
  A. Social Interaction
    1. Geographic Area
      A. Self-sufficiency   1
      B. Common Life   3
      C. Consciousness of Kind   3
      D. Possession of common ends, norms, means   3
      E. Locality group   5

TOTAL DEFINITIONS   94

Despite Hillery's conclusion that there is an absence of agreement, beyond the fact that community involves people, a considerable amount can now be salvaged from his analysis. A perusal of the table should lead to the conclusion that not all the definitions can be correct, that is to say that community cannot be all of these definitions in their entirety. A community cannot be an area and not be an area, though significantly Hillery found that no author denied that area *could* be an element of community. All but three of the definitions clearly mention the presence of a group of people interacting; those that do not have an ecological orientation. This is one reason for examining the ecological approach more closely later in the chapter. Sixty-nine of the ninety-four definitions agree that community includes social interaction, area and some ties or bonds in common. Seventy, or almost three-quarters, agree on the presence of area and social interaction as necessary elements of community; but more than three-quarters (seventy-three) agreed on the joint inclusion of social interaction and common ties. Thus a majority of definitions include, in increasing importance for each element, the following components of community: area, common ties and social interaction.[13]

If the reader now believes that we are achieving a sight of the trees after having hacked away much dead wood, the progress since Hillery's analysis is a salutary warning against optimism. A consideration of a few definitions that have enjoyed wide circulation since Hillery's analysis will serve to show what we mean. Sussman has produced a particularly fine example of an omnibus definition: 'A community is said to exist when interaction between individuals has the purpose of meeting individual needs and obtaining group goals . . . a limited geographical area is another feature of the community. . . . The features of social interaction, structures for the gratification of physical,

[13] *Ibid.*, p. 118.

social and psychological needs, and limited geographical area are basic
to the definition of community.'[14] The utility of this definition is,
however, severely hindered by the fact that the specification of
individual and group goals is an exceedingly troublesome task. This
will be demonstrated in Chapter 7 on community power.

Kaufman's paper, 'Toward an Interactional Conception of Community'[15] argues – in a manner consistent with the traditional formulations discussed above – that centralization, specialization and the increase of impersonal relationships are hastening the decline of the
community. The first two aspects of his formal definition are very
similar to those of Sussman – that community is a place (a relatively
small one at that), and secondly, that community indicates a configuration as to way of life, both as to how people do things and what
they want, that is, their institutions and their collective goals. Kaufman's
third notion is a more radical departure and concerns collective action:
'Persons in a community should not only be able to, but frequently do
act together in the common concern of life.'[16] There are thus three
elements in Kaufman's interactional model of the community: the
community participant, the community groups and associations, and
finally the phases and processes of community action. In other words,
who, with whom, does what, when? This would seem very relevant to
the study of, say, local politics, but of less relevance to the analysis of
the community as an object or unit of study. Kaufman's difficulties
become more apparent later in the paper when he conceptualizes,
again very traditionally, community as an independent rather than
dependent variable: 'One may visualize the community field as a stage
with the particular ethos of the local society determining the players
and the plays.'[17] While Kaufman admits that this is 'much more an
enumeration of elements . . . than a precise statement of their interrelationships',[18] one feels justified in asking where the community is in
all this. Since he refers to the community *field* it is presumably not the
'stage'. Is it then the 'ethos', the 'players', the 'play' or perhaps the most
likely candidate, 'local society'? But the use of 'local society' merely
begs the question: semantic sleight of hand is not substitute for rigorous definition.

Sutton and Kolaja add some variables to the study of action *in* the
community, but do not really elaborate a definition despite the title of

[14] Marvin B. Sussman (ed.), *Community Structure and Analysis*, New York,
Crowell, 1959, pp. 1–2.
[15] Harold F. Kaufman, 'Toward an Interactional Conception of Community',
Social Forces, 38, 1959.
[16] *Ibid.*, p. 9.
[17] *Ibid.*, p. 10.
[18] *Ibid.*, p. 10.

their paper, 'The Concept of Community'.[19] Community is defined in the by-now-familiar way as 'a number of families residing in a relatively small area within which they have developed a more or less complete socio-cultural definition imbued with collective identification and by means of which they solve problems arising from the sharing of an area'.[20] The four crucial variables as they see them are:

1. Number of actors
2. Awareness of action
3. Goal of action
4. Recipients of action

They are attempting a convergence between conceptions of community and conceptions of community action. To do this they cross-classify these four variables and develop a sixteen-fold table which, they argue, can be used to classify community action.

It should be apparent by now that it is impossible to give *the* sociological definition of the community. However, we offer one last attempt at defining the concept, the one which, at least to us, seems to have the most to commend it: that of Talcott Parsons. Earlier, when discussing the sociological tradition out of which emerged Parsons' pattern variables, it was pointed out that particularism, ascription, diffuseness and affectivity (and their opposites) are categories of social action with no necessary local reference. Without this territorial reference it is difficult to distinguish social action within, say, a family from that within a village. So Gidean Sjoberg has found it necessary to significantly modify Parsons' definition in *The Social System*[21] and to call a community 'a collectivity of actors sharing in a limited territorial area as the base for carrying out the greatest share of their daily activities.'[22] Parsons originally wrote 'common' not 'limited' so Sjoberg obviously feels that he wants to include some notion of size in his definition, yet does not build into his definition any notion of what the limit to this size should be.

Parsons, in a more recent paper entitled 'The Principal Structures of Community',[23] avoids begging this question as well as others just as crucial. There has been, as Hillery's discussion showed – and it is more

[19] Willis A. Sutton and Jivi Kolaja, 'The Concept of Community', *Rural Sociology*, 25, 1960.

[20] *Ibid.*, p. 197.

[21] Talcott Parsons, *The Social System*, London, Tavistock Publications, 1952.

[22] Gideon Sjoberg, 'Community' in J. Gould & W. L. Kolb, *Dictionary of Sociology*, London, Tavistock, 1965, p. 115.

[23] Talcott Parsons, 'The Principal Structures of Community', in his *Structure and Process in Modern Society*, but originally in Carl J. Friedrich, *Community*, New York, Liberal Arts Press, 1959.

marked than he implied – a dichotomy in community studies between those which focus, to put it crudely, on the people, and those which focus on the territory. Parsons avoids forcing a choice between the two. His tentative definition (which should be treated as such) is as follows: '. . . that aspect of the structure of social systems which is referable to the territorial location of persons (i.e. human individuals as organisms) and their activities'.[24] There follows an important qualification. 'When I say "referable to" I do not mean determined exclusively or predominantly by, but rather *observable and analysable with reference to location as a focus of attention* (and of course a partial determinant).'[25] As Parsons states, the territorial reference is central, though it is necessary to stress, with him, that we should be concerned with 'persons acting in territorial locations' and, in addition, 'since the reference is to *social* relations, persons acting in relation to other persons in respect to the territorial location of both parties. . . . The *population*, then, is just as much a focus of the study of community as is the territorial location.'[26]

Our motive in discussing these definitional exercises is partially the negative one of demonstrating the non-cumulative nature of so much of the work on community. It is also hoped that it has had the positive function of showing the catholicity of the field despite these terminological arguments. It now appears that something of an impasse has been reached concerning the definition of community – some might even call it exhaustion. This must lead us to examine the theory of community from other points of view. After all, as Hillery has rightly observed 'The significant question concerns the nature of social groups, not whether a ninety-fifth definition of community is possible.'[27] It would now seem more profitable to consider some distinct streams or approaches to community studies rather than to pursue or attempt to resolve the definitional debate. Rather as intelligence is what intelligence tests measure perhaps we can, for the time being at any rate, merely treat community as what community studies analyse.

The Ecological Approach

The substantive contributions of some of the ecologists will be considered in Chapter 4; in this chapter we wish only to outline their theoretical approach. It will be recalled that in Hillery's definitional exercise discussed above, some of the ecological definitions of com-

[24] *Ibid*. (Friedrich), p. 250.
[25] *Ibid*., p. 250 (our emphasis).
[26] *Ibid*., p. 250 (emphasis in the original).
[27] G. A. Hillery, *Communal Organizations*, Chicago, Chicago U.P., 1969, p. 4.

munity specifically exclude notions of social interaction. The ecologists, then, have a distinctive view of community, regarding the solidarity and shared interests of community members as a function of their common residence. Indeed, there is often a great emphasis in their writings on the physical nature of the neighbourhoods in which the residents live, so much so that it is difficult to remember, as Don Martindale has pointed out, that social life is a 'structure of interaction, not a structure of stone, steel, cement and asphalt, etc'.[28] The ecological approach has as one of its major premises 'that there is a continuity in the life patterns of all organic forms'.[29] The term *human ecology* was, in fact, coined in 1921 in Park and Burgess' *An Introduction to the Science of Sociology* and the tendency of the ecologists to stress biological analogies and to use biological terms (at least as metaphors) has remained ever since. The other distinctive aspect of the work of the ecologists is their stress on the *spatial* consequences of social organization.

Amos Hawley's *Human Ecology: A theory of Community Structure* is the most carefully developed and comprehensive statement of the ecologists' theoretical position. In it he wrote that 'the community has often been likened to an individual organism. So intimate and so necessary are the interrelations of its parts . . . that any influence felt at one point is almost immediately transmitted throughout. Further, not only is the community a more or less self-sufficient entity, having inherent in it the principle of its own life process, it has also a growth or natural history with well-defined stages of youth, maturity and senescence. It is therefore a whole which is something different from the sum of its parts, possessing powers and potentialities not present in any of its components. If not an organism, it is at least a superorganism.'[30] All the key elements of the ecological analogy with biology are here. Hawley goes on to discuss both the nature of the biotic community and man's place in it. He says of the biological community (though he could, as far as many ecologists are concerned, be writing of the human community) 'that it is the patterns of symbiotic and commonalistic relations that develop in a population, it is in the nature of a collective response to the habitat, it constitutes the adjustment of organism to the environment'.[31] Clearly Hawley and other ecologists feel that the customary sociological stress on the uniqueness of man – for example, because of his culture-producing capacity – is an over-

[28] Don Martindale, 'Introduction' to Max Weber, *The City*, New York, Free Press, 1958, p. 29.

[29] Amos Hawley, *Human Ecology: A Theory of Community Structure*, New York, Ronald, 1950, p. v.

[30] *Ibid.*, p. 50.

[31] *Ibid.*, p. 87.

emphasis. Ecology at its finest provided sharp and accurate descriptions of the spatial aspects of communities. In some cases it could be justly claimed that 'The question of how men relate themselves to another in order to live in their habitat yields a description of community structure in terms of its overt and measurable features.'[32] What ecology so often fails to do, however, is to provide explanations of these relationships. Ecology, then, renders itself only a fruitful source of hypotheses concerning the community rather than a testing of them.

When the classical ecological approach (meaning that practised in Chicago in the 1930s and the subject of part of Chapter 4) has been combined with other approaches, say that of Weber on social class, more dynamic, sociologically satisfying explanations of spatial patterns and processes can be elaborated. One such example is that of Rex and Moore in their analysis of Sparkbrook in Birmingham,[33] which will be discussed in more detail in Chapter 6. In their spatial analysis the ecologists have located in the urban spatial structure what they call 'natural areas' and these are occupied by 'sub-communities'. These 'sub-communities' in Chicago were the subject of separate monographs, e.g. Thrasher on the gangs, Zorbaugh on the 'Gold Coast' and the 'Slum'.[34] There is a belief in the work of Thrasher 'that there is a tendency for human behaviour to reflect in one way or another the physical characteristics of the area in which it occurs. Man lives life close to the ground and must of necessity relate his activities to his physical milieu.'[35] The ecologists, in fact, produce a definition of community not dissimilar to many other sociologists – although, as noted above, they do tend to omit notions of social 'interaction'. Hawley, for example, writes 'Formally defined, community refers to the structure of relationships through which a localized population provides its daily requirements.'[36] This is strikingly similar to that produced by Parsons, and yet the consequences of their different interests produce a radically different account of communities. Like many other sociologists ecologists also stress the great advantage of dealing with the relatively small and convenient unit for investigation presented by the community. In addition Hawley disarms criticism by writing that ecology makes no attempt to exhaust the possibilities of community analysis, for ecologists are not concerned with 'psychology, attitudes,

[32] *Ibid.*, p. 73.
[33] J. Rex and R. Moore, *Race, Community and Conflict*, London, Oxford U.P., 1967.
[34] F. M. Thrasher, *One Thousand Boys' Gangs in Chicago*, Chicago (and London), Chicago U.P. 1963. Harvey Zorbaugh, *The Gold Coast and the Slum*, Chicago (and London), Chicago U.P., 1929.
[35] Thrasher, *op. cit.*
[36] Hawley, *op. cit.*, p. 180

sentiments, motivations and the like . . . not because they are unimportant but because the assumptions and points of view of human
ecology are not adapted to their treatment. On the other hand, the
results of ecological research provide a framework, i.e. knowledge of
community structure, which should prove useful to psychological
study.'[37]

What exactly do the ecologists mean by community structure?
Clearly it does not refer to the attitudes of individuals but is a property
of the aggregate. Indeed, what is now known as the 'ecological fallacy'
in sociology refers to making statements about individuals from
aggregate data.[38] Hawley states that community structure connotes some
sort of 'orderly arrangement of discrete or at any rate distinguishable
parts . . . to all the essential functions and their interrelations by which
a local population maintains itself'.[39] The community structure exists
independently of particular individuals for 'generations succeed generations without disrupting the pattern of interdependence that constitutes
the community'.[40] Hawley lists the 'parts that make up the whole' –
for example, families, associational corporate units, territorial corporate
units, categoric units (age, sex and, more dubiously, class), cliques,
clubs, societies, and neighbourhood associations. In an important and
pregnant footnote Hawley states the central problem, but makes no
attempt to answer it: 'To what extent are they units of the community?
The test, no doubt, is the degree to which they affect the functioning
of the community as a whole.[41] This may be difficult to determine.
What is at issue here, of course, is the matter or relevance, clearly one
of the most crucial problems in social science. It hinges, in this case,
upon the clarity and demonstrability of the definition of the communal
unit. That, in turn, requires a great deal more exploratory research
than community structure has received to date.'[42] Thus, the ecologists
themselves are not unaware of some of the problems that emerge from
their approach.

Communities as Organizations

The ecological approach relies heavily on analogies with biological
organization. There is another approach that also treats communities

[37] *Ibid.*

[38] See W. S. Robinson's classic statement, 'Ecological Correlations and the
Behaviour of Individuals', *American Sociological Review*, 15, 1950.

[39] Hawley, *op. cit.*, p. 206.

[40] *Ibid.*, p. 206.

[41] This seems to us to show that Hawley recognizes that power is differentially
distributed and can affect 'the collective response to the habitat'.

[42] Hawley, *op. cit.*, p. 218.

as organizations, but organizations in the sociological sense. Earlier in this chapter it was noted that several definitions of the community, for example the recent ones of Sussman, Kaufman, and Sutton and Kolaja, include some notion of goals or action. Organizations, unlike communities, are social arrangements for achieving desired goals. Therefore some sociologists have found it useful to treat communities as organizations.

Hillery has continued and expanded the definitional exercise outlined above in a more recent book, *Communal Organizations: A study of Local Societies* In this he takes three social systems – the village, the city and the total or custodial institution – in order to compare and contrast them. Hillery takes the village to be a small agricultural settlement[43] while, following Louis Wirth, the city is defined as 'a relatively large, dense, and permanent settlement of socially hetero-geneous individuals'.[44] In his definition of the total institution, Hillery followed Goffman's use of the term, 'being a social system that not only tended to regulate the total lives of the inmates but which also set barriers to social interaction with the outside'.[45] Using these three types of organization, Hillery's aim, then, is to develop a theory of community.

What relation does community bear to these three social systems? This is Hillery's first problem because no one has developed a satis-factory taxonomy of community. Hillery decides to confer the term community on the village, on the grounds that 'no definition could be found which clearly stated that the phenomenon of community was *not* to be found in such a social system'.[46] The village, then, is assumed to *be* community, though community *could* be found in other types of social system. It is used as an object of comparison with other social systems whose status as communities is more questionable – the city and the total institution. Once Hillery establishes the village as community, he appends the adjective 'folk'.[47] Hillery, treating communities in this way as *objects*, neatly sets up the eight logically possible hypotheses to test against the data concerning the three social systems. As can be seen from the diagram, these hypotheses concern the differences, quantita-tive and qualitative, between the folk village, the city and the total institution.

Hillery's procedure is similar to that in his paper on the definitions

[43] Hillery, *op. cit.*, p. 12.
[44] *Ibid.*, p. 14.
[45] *Ibid.*, p. 14.
[46] *Ibid.*, p. 12.
[47] This is derived from the work of Robert Redfield and is considered in more detail later in this chapter.

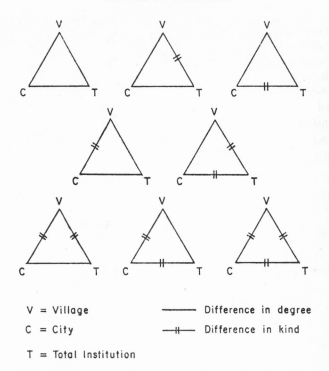

V = Village

C = City

T = Total Institution

——— Difference in degree

—‖— Difference in kind

Hillery's Typology of Communal Organizations (from Hillery [1968] p. 15)

of community. He lists nineteen 'components' or 'traits' of the folk village[48] which are integrated by three concepts: space, co-operation and the family. The nineteen components are then applied in turn to the examination of the city and the total institution. With regard to the city, Hillery concludes that the differences are only of degree, not of kind – in other words the folk village and the city can be regarded as 'variations of the same type of thing . . . as existing on continua'.[49] Taking his nineteen components of the total institution, however, he found that on only three are the differences qualitative. Total institutions, then, are a different *kind* of entity from the city and the folk village. Quoting Parsons, Hillery writes that 'The defining characteristic of an organization . . . is the "primacy of orientation to the attainment of specific goals". This feature distinguishes organizations

[48] Hillery, *op. cit.*, pp. 29–30.
[49] *Ibid.*, p. 61.

from such groups as the family, which "is only partly an organization: most other kinship groups are even less so. The same is certainly true of local communities, regional sub-societies and of a society conceived as a whole, for example, as a nation". '50

Nevertheless Hillery is moving forward towards a theory of communal organizations, as the title of his book suggests. A communal organization, as he sees it, refers primarily to a system of institutions formed by people who live together. Only it has no goal: 'The reasons for living together are often no more than that of being born in the locality – for all communal organizations occupy a particular territory.'51 He recognizes that specific reasons (or goals?) draw people together in some communal organizations, but the inhabitants of a locality always engage in activities unrelated to the initial attraction. 'Thus', he writes, 'the migrant may enter a city specifically for a job, but he also marries, plays, goes to church, etc.'52 Here, in considering migration, Hillery approaches the problem of the impingement of the national on the local. He recognizes that communal organizations include a wide range of social groups, some of which are nationally oriented while others are locally-oriented.53 But while this distinction is acknowledged the existence of the two types of group, and their interrelationship, is never fully examined.

Communities as Microcosms

Unlike those who have studied communities as ecologies or as organizations, this approach is specifically concerned with what can be learned from community studies about macro-social processes. Maurice Stein's book, *The Eclipse of Community*54 discusses, as the title suggests, the increased interdependence and decreased local autonomy that have resulted from the social processes of urbanization, industrialization and bureaucratization. Stein's book represents a general tendency within the field of community studies to come to grips with two related problems – the difficulty of generalizing from individual community studies and the need for an adequate theoretical framework within which to locate the community studied in a sequence of change.

At the beginning of his book, Stein deals with some of the American

50 *Ibid.*, p. 142, quoting Parsons, *The Structure and Process of Modern Society*, p. 17.
51 Hillery, *op. cit.*, pp. 185–6.
52 *Ibid.*, p. 186.
53 In Hillery's terminology, 'those that include vills and that vills include', *ibid.*, p. 186.
54 Maurice Stein, *The Eclipse of Community*, New York (and London), Harper Row, 1964.

studies that will be examined in more detail in Chapter 4 – namely those of Robert Park and the other Chicago ecologists, the Lynds' 'Middletown' and Lloyd Warner's 'Yankee City', all of which were written in the 1920s and 30s. Stein uses their work 'as case studies showing the ways in which large-scale social processes shaped human affairs in local settings'.[55] These processes are urbanization, elaborated with Chicago data,[56] industrialization, elaborated with data from the two Middletown[57] studies, and the growth of bureaucracy, with data from the five Yankee City volumes.[58] Stein would be the first to admit that his are selective accounts and that, in any case, community studies are always confined in time and space. The studies he used are not 'representative' in any statistical sense, but Stein claims that these communities 'were undergoing processes of structural transformation that affected all American cities and towns to one or another degree, and therefore could be used as laboratories in which to study these representative social processes'.[59] And the best community studies have always been of transitional processes. After dealing with those classic American studies, Stein analyses the slum (through William Whyte's *Street Corner Society*),[60] bohemia (through Caroline Ware's *Greenwich Village*),[61] the Deep South (through Davis's and Gardner's *Deep South* and Dollard's *Caste and Class in a Southern Town*),[62] the US army (through *The American Soldier* by Samuel Stouffer *et al*)[63] and Suburbia (through Seeley, Sim, and Loosley's *Crestwood Heights* and William Whyte's *The Organization Man*)[64] Stein has 'reflected' on *The Eclipse of Community* and makes it clear that the book is a kind of sociological autobiography, most of the communities having personal and symbolic significance for him. He enthusiastically quotes Robert Park, who insisted that the student should deeply involve himself in the life of a particular community whose problems he should take over and make his own. Whilst the precise consequences of this sort of approach will be discussed in the next chapter, it should be noted here that, though Stein is clearly deeply involved, albeit *at second hand* in the communities mentioned above, that is no substitute for reading the original. So rather than increase the distance from these studies –

---

[55] *Ibid.*, p. 1.
[56] See below, pp. 91-101.
[57] See below, pp. 82-91.
[58] See below, pp. 101-111.
[59] Stein, *op. cit.*, p. 94.
[60] Published in 1955, Chicago (and London), Chicago U.P.
[61] Published in 1935, New York, Houghton Mifflin.
[62] See Chapter 4, below pp. 111-116.
[63] Published in 1949, Princeton, Princeton U.P.
[64] See Chapter 4, below pp. 121-130.

Bell and Newby on Stein on Warner! – some comments will be made
on the weaknesses of this approach.

There is a connection between the three processes and the title of
Stein's book. Stein wrote: 'American communities can be seen continuing the vital processes uncovered in Muncie by the Lynds.
Substantive values and traditional patterns are continually being discarded. . . . Community ties become increasingly dependent upon
centralized authorities and agencies in all areas of life. On the other
hand, personal loyalties decrease their range with the successive
weakening of national ties, regional ties, community ties, family ties,
and finally ties to a coherent image of one's self. . . . Suburbia is so
fascinating just because it reveals the "eclipse" of community at one of
its darkest moments.'[65] For the moment we shall ignore the empirical
falsity of this last statement;[66] the argument, however, is clear: the
three processes of urbanization, industrialization and bureaucratization
are breaking up the above-mentioned complexes of primary group
relationships and resulting in the community's 'eclipse'. Martindale
has pointed out in a splendidly vitriolic article, however, that Stein uses
the term 'community' as though it refers to everything that has been
described as such, including cities. 'At the same time, urbanization is
inconsistently treated as one of the processes which bring the community into "eclipse". If the city is a community and if urbanization
represents the extension of patterns typical of a city, urbanization ought
more logically to represent a peculiar kind of community formation
rather than community destruction.'[67] Thus Stein can be seen to be
guilty not only of blurring the distinction between communities and
descriptions of them, but of the familiar interference of value judgements in the definition of community. This is a pity, for attempts to
synthesize the detailed knowledge contained in community studies of
particular, circumscribed and seemingly parochial social forces are
rare, but are nevertheless capable of contributing to a formulation of a
more general theory of societal processes.

Community Study as Method[68]

We have noted that Stein's interest in community studies was not
simply a seminal one, but an interest in what they could tell him about

[65] Stein, *op. cit.*, p. 329.

[66] See below, pp. 121-130.

[67] Don Martindale, 'The Formation and Destruction of Communities', in
G. K. Zollschan and W. Hirsch, *Explorations in Social Change*, Routledge,
London, 1964, p. 66.

[68] Since Chapter 3 explicitly deals with the methodological problems of
community studies, a more detailed elaboration is found there.

wider societal processes. In other words. Stein was less interested in the community as an *object of study* as in community studies being a *method* of elucidating data illustrative of some wider generalization. Such a view is echoed by Havinghurst and Jansen in their 'trend report' on Community Research, published as an edition of *Current Sociology* in 1967: 'A community study is not a branch of sociology, such as ecology, demography and social psychology. Rather it is *a form of sociological research* that is useful for a variety of research purposes.'[69] This approach to community studies leads the sociologist to ask a different series of questions in and of the community from those which are asked when the community is treated as an object. As Arensberg and Kimball remark 'The traditional community study has as its goal the enumeration of the attributes that distinguish it.'[70] They, on the other hand, are the principal proponents of the alternative approach of viewing the community study as a way, in their graphic phrase, of 'getting to grips with social and psychological facts in the raw'.[71] The community study is therefore seen as an example of the empirical, inductive tradition, the models created being 'won from raw data themselves, as knowledge of their interconnectedness and processes unfold from the facts gained in observational research. . . . The researcher must often learn within the field situation itself the questions he must ask.'[72] There will always be, therefore, a particularly close, hazardous, but potentially rewarding relationship between theory and method in community studies but, needless to say, such an approach is not without its difficulties. One is a methodological difficulty about proof (this will be dealt with in the next chapter). Another arises from the fact that, as Arensberg and Kimball argue, 'the thing-in-itself, the community as object, is imperfectly separated, in concept and in practice, from the use of it, as field or sample, where the community is that within which work is done, observations made, relationships traced out'.[73]

As a method, the community study is just one of a number of observational techniques, central to which is the 'massive immersion' (again to use Arensberg and Kimball's words) of the researcher. This will have certain rather problematical consequences for the researchers' data, not the least of which is how reliable and valid they are. An observational, rather than a statistical or experimental method, means

[69] R. J. Havighurst and A. J. Jansen, 'Community Research', *Current Sociology*, XV, 1967, p. 7 (our emphasis).
[70] Arensberg and Kimball, *op. cit.*, p. 30.
[71] *Ibid.*, p. 8.
[72] *Ibid.*, p. 8.
[73] *Ibid.*, p.8.

that the usual procedures of control, verification and reliability are quite different from those of, for example, survey research or small group experiments. These problems are again dealt with more fully in the following chapter. At its best, however, the community study is eclectic, utilizing whole batteries of techniques over and above the central one of observation. In bringing the researcher closer and closer to the interconnections of the data, the community study as a method has some clear advantages, but it does tend to produce idiosyncratic and non-comparable monographs, In conclusion it can be stated that unlike the ethnographer of primitive groups, the community sociologist rarely wants to study the whole community. Community study concerns, as Arensberg has written, 'the study of human behaviour *in* communities'.[74] What the field worker needs to know, therefore, is not 'everything' about a community, but how the data which he collects are related to his theory before, during and after his 'massive immersion'.

Communities as Types – the Rural-Urban Continuum

Treating communities as types is the closest approach to the classical tradition of Tönnies. It is also the most pervasive – the rural-urban dichotomy having passed into everyday usage – and, though put to death by several writers on the subject, it still refuses to lie down.[75] When dealing with community typologies we are dealing centrally with the rural-urban continuum, for all others have essentially taken this as their starting-point, either to present some variation on it or to set themselves up against it. It should be realized that this typological approach to communities is also a theory of social change – its aim is not merely to classify communities like so many butterflies, but also to say something about the nature and direction of social processes.

The idea behind the rural-urban continuum is a familiar one – we have met it already in our discussion of Tönnies' *Gemeinschaft and Gesellschaft*, and in Hillery's village-city continuum in the section on organizations. Perhaps the most famous recent figure in this tradition is Robert Redfield. Redfield, in his book *The Folk Culture of Yucatan*, published in 1941, drew up a list of five characteristics to be found in a folk society. What he used his community studies to test was the general thesis that the progressive loss of isolation, when associated with an increase in heterogeneity, produces social disorganization, secularization and individualization. He is postulating a continuum, from 'folk'

---

[74] *Ibid.*, p. 42.
[75] See for example Ray Pahl's, 'The Rural-Urban Continuum', *Sociologia Ruralis*, IV, 1966. Reprinted in his *Readings in Urban Sociology*, Oxford, Pergamon, 1968.

to urban, on which communities can be placed. His characterization of folk society is, however, much more complete than that of urban society-the latter being seen as the antithesis of the former. He summarized the traits of 'the folk society' in a paper with that title written in 1947: 'Such a society is small, isolated, non-literate and homogeneous, with a strong sense of group solidarity. The ways of living are conventional-ized into the coherent system which we call "a culture". Behaviour is traditional, spontaneous, uncritical and personal: there is no legislation or habit of experiment and reflection for intellectual ends. Kinship, its relations and institutions, are the type categories of experience and the familial group is the unit of action. The sacred prevails over the secular; the economy is one of status rather than the market.'[76] As a typology of community this lacks both specificity and focus, something which could be seen both as a strength and as a weakness. Its strength is that with such a multiplicity of traits a variety of causal relationships are suggested. Its great weakness is that it is not clear which are causes and which are effects, which should have the status of dependent variables and which should have the status of independent variables. However, as a supporter of this typology Minar has remarked: 'If we had the answer to all these questions, there would be no need for the ideal types.'[77]

In his paper, Redfield is quite explicit that 'the type (i.e. the Folk Society) is an imagined entity, created only because through it we may hope to understand reality'.[78] If the folk society is placed at one end of a continuum and its characteristics are very similar to those usually associated more generally with the concept of 'community', it is difficult to escape the conclusion that as 'villages/settlements' (here an attempt has been made to deliberately avoid a 'loaded' term) are placed on this continuum further away from the folk society end, they are less and less 'communities'. The characterization of folk society can be con-sidered again with this point in mind. 'The folk society is a small society':[79] so in the folk-urban continuum, the larger the community, the more urban it is. 'The folk society is an isolated society':[80] therefore, the less isolated the more urban. 'This isolation is one half of a whole of which the other half is intimate communication among the members of a society':[81] so the less intimate the communication the more urban

[76] Robert Redfield, 'The Folk Society', *American Journal of Sociology*, 52, 1947, p. 293.
[77] H. Minar, 'Community-Society Continua', *International Encyclopaedia of the Social Sciences*, Vol. 3, p. 177.
[78] Redfield, *op. cit.*, p. 295.
[79] *Ibid.*, p. 295.
[80] *Ibid.*, p. 296.
[81] *Ibid.*, p. 296.

a community, presumably the ultimate being the stereotype of urban anonymity. 'We may conceive the members of the [folk] society as remaining always within the small territory they occupy':[82] so the more physical mobility, the more urban the locality. 'The people who make up a folk society are much alike':[83] so the more heterogeneous a community the more urban it is. Redfield also states that 'In such a society there is little change':[84] so the more change, the more urban a society. 'The members of the folk society have a strong sense of belonging together':[85] so, presumably, urban society is 'anomic'. 'Thus we characterize the folk society as small, isolated, non-literate and homogeneous with a strong sense of group solidarity;[86] and if we characterize urban society as the opposite – large, non-isolated, literate, heterogeneous, lacking a strong sense of group solidarity – we come close to Wirth's famous characterization of 'urbanism as a way of life'.[87]

There are a number of criticisms that can be made of this typology and of the rural-urban continuum conceptualization of social change. It is important to note that its purpose, as far as community studies are concerned, is to locate them both relative to each other and to some overarching theoretical schema. The main point against it is that it locates *social* relationships in a specific *locale*; this point will be taken up again in the next section on locality and networks, but it should also be noted that it was a problem presented to, but never reconciled by, the ecologists. This typology also focuses attention on the city as a source of social change and obscures the wide range of values and ways of life of individuals at the folk end of the continuum (and, for that matter, the urban end). Oscar Lewis, a significant critic of Redfield has written that ' . . . the question posed by Redfield, namely, what happens to an isolated homogeneous society when it comes into contact with an urbanized society, cannot possibly be answered in a scientific way, because the question is too general and in the terms used do not give us the necessary data. What we need to know is what kind of an urban society, under what conditions of contact and a host of other specific historical data.'[88] Redfield, indeed, so framed his basic questions that folk societies would necessarily appear more organized than cities. His typology overlooks the stability and success of city life, which has been

[82] *Ibid.*, p. 296. [83] *Ibid.*, p. 297.
[84] *Ibid.*, p. 297. [85] *Ibid.*, p. 297.
[86] *Ibid.*, p. 297.
[87] Louis Wirth, 'Urbanism as a Way of Life', *Amercian Journal of Sociology*, 44, 1938. See the elaborate discussion of this famous paper in R. N. Morris's *Urban Sociology*, London, Allen & Unwin, 1968.
[88] Oscar Lewis, *Life in a Mexican Village: Tepoztlan Restudied*, Urbana, University of Illinois Press, 1951, p. 434.

with us for thousands of years. It may also be argued that, in the tradition of the classical writers on community, Redfield's 'folk society' is riddled with value judgements. As Lewis states 'It contains the old Rousseauan notion of primitive peoples as noble savages and the corollary that with civilization comes the fall of man.'[89]

Joseph Gusfield documents the 'misplaced polarities' of the rural-urban continuum with data mainly from India.[90] He argues that it is fallacious to assume that a so-called folk society or traditional society has always existed in its present form or that its recent past represents an unchanged situation. It is similarly fallacious to believe that folk society has an homogeneous social structure. The old is not necessarily replaced by the new, there seems to be a great capacity for folk and urban cultures – so-called – to co-exist even with mutual adaptations. Urban culture, indeed, does not necessarily weaken folk culture – it may strengthen it. Manuel Avila's study of four 'traditional' rural Mexican communities, also provides a corrective to some of Redfield's misconceptions.[91] Avila found, for example, that these communities had a considerable capacity for economic growth, the peasants being neither unresponsive to market forces nor uninterested in improving their condition. Two of the four communities examined were also those studied by Redfield in the 1930s. And far from agreeing with the folk conceptions of Redfield he concludes: 'Contrary to the popular notions, neither stagnation, nor lack of interest have characterized [the four villages]. For the truth is that the villages have not been mere bystanders passively contemplating outside events. Instead they have been active promoters and development seekers, very much interested in working towards a better life.'[92] This is a far cry from the 'folk society'.

While it can thus be shown that the rural 'end' of the continuum is not a single type of unchanging entity, the urban end too, despite the writings of Wirth, is extraordinarily difficult to conceptualize as a single way of life. Particularly troublesome are the so-called 'urban villages'. Lewis' work in Mexico City[93] has shown that peasants adapted to city life much more easily than folk-urban theory would suggest: Mayer has coined the term *encapsulation* to describe the situation of migrants in East London who live in the city but are not of the city.

[89] *Ibid.*, p. 435.
[90] Joseph Gusfield, 'Tradition and Modernity; misplaced polarities in the study of social change', *American Journal of Sociology*, 72, 1967.
[91] Manuel Avila, *Tradition and Growth*, Chicago, University of Chicago Press, 1969.
[92] *Ibid.*, p. 165.
[93] Oscar Lewis, 'Urbanization without Breakdown', *Scientific Monthly*, 75, 1965, *Children of Sanchez*, Penguin Books, 1964.

Thus, 'while some are born "urban" and others achieve urbanization, none can be said to have urbanization thrust upon them.'[94] Gans' paper, 'Urbanism and Suburbanism as Ways of Life'[95] is an important addition to this debate. In it he argues that, apart from urban villages, the central areas of cities are anyway by no means homogeneous, and he concludes that ecological and typological approaches are in no way sensitive enough. He maintains instead that *class* and *family cycle* have more value – the former is the best indicator of individuals' ability to *choose* and the latter determines the area of choice which is most likely. Gans concludes, 'If ways of life do not coincide with settlement type and if these ways are functions of class and life cycle rather than of the ecological attributes of the settlement, a sociological definition of the city cannot be formulated.'[96] This implies that no sociological definition of any settlement type can be formulated, and if this is true it would destroy notions of a rural-urban or any other continuum.

Despite these criticisms of Redfield's typology, it has continued to exert its influence. It clearly has the heuristic appeal of being a relatively simple way of conceptualizing social change and of classifying communities. Indeed there have been recent variations of this typology, which nevertheless take the folk-urban continuum as the starting point. Nancie L. Gonzalez, for example, has used the term 'neoteric society'[97] for the communities of Caribs she studied in the West Indies. She claims that this type cuts across the rural-urban or folk-urban continuum. The *barrios*, or shanty towns, surrounding the large cities of the West Indies and Latin America contain neither primitive nor peasant inhabitants and their traditions are either absent or very shallow and contemporary. The characteristics of the neoteric communities are their varied ethic or national origins, relative poverty, openness, secularity, face-to-face interpersonal relations and *lack* of apathy on the part of the people concerning the world and their future. They also tend to be matrifocal in their kinship organization. As she sums up, 'It may be a mistake to look for rural social organizational parallels in the city *barrios*. What we see may be new types of social organizations which only appear on the surface to be like that of the country, but which are structurally and functionally quite different precisely in terms of their relationships to higher levels of integration,'[98] i.e. the

[94] P. Mayer, 'Migrancy and the Study of Africans in Towns', *American Anthropologist*, 64, 1962, p. 591.

[95] H. J. Gans, 'Urbanism and Suburbanism as Ways of Life', in A. M. Rose (ed.), *Human Behaviour and Social Processes*, London, Routledge, 1952.

[96] *Ibid.*, p, 643.

[97] Nancie L. Gonzalez, 'The Neoteric Society', *Comparative Studies in Society and History*, 12, 1970.

[98] *Ibid.*, p. 13.

cities themselves. Gonzalez nevertheless clearly finds it useful to create an ideal type for the communities she has studied.

In contrast, Anthony Richmond has expanded the rural-urban continuum to include 'post-industrial' society,[99] developing it to include a number of traits, as shown in the table:

	Traditional	Industrial	Post-Industrial
Form of organizations	Gemeinschaft	Gesellschaft	Verbindingouretzschaft
Typical way of interaction	Communities	Associations	Social Networks
Principle mode of production	Agricultural	Mechanical	Automated
System of stratification	Quasi-feudal	Class	Meritocracy
Main means of communication	Oral	Written	Electronic
Main means of transport	Horse & sail	Rural-Urban	Inter-urban
Type of migration	Forced (push)	Voluntary (pull)	Transilient (two-way)
Mode of migration of migrants	Assimilation/ isolation	Pluralistic	Active mobilization

In his work, the post-industrial community, or rather social networks, are 'social systems in which the characteristic forms of social interaction take place through networks of communication maintained by means of telephone, teleprinter, television and high-speed aircraft and spacecraft, etc. Such relationships are not dependent upon a territorial base or face-to-face contact, nor do they involve participation in formal organization. Behaviour is governed by a constant feed-back from highly efficient information storage and retrieval processes based upon diffuse networks of interdependent communications systems.'[100] Its advantage as an ideal type for a student of migration, which Richmond is, is that, unlike the folk society, it does not propagate the myth of the static society. Its fundamental misconception is the equally fallacious one of the totally mobile, 'McLuhanized' society. It is worthwhile repeating the objection briefly touched upon in our Introduction – that people still live and breed somewhere.

The current 'neo-ecological' school of American sociologists, Schnore and Duncan[101] in particular, also suggests that there is a multi-

[99] Anthony Richmond; 'Migration in Industrial Societies', in J. A. Jackson (ed.), *Migration*, London, Cambridge U.P., 1969, p. 272.

[100] *Ibid.*, p. 278

[101] See for example Leo F. Schnore, 'The Rural-Urban Variable', *Rural Sociology*, 31, 1966; and Otis Dudley Duncan, 'Community Size and the Rural-Urban Continuum', in Paul K. Hatt and Albert J. Reiss (eds), *Cities and Society*, Glencoe, Free Press, 1957 (London, Collier-Macmillan, 1957).

dimensional continuum between rural and urban communities. Indeed there is a great deal of data, some of which will be discussed in later chapters, to suggest, in the words of Leo Schnore, that rural-urban differences 'while clearly diminishing are still crucial'.[102]   They have demonstrated this with the use of demographic data on the size of community and its rate of change, its density, the age of the settlement and its independence (is it dependent on other communities?), its sex and age composition and the rates of migration. Yet when they turn to the 'structural aspects of community', which are not so readily amenable to ecological mapping, they do not really demonstrate that there are rural-urban differences. Schnore says that '. . . it is no wonder that the sociological understanding of community is at a fairly primitive level' because the 'manifold threads of interrelationships make the community very complex system'. He writes that 'the analysis of community structure remains an important task of sociological effort'[103] – a plea reminiscent of that of Hawley's on p. 35. In fact, neither need have been so pessimistic, for out of the idea of the rural-urban continuum has come some of the more promising advances in the analysis of community. These will be dealt with in the final section.

Community, Locality and Network

The final section of this chapter attempts to show the directions in which sociological thought on the concept of community is moving. A consensus on the theory of community appears as remote as ever, though this is not to say that the area of discourse has not shifted somewhat. The broad lines of debate are now between those who regard the community as a legitimate *object* of sociological inquiry, while at the same time, perhaps, wishing to alter the nomenclature, and those who do not.

Those who regard the community as a legitimate object of sociological enquiry clearly have to resolve the problems of definition and value judgements. There must be a departure from the *Gemeinschaft* conceptualizations of communities where, as John Jackson has written, there is a 'harking back to some pre-existing rural utopia' in which 'the natural condition of man is sedentary',[104] and movement away from which is a deviant activity 'associated with disorganization and a threat to the established harmony of *Gemeinschaft* relationships which are

[102] Schnore, *op. cit.*, p. 131.

[103] Schnore, 'Community', in N. Smelser (ed.), *Sociology*, New York, Wiley, 1967, p. 114.

[104] Jackson, *op. cit.*, p. 3.

implied by a life lived within a fixed social framework'.[105] Value judgements are one problem, ambiguity is another: König has shown that 'there is a good deal of very obvious ambiguity', even in the German derivation of the word (*Gemeinschaft, Gemeinde, Gemeinderschaft*) and particularly between the 'community as an administrative unit and the community as a social reality'.[106]

One solution to the problems of the definition of community, indeed an avoidance of the term 'community' altogether, has been proposed by Margaret Stacey.[107] If institutions are locality based *and* interrelated there may well be, she argues, a *local social system* that is worthy of sociological attention. She does not want to call this local social system a 'community' for the latter, she feels, is a non-concept. In other words, Stacey claims that the definitional debate about community is something more; it represents a much more serious conceptual disagreement about whether the community is a geographical area, or a sense of belonging, or non-work relations and so on. Instead, sociologists should concentrate on institutions and their interrelations in specific localities. Stacey is not concerned whether a locality is isolated or not. She writes, for example, that 'the consequences for the social relations within a locality of changes introduced from outside have after all produced some interesting studies'.[108] Stacey's approach brings a welcome rigour to the field and she writes that it is possible to talk with some certainty about '(i) the establishment and maintenance of a local social system; (ii) local conditions where no such system can be expected; (iii) some circumstances under which an existing system might be modified or destroyed; (iv) certain interrelations between systems and their parts; (v) the interaction of local and national systems'.[109]

Stacey's concept of a 'local social system' will obviously be empirically varied, for the nature and configuration of the interrelations of social institutions are very diverse. Rarely will there be a completely inter-related social system, with all institutions present: in any given locality it is likely, as she says, that 'there will either be no local social system, or some kind of partial local social system'.[110] Stacey does not intend that the 'complete local social system' should be open to the same sort of objections as the concept of 'community' or, for that matter, 'folk society'. She is arguing that it is theoretically possible to list systematically the social institutions which might be present in a locality with all

[105] *Ibid.*, p. 3.
[106] Rene Konig, *The Community*, London, Routledge, 1968., p. 1.
[107] Margaret Stacey, 'The Myth of Community Studies', *British Journal of Sociology*, 20, 1969.
[108] *Ibid.*, p. 139.
[109] *Ibid.*, p. 139.
[110] *Ibid.*, p. 141.

their interconnections. This can be regarded as a model and against it the empirically observed presence and absence of institutions and connections can be plotted. Another significant aspect of Stacey's argument is her insistence on the inclusion of time as a dimension – '. . . the state of a system at a given moment in time will be considered and the temporal conditions which have led to that state and what may follow will be indicated'.[111]

She concludes her paper with thirty-one interrelated propositions about local social systems. It is not possible here fully to reproduce her argument in all its complexity, but two examples of the kind of propositions about local social systems that she makes can be given:

Proposition 9:   'Where any substantial institutions are greatly changed the system cannot work as it did previously, as in Banbury where new economic relations were introduced'.[112]

Proposition 18:   'In localities where there is a local social system there will also be elements of other social systems present in the locality, i.e. the local social system will not totally encompass all institutions and relationships present, e.g. migrants bring with them *nationally legitimated* rights to vote for *local* political bodies'.[113]

Central to Stacey's case is her argument that because the totality of social relations may not be found in the locality, this does not necessarily mean that there is nothing worth studying. The 'eclipse' of the local system is highly unlikely, though these propositions make it clear that it is going to be necessary to consider some social processes working from outside the locality.

How can this be done? Robert Warren, in his book, *The Community in America*,[114] calls the national and local dimensions of the local social system the 'vertical' and the 'horizontal'. Warren argues that the locally based intertwining of lives provides an important social reality and focus of study but that a 'great change' has come over the American community involving the increasing orientation of local community units towards extra-community systems. Warren sees in this a corresponding decline in community cohesion and autonomy. Warren defines a community's 'vertical' pattern as 'the structural and functional relation of

[111] *Ibid.*, p. 141.
[112] *Ibid.*, p. 142. The reference here is to her own *Tradition and change*, 1961, which is discussed in more detail in Chapter 5.
[113] *Ibid.*, pp. 143–4.
[114] Robert Warren, *The Community in America*, Chicago, Rand McNally, 1963.

its various social units and sub-systems to extra-community systems',[115]
while the 'horizontal' pattern is 'the structural and functional relation
of its various social units and sub-systems to each other'.[116] The
'great change' involves the increasing vertical orientation of local communities and Warren examines it in terms of seven aspects: the division
of labour, differentiation of interests and associations, increasing systematic relationships to a larger society, bureaucratization and imper-
sonalization, transfer of functions to profit enterprise and government,
urbanization and suburbanization, and finally, changing values. Within
the locality will be individuals, those, for example, Merton has called
'cosmopolitans'[117] and Stacey 'non-traditionalists', who are in Warren's
terms more strongly oriented vertically in the community participation,
and others, those Merton calls 'locals' and Stacey 'traditionalists', who
are more strongly oriented horizontally.[118]

Warren's schema presents a framework within which the study of
social processes impinging on the locality from outside can be ac-
commodated, and this provides a complementary addition to Stacey's
approach. It should be recognized, however, that Stacey remains in the
mainstream of community sociologists, despite her denunciation of the
term, for considering the local social system, or what others have
termed the community, as an object of study. Other recent approaches
that have emerged from the declining influence of the rural-urban
continuum, however, deny even this. Both Gans and Pahl,[119] for
example, doubt the *sociological* relevance of the physical differences
between 'rural' and 'urban' in highly complex industrial societies. We
are being asked to consider, in other words, whether the community is a
sociological variable at all or merely a 'geographical expression'. Such
an approach has resulted from recent detailed work on communities
which has shown that, far from there being an exclusive continuum
from *Gemeinschaft* to *Gesellschaft*, relationships of *both* types are found
in the *same* community. The Parsonian pattern-variables, breaking
down as they do the solidary concepts of *Gemeinschaft* and *Gesellschaft*,
have opened the way for analysis along these lines. As Gans has
observed, 'Ways of life do not coincide with settlement patterns.'[120]
The emphasis for the sociologist, then, should not be on geographical
demographic or economic indicators but on *changing social relations*.
Pahl in his important critical article on the rural-urban continuum[121]

[115] *Ibid.*, p. 151.   [116] *Ibid.*, p. 162.
[117] R. K. Merton, *Social Theory & Social Structure*, Glencoe, Free Press
1957.
[118] Stacey (1961), *op. cit.*
[119] Pahl (1966), *op. cit.*
[120] Gans (1962), *op. cit.*, p. 643.
[121] Pahl (1966), *op. cit.*

even concludes that he can find little universal evidence for such a continuum and he doubts its value as a classificatory device. He points out that there are a number of non-overlapping continua in the complex social relationships that should be examined, and that the isolation of one process is misleading. 'Whether we call the process acting on the local community "urbanization", "differentiation", "modernization", "mass society" or whatever, it is clear that it is not so much *communities* that are acted upon as groups and individuals at particular places in the social structure. Any attempt to tie patterns of social relationships to specific geographical milieux is a singularly fruitless exercise.'[122] He echoes Clifford Geertz[123] when he writes, 'Of much greater importance is the action of a fundamental distinction between the *local* and the *national* . . . '[124] and 'between the *small scale* and the *large scale*. . . .'[125] The local and the national confront each other in towns *and* in villages, and the same concepts and analytical tools can be used to analyse the consequent social processes in either. Here Pahl appears to be approaching a rapprochement with Warren but, whereas Warren regards the community as an object undergoing infiltration by and reorientation towards super-community systems, Pahl denies the existence of community altogether and is concerned only with nationally and locally oriented social groups.

The concept for analysing, indeed for conceptualizing, these social groups is the 'social network'. The 'social network' as an analytical tool stems from John Barnes' famous paper published in 1954,[126] in which he wrote that 'the image I have is of a set of points some of which are joined by lines. The points of the image are people, or sometimes groups, and the lines indicate which people interact with each other.'[127] This usage of the term social network has been followed by Elizabeth Bott in her book *Family and Social Network*.[128] She suggests that 'the immediate social environment of urban[129] families is best considered not as the local area in which they live, but rather as the network of actual social relationships they maintain, regardless of whether these are confined to the local area or run beyond its boundaries.'[130]

[122] Pahl, in his *Readings* (1968), *op. cit.*, p. 293.

[123] Clifford Geertz, *The Social History of an Indonesian Town*, Cambridge, M.I.T. Press, 1965.

[124] Pahl (1968), *op. cit.*, p. 285 (our emphasis).

[125] *Ibid.*, p. 286 (our emphasis).

[126] John Barnes, 'Class and Committees in a Norwegian Island Parish', *Human Relations*, 7, 1954.

[127] *Ibid.*, p. 43.

[128] Elizabeth Bott, *Family and Social Network*, London, Tavistock, 1957.

[129] There does not seem to us to be anything against changing the word 'urban' to 'all'.

[130] Bott, *op. cit.*, p. 99.

Two aspects of the concept are particularly relevant in the light of the foregoing discussion. Firstly, the 'mesh' or the 'connectedness' of the network clearly varies from locality to locality. Secondly, the 'range' or 'spread' of the network will vary from individual to individual. We would dispute the utility of Pahl's notion of networks as 'non-place communities'[131] and Bott's conceptualization of social change as 'from community to network'.[132] The latter we fail to understand as meaning anything but a move from one sort of network to another – perhaps from a 'close-knit' – meaning both a high proportion of connectedness and multiplexity – to a loose-knit network. Networks for some people will be locality bound, for others less so. Traditional notions of community may be subsumed under the label of a 'locality bound, close-knit network'. Indeed one of the changes that is occurring for many, but not all social groups is that social networks are becoming less locality bound and less close-knit. What the precise change has been will only be discoverable from detailed and painstaking empirical work, but it will certainly be more complex than the 'vulgar Tönniesism' of 'from community to network'. A battery of concepts has recently been elaborated by Clyde Mitchell and his colleagues[133] to analyse networks that carefully distinguishes between their morphological or structural characteristics, and their content.

What little empirical data there is directly relating to social networks leads us to believe that it is indeed a powerful analytical tool and that the two most powerful independent variables working on the structure and content of the social network are class and family cycle. When a satisfactory way of recording social networks has been worked out, then we will be well on the way to having comparable and theoretically relevant data on communities. How far we are from this position will be seen in the next chapter.

[131] Ray Pahl, 'Patterns of Urban Life', London, Longmans, 1970, p. 106.

[132] Elizabeth Bott, 'Family, Kinship & Marriage' in Mary Douglas et al. (eds), Man in Society, London, Macdonald, 1962, p. 102.

[133] J. Clyde Mitchell (ed.), Social Networks in an Urban Situation, Manchester, Manchester U.P., 1969.

Community Study as a Method of Empirical Investigation

IN the previous chapter we discussed the view that communities, unlike organizations, such as factories and schools, or institutions, such as the family, should not and cannot be objects of study for social scientists. Nevertheless, some sociologists who hold this view have still produced community studies, not as *objects* in their own right, but as *samples* of cultures: they have used the community study as a *method*, in the words of Arensberg and Kimball, for 'getting to grips with social and psychological facts in the raw'. This is one reason for considering community study, in some detail as a method of investigation before examining what has been discovered, both *about* and *in* communities.

It would be considered alarming if a scientist's results were the product of his methods of research rather than the phenomena under study–although some techniques *are* more suitable for some phenomena than others. It would be reasonable in the first instance, though, to suggest that if phenomena of class A, located (in time and space) at B, can be studied with a set of techniques T, then all phenomena A, regardless of B, could be studied with techniques T. Put like that, and letting A = community, it quickly becomes apparent that T has varied enormously, so much so that it is doubtful about the unity of A. Community study as a method has been so varied and eclectic, and so determined by the object of study, that some doubt must be cast on whether there is a single community study method. There seem to be as many community study methods as there have been community studies. Nevertheless it is possible to make some generalizations and to underline both the strengths and weaknesses of such eclecticism.

The first and most important generalization, from which much else follows, is that community sociologists have usually gone, sometimes for only a short while, to *live* in *their* community. Community sociologists are fieldworkers: they have shared *some* of the experience of *some* of the inhabitants of the locality in which they are interested. This sharing of experience is not, of course, always conducive to the supposed ideal detachment of the scientist. It accounts for the fact that, unlike much of contemporary sociology, community studies are often so vivid and alive. It also accounts for the fact that so many other sociologists are so impatient with these studies – impatient with their idiosyncrasy, their non-cumulative nature – and why it has been said that community studies are the poor sociologist's substitute for the novel. It is not to be expected that two novels by two different authors will be cumulative in the normal sense of the word. Similarly no one expects scientific detachment from the novelist. Yet there are ways of evaluating the procedures and techniques of the community sociologist – ways that will help test the validity of the substantive findings of the many monographs on many communities.

The sociologist of the community is prepared to leave the cloister or plate glass tower of his academic institution for a short while, rarely for more than a year or so, and live in a community. Some have managed to avoid this fate and have studied aspects of their university town. The major example of this is the Chicago school, who will be discussed in more detail below (see Chapter 4). However, even the Chicago ecologists were great pounders of the streets and frequenters of taxi-dancehalls. They talked and listened to, and watched people in their natural habitat, to use their own analogy. They were very close, physically and emotionally to what they were studying. This is true of most community sociologists and one frequent criticism that is made, therefore, of community studies is that they are over-involved and not detached. This usually means that community studies are very sympathetic – critics would say, over-sympathetic – portraits of a locality.

Communities can be understood as on-going systems of interaction, usually within a locality, that have some degree of permanence. This interaction occurred before the sociologist arrived (though in some new communities the sociologist has arrived with the first inhabitants) and will continue after he has left – unless he 'goes native', a rare but not unknown occurrence. The implication of this is that usually the sociologist must somehow both 'fit-in' and be 'fitted-in' with this on-going system of interaction. Whilst some North American Indian groups are now said to have put their anthropologist on their genealogies, most communities have no place in their social structure for the sociologist. When community studies involve fieldwork – and most do – and as fieldwork involves role-playing, then a prime consideration must be the role of the fieldworker in the community.

This is especially paramount when the community which is studied is small – if nothing else has been learned from the study of small communities it is that 'everybody knows everybody else'. They are what are usually known as face-to-face societies. And in this case the community sociologist will also have to be face-to-face with the inhabitants of the locality. He will have to become 'known' and be able to be 'placed' in the local social structure. There are hardly any communities, no matter how small and isolated, that have no place for an outsider or stranger. It is to this position that the community sociologist is likely to be allocated in the first instance. And outsiders or strangers are treated in particular ways – ways that do not necessarily facilitate field work and the collection of data. Outsiders in the small and isolated Irish community described by John Messenger called Inis Beag were not that infrequent.[1] However, past experience had taught the islanders that outsiders fell into four broad categories. The first he clearly was not – that of priest, though Messenger shows that if the priest had turned anthropologist he would certainly not have had full access to information about the islands' culture, especially the belief system. There were things that you told priests and things that you did not. The next two categories of outsider were taxman or tourist. Taxman was an omnibus category that covered any representative from Dublin, be it an excise man looking for illicit stills and preventing smuggling, a 'dole' man checking whether those in receipt of assistance were actually unemployed or not, or the man who measured the height of the stone walls for which subsidies were paid by the foot. Messenger was not one of those, it turned out, because he brought his wife to the island. There was, therefore, a strong possibility that he fell into the third category, that of tourist. Just as there were ways of reacting to priests and taxmen, so there were to tourists. They were to be told folky tales, sold curios at exorbitant prices and importuned to stand rounds in the bar. However, Messenger was lucky in the fourth category into which the islanders placed strangers: Inis Beag is part of the Gaelic-speaking Atlantic fringe with the whole region under the critical eye of Irish folklorists and the islanders were used to schoolmasterly interest in customs and beliefs – though not into questions about the family and sexual practices. However, Messenger was an American, and though the islanders had initially reacted to him as a folklorist and therefore overemphasized their interest in their history and their ability in Gaelic, they eventually had to invent another category for him. Beattie, when he was studying

[1] John Messenger, *Inis Beag: Isle of Ireland*, New York, Holt, Rinehart & Winston, 1969.

the Bunyoro, wanted to distinguish himself from the colonial administration and the missionaries – the white men with whom the Bunyoro were familiar. To do this he grew a beard and lived in a tent, both of which had the desired effect.[2]

In any community, then, the community sociologist or anthropologist must be categorized by the locality. This may imply teaching the locality a role that is new to them. The components of this role will have to be elaborated to the community. Naturally it will seem strange to them that here is someone who is paid for apparently doing nothing but gossiping and chatting. It will mean that the 'rules of gossip', as Max Gluckman[3] has called them, must first be learned and then kept. Initially, fieldwork is always difficult and these difficulties will not be resolved until some satisfactory position has been adopted in the local social structure. These difficulties might be called 'entry' problems.

Indeed, social systems can be categorized by the degree of difficulty of entry for the fieldworker. The importance of this period cannot be overemphasized for on it depends both the success or failure of the whole project and also the nature of the results. For entry determines the position into which the fieldworker is adopted. Once the fieldworker is 'placed' it will be difficult – in a small community at least – to change positions. And his position in the local structure will determine what he sees.

To do fieldwork, to collect data in a factory, for instance, involves the initial decision of whether the fieldworker is going to be open about what he is doing or not. If it is decided not to be open about the research project there is nothing, save the ethics of the fieldworker, to prevent him being hired by the firm and covertly collecting data. There are several examples of this, notably Melville Dalton's *Men who Manage*.[4] The usual justifications for this procedure are that the data wanted would not have been available to the open fieldworker, or that if it was known by those being studied that they were in fact being studied, they would behave differently in some way. It is questionable, though, how far the legitimate desire to be unobtrusive makes recompense for misleading – usually a sin of omission rather than commission – the people studied. However, if it is decided to work openly, either for pragmatic reasons – because the data will be fuller or better – or 'ethical' reasons – because it's proper – some degree of sponsorship is necessary. Permission will have to be asked for and may only be granted with certain conditions – which may include, of course, suppression of results that the sponsors find unpleasant. Sponsorship

[2] John Beattie, *Understanding an African Kingdom: Bunyoro*, New York (and London), Holt, Rinehart & Winston, 1965.

[3] Max Gluckman, 'Gossip and Scandal', *Current Anthropology*, 4, 1963.

[4] Melville Dalton, *Men Who Manage*, New York (and London), Wiley, 1959.

may therefore imply some degree of control and perhaps some degree of identification with the sponsors. In the example of studying a factory it will be the management and/or the owners that will have to be approached first, albeit in consultation with the trade unions. There may thereafter be some identification with the management of the research workers. This may mean that in a conflict situation behaviour will be seriously biased – the fieldworkers will be told only things that the employees want the management to know. Indeed, unless the sociologists are very careful they will be seen as a branch of management: say as work-study consultants brought in to extract more work for less pay. Put like this it is easier to see why some industrial sociologists operate by stealth. Factories are closed systems – though less closed than say mental hospitals, prisons and ships. For a fieldworker to gain entry requires either guile or sponsorship. Once in and sponsored, it is possible, with managements' and unions' permission, to choose to work openly or covertly. In the case of having gained entry by guile the fieldworker can only work covertly or be excluded from the factory.

Communities in most western societies are open systems – at least when compared to factories or total institutions. The fieldworker is, however, still faced with the basic choice of working openly or working covertly. As long as the fieldworker can find somewhere to live – and this alone can sometimes be an insuperable obstacle – he can study the locality. Unlike studying a factory, sponsorship is not necessary. However, if the fieldworker wishes to work openly, publicity will be required for everybody in the community to know what he is doing. A condition laid down by the grant-giving foundations for the second study of Banbury was that the town should give its permission. But who is the town? The town clerk was asked, but he was responsible to the town council and so they had to be asked. The whole study became a matter for political debate in the council chamber, for it was unreasonable to expect two political parties divided on so many other issues to agree on this one. After the study had been going a few months a public meeting was held to explain to the people of Banbury what was happening. This was only really attended by town leaders and so the town as a whole was not informed. The press reported the activities of the research team and so, in a way, the fieldworkers lost control of their own publicity. This was in a relatively large town of 26,000 people, but there have been similar difficulties in smaller communities.

Entry into the community, into local social groups, may well involve something very similar to sponsorship. When William Whyte Jr first went in search of Street Corner Society,[5] he totally failed to connect

[5] William J. Whyte *Street Corner Society*, 2nd edition and his essay in Vidich, Bensman and Stein *op. cit.*

with it – nobody would talk to him and he could see nothing of significance going on. It was not until he was adopted by one of the most famous figures in sociological field work, 'Doc', that Whyte literally got anywhere. Whyte was accepted in Boston's East End because of his relationship to 'Doc'. Luckily for Whyte 'Doc' was a central figure, the leader of a gang. Whyte therefore saw what 'Doc' saw, and 'Doc' being the leader, saw most things. Though Whyte was adopted into the structure of social relations in a group that 'hung out' on street corners and in settlement houses, he did not have to totally alter his behaviour. True he found himself behaving in ways which, as an upper-middle-class Boston WASP, he found reprehensible and surprising: he 'repeated' in local elections – voted several times like the rest of the political racketeers. Yet when he swore in the company of a gang who swore all the time, there was a shocked silence. He was told that he did not have to talk like that.

'Doc' was Whyte's 'key informant' on the local social structure and clearly was central in that social structure. That was why he was able to help Whyte so much – as Whyte recognizes, 'Doc' is really a co-author of *Street Corner Society*. But what if Whyte had been adopted by someone else, say in a gang that was about to split – would he then have had such insight into the other half of the gang? Or if he had been adopted by a marginal character? It is by no means certain that in a fieldwork situation the fieldworker will be adopted by the most prominent individual – he may get attached to less socially secure characters lower in the social pecking order. And once attached this may take him below the level of recognition for the leader – anyone friendly with a marginal figure in 'Doc's' gang might not have been seen as worth befriending by 'Doc'.

Yet some community sociologists have advocated seeking out marginal men for informants. Vidich and Bensman,[6] for example, suggest that alienated small town intellectuals, say newspapermen, are sufficiently detached from the local social structure to be able to articulate it for the fieldworker. This point of view has a great deal to recommend it: marginal individuals will not be so involved, will not accept, or will at least be prepared to question, the prevailing normative structure – the small town ethos. Vidich and Bensman obviously feel that they saw behaviour for what it actually was in Springdale, having cut through the mystifying ideology of many of the town's inhabitants. All that can be suggested at this point is that perhaps one consequence of their use of marginal informants is the shrill tone of *Small Town and Mass Society*

[6] Arthur J. Vidich and Joseph Bensman, 'Participant Observation and the Collection and Interpretation of Data', *American Journal of Sociology*, 1955; reprinted in 2nd edition of *Small Town in Mass Society*, 1968.

compared to the sympathetic analysis of Whyte's *Street Corner Society*. Marginal informants are marginal, central informants are central, their view of the local social system will differ, hence the sociologist's findings differ. This is one reason why it is necessary to consider in detail in this book the methods used by sociologists to study the community.

It was said at the beginning of this chapter that techniques of community study varied so much that it could reasonably be wondered whether the same phenomenon was being studied. The problem that must be faced here is that of the size of the community. If there is a qualitative change in the nature of social relations between small and large communities then naturally techniques appropriate for studying them may also change. Frankenberg has claimed that on the one hand there are those communities (small ones) best studied by what he calls face-to-face methods, in which the research worker should supplement his findings by what are normally understood as survey methods, and on the other there are those communities (larger ones) which are best studied by survey methods supplemented by face-to-face methods,[7] the obvious point being that some communities are too large to study by face-to-face methods. This all seems very unexceptional, at least until it is remembered that it is also at this point (there is no agreement on precisely what this point should be, but there is some consensus that it lies in communities between 10,000 and 30,000 in population) beyond which it is doubted whether 'community' exists. 'Community' is found in small localities studied by face-to-face methods and tends not to be found in large localities studied by survey methods of social investigation. This looks very suspicious and must be considered carefully.

The desire to give a total and inclusive portrait of a locality, which if it is a town means to the edge of the built-up area, has naturally led the sociologist of the larger locality to use survey techniques. This forecloses on certain important questions – the most important of which is whether the built-up area is a significant social universe for its inhabitants. The fact is that for most of the inhabitants of the town it is far less than the built-up area that is significant, and that for others, especially those of higher social status, it is a far larger area that should be considered.[8] Delimiting an administrative area and sampling within it seems a very good way of not getting at something called 'community'.

[7] R. Frankenberg, *Communities in Britain*, Harmondsworth, Penguin Books, 1966.

[8] For evidence supporting the first point see the *Community Attitude Survey* of the Royal Commission on Local Government (the 'Maud Report'); on the second point see Margaret Stacey, *Tradition and Change* and James Littlejohn, *Westrigg*, London, Routledge, 1963.

The sample survey as normally carried out by sociologists is a wonderful instrument for collecting facts about individuals. It facilitates the collection of these facts by bureaucratically convenient categories and allows them to be statistically described. This is obviously worthwhile and valuable, especially for providing descriptive parameters for the locality, yet the survey is arguably of marginal relevance for studying the community. Despite there being little agreement on what community is, most sociologists include within their definition of community, and for that matter their subject, something about interaction. Interaction implies that there are groups, persistently patterned interaction implies social institutions and their interrelation implies social systems. This is the subject matter of the sociologists, not individuals. So when the sociologist studying a locality uses as his major or sole data collection instrument the sample survey and concludes that it is not a 'community', it is hardly surprising and could hardly have been otherwise. Indeed it is even more suspicious when survey analysists do find something called 'community', for it must have been despite, rather than because of, their research instruments. Survey analysists sometimes have a peculiar view of fieldwork techniques. Lois R. Dean, in her *Five Towns: A Comparative Community Study* (the data on which it is based is almost entirely survey data) wrote of her methods ' . . . and finally: much of our method was anthropological. That is, we spent as much time as we could just wandering about, soaking up the community atmosphere. We stayed in the principal hotel if there was one, read the local papers regularly, collected documents from the Chamber of Commerce and drank in the hotel lounge.'[9] This should not be confused with social science.

These critical comments on survey techniques imply that there is a limit to the size of locality that can be studied by the community sociologist. It does *not* necessarily imply that there is a limit to the size of community – just that one sociologist or even a team of sociologists are, not unnaturally, limited in what they can cover. These seemingly simple points have not always been understood, but once they are it is possible to move beyond notions of rural-urban dichotomies, or even continua, that have so bedevilled the sociology of community. Theory and methods have for once been interrelated and in this case to the detriment of sociology. Inappropriate methods have been used to buttress an unsound theoretical position. Community sociologists will always have to delimit their area of investigation, though they should do so in socially significant terms – to those they study, that is. They will go on studying the small town, but when they turn, for

[9] Lois R. Dean, *Five Towns: A Comparative Community Study*, New York, Random House, 1967, p. 21.

example, to a great metropolis, just because they cannot study all the local interaction, they cannot say that there is no community. True there is no single community, but nor is there in many small towns, as will be shown in the succeeding chapters. There are many communities in London or New York or Johannesburg or Cairo or Calcutta, not a lack of community.[10]

If there are good reasons for doubting the suitability of the social survey for the community sociologist what, then, should be his research tools? And what should be his procedures? It is in answering these questions that most of the rest of this chapter will be concerned. The answer has already been implied earlier when it was said that the one common feature of most community studies was that the sociologist went to live in his community. He is his own research instrument. It is how *he* reacts, it is what *he* sees and what *he* records. The positivist analogies with litmus paper or a thermometer are far too crude – it is clearly understood how litmus paper works and what it measures. It can be guaranteed to do so in the same way over and over again. That is also what is so good about thermometers. It is not possible always to know what the fieldworker in a community measures, or how, or whether he, let alone anybody else, would do so again. What *is* possible is to produce a general discussion that will sensitize both future community sociologists and the readers of their monographs to the main problems.

It quickly becomes apparent from a cursory examination of the field of community studies that many have been carried out using the techniques of classical social anthropology established by Malinowski. Indeed, in most of this book the labels sociologist and anthropologist are used almost interchangeably and tend more than anything else to reflect the institutional and academic allegiance of the social scientist. It is not a distinction that we find very useful. However, it is necessary to point out the limitations of traditional anthropological techniques when they are used uncritically in communities of advanced industrial societies. One of the baldest statements of intent and practice is that made by Lloyd Warner when he wrote that he had 'studied American communities with the techniques [he] previously used in the investigation of Australian tribes, and other anthropologists have used in Africa, Polynesia and New Guinea'.[11] The specific consequences of this

[10] As Janet Abu-Lughod wrote, '. . . Cairo is not one community but, rather, many separate social communities. . . . A member of one community may pass daily through the physical site of communities other than his own, neither "seeing" them nor admitting their relevance to his own life. But, within his own community, there is little if any anonymity.' 'Migrant Adjustment to City Life: The Egyptian Case,' *American Journal of Sociology*, 67, 1961, p. 31.

[11] W. Lloyd Warner, *Yankee City*, Yale (and London), Yale U.P., 1963.

for his findings in Yankee City will be discussed in the next chapter. It should, however, be remembered that anthropological methods were designed to study non-literate peoples. Communities in more advanced societies will have records that are also data – the social scientist may be in possession of the whole book not just the last page. If these records are treated as data, that is to say, to be questioned and checked like any other fieldwork data, they will give a dimension to community studies in advanced societies almost totally lacking in studies of communities without records. Warner specifically ignored the records of Yankee City, to his considerable cost. Anthropological studies are often 'historyless'. There is no excuse for this in community studies in advanced societies. Also anthropological studies usually treat communities as isolates – this is a great deal more hazardous in advanced societies where community studies must face the problem of the interrelationship of a particular community with the wider society.

One often stressed reason for following traditional anthropological methods is that it lays the ghost of ethnocentrism. Instead, anthropological methods suffer from what Robert Bierstedt has called 'temporocentrism'. This he defines as 'the unexamined and largely unconscious acceptance of one's own lifetime, as the centre of sociological significance, as the focus to which all other periods of historical time are related, and as the criterion by which they are judged'.[12] Though many community studies have adapted their techniques to studying larger, more complex, literate, interconnected communities with a history, there is one final drawback to using uncritically anthropological techniques. This is their 'localism', the belief in both the uniqueness of the community studied and its generality: as samples or microcosms of culture. Clearly a great deal of effort must be expended to show in what way a community is representative and it cannot be taken for granted that 'all America is in Jonesville' as Lloyd Warner once claimed.

Earlier, communities were compared to factories and the problems of entry for the fieldworker were discussed. Unfortunately there are crucial problems that precede this. A canon of scientific method is that explanations should not be imposed on data – that inconvenient facts cannot be ignored. In community studies they may not have been collected in the first place. Regardless of what sociologists claim, when they do empirical work many of them have a shrewd suspicion of what they are going to find. Indeed they may have a well worked out theoretical scheme before they start their research. Once in the field, theory acts like a pair of blinkers – it defines the field of vision. Theory

[12] Robert Bierstadt, 'The Limitations of Anthropological Methods in Sociology' *American Journal of Sociology*, 1948–9, pp. 27–8.

defines what is relevant and what is not; in a very real sense it determines what is seen. In many cases the rules of thumb that working sociologists use in the field cannot really be called 'theory' as such. But every sociologist brings to the fieldwork situation some expectations. For example, when W. M. Williams went to Gosforth. he was a postgraduate student in a department which used Fox's *Personality of Britain*. This work adopts an extreme geographical determinist position. Briefly it argues – from the evidence of the material remains of prehistoric peoples – that in Lowland Britain there was a replacement of cultures, whereas in Highland Britain there was a continuity of cultures. The first farmer Williams interviewed in Gosforth – which is, of course, in the Highland Zone – was living on a farm occupied continuously by his family since the sixteenth century. 'Continuity in the Highland Zone,' thought Williams. Indeed continuity of occupation is stressed when he discusses all farmers in Gosforth. However, when doing fieldwork in Ashworthy he discovered a system which he calls one of 'dynamic equilibrium' – a great deal of movement between farms, and farms changing shape. This led him to look again at both his Gosforth data and that of Arensberg and Kimball and to realize that he overstates the amount of continuity. In this case it was not that data were not collected but that they were interpreted in a particular way consistent with his preconceptions. It is necessary, then, to know the fieldworkers' preconceptions. Once entry has been effected into the community, the most frequently used techniques are those of participant observation.

Everett Hughes caught the strains and tensions of participant-observation well when he wrote that it was a dialectic between field-worker as stranger and fieldworker as friend.[13] That the community sociologist will initially be classified as 'stranger' is natural and has already been discussed. What is often forgotten is that to a great extent he remains a stranger, no matter how friendly he is with individuals he meets in the field. William Whyte is still in contact with individuals that he first met over thirty years ago in Boston's East End and yet he must remain a stranger. He and every other community sociologist *translate* the culture of the community studied into the language of their other culture: the current intellectual academic culture. This is what traditional anthropologists, at least until recently, have always done. This fact is more often forgotten when the community is also part of the same culture as the sociologist and the readers of his monograph. The fieldworker is a broker between two cultures and often his work shows the strains of this position.

13 Everett Hughes, 'Introduction' to Burford Junker, *Fieldwork*, Chicago (and London), University of Chicago Press, 1960.

Having gone to live in his community, having entered it and started to work there, he cannot but observe what goes on. What he sees, as already explained, depends in part on his preconceptions, sometimes rather grandly called his theory, and in part on his position in the ongoing system of social relations. If he does not have a position he can only observe; when he has a position, i.e. when he has 'got in' or has been adopted, he can become a participant observer as well. Participant observation in a social system as complex as most communities cannot be a single technique but is rather variable depending on the social situation. Put rather crudely, participant observation varies along a continuum from observation with no participation, to participation with no observation. It has been observed that the central paradox of the participant observation method is to seek information without asking questions. The questions that the fieldworker is asked are sometimes more important than the questions he himself asks.

In more advanced industrial societies the classical anthropological techniques – the 'I am a camera' approach – has serious limitations, for a great deal of social action takes place privately. Frankenberg has told us wistfully of how he would climb the hills about Glynceiriog – his *Village on the Border* – and envy his anthropological colleagues who just sat in the middle of their villages and watched what went on.[14] He gazed at the roofs of the council estate and wondered what went on inside them. Even in as small a community as this one there may well have been too much going on for him to study everything anyway, but much of what was happening, and he tells us that he was very busy, was happening behind closed doors. Entry problems have not ended for the community sociologist once he has set up house in the community and people have started to talk to him.

The fieldworker can observe but not really participate with people walking the streets or drinking in the pubs. He may feel, however, that this is not where the action is. Aiming to study political institutions in a locality when all that can be observed are council meetings will not be satisfactory. The example has been chosen deliberately, for it exemplifies many of the problems faced by the community sociologist whilst in the field. If he wishes to become more than a passive observer of poorly comprehended public behaviour he must move this technique along the continuum a way and include some participation. He will approach the political leaders and talk to them: no doubt at this stage he will be grilled as to his objectives and motives. He will want to attend meetings and watch the parties electioneering. The difficulties should now become apparent. It will be impossible to watch both parties

[14] Frankenberg, *op. cit.*

closely during an election as they will be in conflict. Even if they were always conveniently to hold important meetings at different times, political parties are unlikely to be willing to allow the same observer to be present. No matter how much the fieldworker stresses his stranger or scientist role, friendship – or what appears to be friendship – with members of one party will prevent close relationships with the opposition. The more polarized the situation, the more this will be true. It is virtually impossible to be friendly with both Catholics and Protestants in small towns in Northern Ireland. And in a small town in Co. Down for example, it would soon be known if one was talking to the other side. Once this was known the fieldworkers' information would dry up. There is no neutral ground and even complete outsiders – Scandinavian sociologists – in Northern Ireland have found it impossible for a single fieldworker to gather data on both sides. This was also the case in *Deep South*, a community divided radically in the Southern United States.[15] Whereas in Northern Ireland, it is possible for fieldworkers to avoid being thought of as 'green' or 'orange' as there are other categories such as 'English' or 'foreign', in the Deep South the fieldworker is either black or white. A white fieldworker cannot collect full data from blacks – though he can collect some, as the power structure favours his position, but a black fieldworker cannot talk to or observe whites. Certainly a lone fieldworker would be very limited as to what data he could collect. One solution to this problem, the one adopted in *Deep South*, was to have two couples, one black and one white. They found that they could not meet to discuss their research or findings in the town they were studying, but had to meet in neighbouring 'Big City' where they could do so more anonymously.

Whilst many communities are not so polarized as those in the Deep South of the United States, few are totally homogeneous and conflict free. In a conflict situation, even if it is possible for the fieldworker to remain personally detached (he may genuinely not care about the issues), it will be difficult for him to retain the appearances of detachment. And once this has happened it is probable that the other side will cease to talk to him and refuse him admittance to their meetings. It is necessary to add that many fieldworkers, for all their protestations, do not remain detached and feel as deeply on issues that divide a community as do the natives. In any case some semblance of concern will have to be shown, for it is virtually impossible to retain an air of indifference. This will eventually be suspected to mask opposition by informants who care deeply about an issue.

In short, in almost any community it will be impossible for a lone

[15] Alison Davis, B. B. and M. R. Gardner, *Deep South*, Chicago, University of Chicago Press, 1944; abridged edition, London, 1965.

fieldworker to collect full data from every side. Team work is essential. This does not mean that nothing of value can be produced by a lone fieldworker: that is obviously untrue, but he will find it difficult to write about both sides where there is any conflict. In the second Banbury study the two male fieldworkers studied one major political party each. This was not just for the pragmatic reason that there was too much for a single researcher to do, but because in the political situation existing in the town it was impossible to maintain good *rapport* with both sides: it was impossible not to be seen. The political parties, in fact, knew they were both being studied and appeared to accept this situation, for a prominent local politician once telephoned the research office in the town and asked whether he was speaking to the Tory or the Socialist fieldworker.[16]

There will be other divisions in the community which will make the task of the lone fieldworker difficult. One that is often overlooked is the sex division. The collection of data by women on some male activities is well-nigh impossible, and certainly the opposite is also true. The oft-thanked wife who appears in the last line of the acknowledgements of a monograph has, in fact, in many community studies been responsible for more than the index. The male fieldworker will have been dependent upon her for much of his data. Community study research teams should always have at least one female member.

Some of these problems can be planned for in advance. What it is useful to produce for the community about to be studied is the equivalent of what the social surveyors call 'quota controls', i.e. the major parameters of the community. Rarely is so little known in advance about a community that this cannot be done. This means drawing up schematically the crude outline of the social structure of the locality. Let a rectangle represent the community and then represent the major divisions known to be present. (See diagram on next page.) It is then possible to plan whether fieldwork can be done, say, on both sides of an ethnic divide, on men and women, on old and young, on the high status and the low. It has, for example, been found possible for the same fieldworker to collect data from the local aristocracy and the 'rough' working class, but not from the middle class and either. The fact that the aristocracy and the working class did not mix allowed the fieldworker, with appropriate behavioural changes, to work with both. The middle classes were not so sure about his activities when they extended above and below them in the social hierarchy.

Another reason for schematizing the community has to do with the

[16] It was later discovered that this was a much repeated joke on his side, as well as ours.

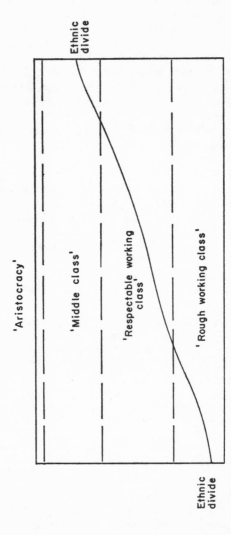

'Aristocracy'

'Middle class'

'Respectable working class'

'Rough working class'

Ethnic divide

Ethnic divide

(This diagram ignores sex, age and ecological distinctions that certainly would be relevant. There may well be in addition religious, political or cultural divides that should be acknowledged.)

vexed question of the representativeness of informants. It is as well during the fieldwork to occasionally stop and list the people that are providing most data and to categorize their data. The questions that must then be asked include, what groups do they represent? Who are not represented? For example, a group that many community sociologists have had most difficulty with are 'high status locals' – are they as well represented amongst the informants as the small town marginal intellectuals and professionals beloved of Vidich and Bensman? Are both sexes in all social classes and ethnic groups represented? And from all areas of the town? For without these kinds of checks it is difficult for both the fieldworker and the reader of his monograph to know how full and accurate are the data given. Several community sociologists have been accused of being 'captured' by their informants – of giving a view of the community that reflects the view of certain key informants. This would appear to be the case with Lloyd Warner whose LU informants are certainly over-represented in the quotations given in the Yankee City series. In most community studies the representativeness or otherwise of informants is impossible to judge, for little or no systematic information is given about them. A list of informants, together with some descriptive information about them, would seem to be as essential an appendix to community studies as sampling details and the questionnaire for studies produced from sample surveys. They are, however, singularly absent.

A reasonable question to ask at this point would be, if the only general characteristic of community studies is that their authors, or at least their research assistants, have gone to live in the community, that they themselves are their principal research tools, and that the principal technique is the variable one of participant observation, why is there this emphasis on informants? Should not the research workers be their own informants? One reason why they are not just their own informants is that they can only participate in and observe what is going on whilst they are there. This deliberately has two meanings: firstly they are there for only a short time and they must find out what went on before; secondly they cannot be everywhere, too much goes on too quickly, they may still not be admitted or not know something is happening, so they must ask. In addition they will want to know other peoples' reactions to events, and reactions do not always manifest themselves in observed behaviour. The final reason is unfortunately empirically likely to be the most frequent and is most likely to lead to the fieldworker losing the initiative and being captured. It is that it is all too easy to 'coast' with a 'good' informant, good here meaning friendly and having the time and inclination to chat. A 'good' informant is likely to share some of the objectives of the study, why else would he waste so much time? He might even share some of the values and attitudes of the researcher – this would seem to be true of Lloyd Warner's LU informants and Vidich and Bensman's alienated intellectuals. This is the time to get out the schematic diagram of the community to check just how representative these informants are.

It is also likely that by this time the informants have stopped treating the fieldworker as an outsider and have started treating him as a friend. The Everett Hughes dialectic should be remembered. For when this dialectic has ceased to exert a strain on the fieldworker, it is also likely that the fieldworker will begin to report that fieldwork is 'easy' and that he is 'really enjoying it'. Without the thesis and antithesis of stranger and friend continuing in some dialectical relationship it is unlikely that the overall quality of the data being produced will satisfy the scientist – the other role that the fieldworker must keep playing. The bitter pill that fieldworkers have to swallow, and nobody should do fieldwork in a community unless they are prepared to swallow it, is that many social relationships have to be developed for instrumental reasons and that they will not always be understood as such by those with whom the fieldworker has to interrelate in the community.

One reason for the stress so far in this chapter on procedural matters is the belief that these are good data in their own right for the community sociologist. How entry is effected into a community may give more insight into the community than fifty depth interviews. The roles that the community sociologist plays whilst in the field are good data. There is, though, a warning given by Oscar Lewis that needs to be heeded. He said that it was a mistake to believe that the inhabitants of a community necessarily behaved to each other in the same way as they treated him as fieldworker.[17] Lewis was of course a *gringo* outsider in Tepoztlan and so it was unlikely that the villagers would treat him in the same way as they did each other. He found that the villagers were open and trusting and friendly with him, yet were closed and suspicious and hostile with each other.

The fieldworker – as participant observer – will be involved with the people of the community. His position is, of course, curious in many ways – he will, for example, be playing fewer roles to the inhabitants than they play to each other. This means that he may well be in a position to resolve conflicts, though not necessarily willingly. The outsider or stranger can have decisions forced on him. Frankenberg has described the process brilliantly in his *Village on the Border*.[18] This role can also be played by members of the upper class. The stranger can be thrust into the position of appearing to take the decision, and gossip in

Oscar Lewis (1951), *op. cit.*, p. xvii.
[18] Ronald Frankenberg, *Village on the Border*, London, Cohen & West, 1957.

the village can then blame this outsider and allows the community to maintain the appearances and feelings of unity.

Conflicts are in fact resolved by persons who live outside the ordinary round of village life, and the fieldworker, similarly outside the ordinary life of the village, may find himself resolving conflicts in the political groups and voluntary associations into which he has worked his way. Apart from anything else, the fieldworker who is being used in this way has ceased to be unobtrusive. He will be altering the field of study and he must therefore report on his own activities as an actor in the system. Although, as in Frankenberg's case, this can give the fieldworker insight into fundamental social processes, it can be a difficult experience.

Though there are many good accounts of fieldworkers reflecting on their community studies, they are still the exception rather than the rule. It is difficult usually to know the role fieldworkers played or were allocated in the community. Herbert Gans, a sensitive fieldworker who has produced some such notes about his methods, very interestingly describes letting his private opinions show as 'performance breaks'. He was, therefore, very conscious in Levittown of putting on a performance – of playing a role. At any one time, this role was one of three types, which can in fact be seen as points on the participation – observation continuum mentioned above.[19] These roles are:

1. Total researcher,
2. Researcher-participant,
3. Total participant.

What he means by the first category are those occasions where he participated minimally, for example, as a silent member of a public meeting. In the second case he participated – but as a researcher rather than as a Levittowner or resident. The third category – which he claims is the most honest one – was when he acted spontaneously as friend or neighbour. In this case he was also affected by the events in which he participated. He also realized that if one loses consciousness of the research role, one becomes less observant of what is happening. For instance, one of Gans' ascribed roles in Levittown was that of neighbour, a role almost incompatible with that of social scientist. In studying the area in which he resides, it is inevitable that he would be caught up in the gossip: he, like everyone else living there, would be in a gossip cell. And the role of neighbour certainly precludes being given certain data.[20]

Levittown appears to be a particularly open community, however.

[19] H. J. Gans, *The Levittowners*, London, Allen Lane, 1967, pp. 439–40.
[20] See Colin Bell, *Middle Class Families*, London, Routledge, 1968 especially Chapter One.

Gans reported little difficulty in gaining access to all the information he wanted. Yet he states that he 'did not attend many religious functions (except in the Jewish community) partly because of lack of time, partly because people knew I was Jewish and I felt I would be intruding in a Christian religion's service to no useful purpose'.[21] He noted that he would not attend women's meetings either. Levittown was also fairly homogeneous and there were no marked conflicts, so he claims he 'did not have to worry about talking with a representative sample'. He was maintaining contact with at least fifty to seventy-five informants and talked altogether with four or five hundred. He admits, however, that he 'probably talked with proportionately more middle-class people than working-class ones, and with more upper middle-class than lower middle-class ones'.[22]

Gans realizes that he came to Levittown with some hypotheses – for example that critics of suburbia were wrong – and that this might have blinded him to some contradictory data. This hypothesis also meant that he was more sympathetic to Levittowners, but he claims that he avoided over-identification with them. Nevertheless this means that Gans was particularly concerned with the central problem for all participant observers – the concern about the deceptions which are required. This creates guilt and anxiety. Gans catches the dilemma well: 'If the researcher is completely honest with people about his activities, they will try to hide actions and attitudes they consider undesirable, and so will be dishonest. Consequently, the researcher must be dishonest to get honest data.'[23] The strain and tensions are well illustrated when Gans says that 'only when I was involved in activities which I did not expect to produce relevant data would I *relax* into the total participant role'.[24] Gans just wanted to be a total participant in the neighbourhood in which he lived, but not unreasonably his neighbours were very ambivalent about this. Away from where he lived he always announced himself as a researcher as soon as he could, so as to prevent uncertainty about his role. Gans was put in a conflict situation because the people with whom he was interacting in Levittown wanted him to

[21] We know, because of recording difficulties in the field (taking notes), that several fieldworkers have finished up as the secretaries of the associations that they were studying; this gives a satisfactory role although the responsibility of the fieldworker here is great. Minutes are not unbiased records of impartially observed events: they are usually couched in a semi-private language and have to be read between the lines. They may well be a charter for future action for the group. An unbiased record for this group would well be embarrassing – an over-zealous fieldworker records who votes for and against an issue when it was meant to be 'forgotten'.

[22] Gans, *op. cit.*, p. 440.

[23] *Ibid.*, p. 447.

[24] *Ibid.*, p. 445–6 (our emphasis).

take a non-research role – for example, because of his planning background he was under pressure to be on the Planning Board. He was also asked for advice on technical matters, which he did not give. Politically Levittown was 'all Republican and often quite conservative'.[25] Gans himself said that he generally voted Democratic. He was, therefore, very pleased to discover that a branch of the Democratic Party had been formed and he offered to help out, an event which Gans calls one of his 'performance breaks'. But he realized that if he revealed his political sympathies he would no longer get data from the Republicans and so he had to withdraw his offer of help. Gans makes the proud boast that 'no one knew where I stood politically as long as I lived in Levittown'.[26]

Some of the most difficult times a fieldworker can have is when there are status discrepancies between him and his informant. As Gans points out: 'A researcher of higher or lower status than his informant obtains different data than a researcher who is felt to be of equal status.'[27] Though his aim was always to reduce status discrepancies, it is not always clear how this could be done. One vital factor here is that many fieldworkers will be considerably younger than their informants, which makes asking some questions and even being present at some meetings very difficult. On the other hand, dealing with people of similar background and values will lead to the temptation of resorting to 'performance breaks' with them of dropping the role of researcher and acting 'as a person'. The most likely group, as in Gans case, is the cosmopolitans – hence Gans' preponderance of middle-class informants.

Just how can the validity of fieldwork data be checked? This is an acute problem for community sociologists. The research worker will be able to check the data against itself for its internal consistency. Besides this there are three other ways of checking its validity, none of which are particularly satisfactory. Firstly, fieldwork data can be checked against data collected in other ways. Secondly, team research lessens the idiosyncracies or downright eccentricities of the lone research worker. Third, there can be replication by another research worker. Before discussing these points in some detail the most obvious objections to these three checks on the validity of field data ought to be made. Data collected in other ways can be equally biased or invalid. (There is, of course, a distinction between bias and validity: the former is quantative the latter qualitative. Data can be more or less biased but the trouble with validity is that data is either valid or it is not. This distinction is

[25] *Ibid.*, p. 440.
[26] *Ibid.*, p. 443.
[27] *Ibid.*, p. 444.

by no means clear in many discussions of the methods and techniques of sociology). Teams of research workers may support and reinforce misinterpretations of data. So there is no guarantee that teams produce more valid data. Re-studies by definition take place later than the first study and so it is not always clear whether the community or the researcher has changed, or whether the earlier findings were in some way incorrect.

Community studies are nothing if not eclectic in their methods. One of their strengths is that, unlike many surveys, they rely on data from many sources, although participant observation remains central. This technique, as has been explained, relies heavily on the use of informants, but relatively little attention has been given to information variability and distortion due to the informants' motives and position in the social structure. Vidich and Bensman have discussed this in relation to the Springdale Project that eventually produced *Small Town in Mass Society*. They list the wide variety of field techniques used on that project: census-type fact-finding surveys, check-list personality interviews, passive non-participant observation, tape-recorded interviews with spouses, depth interviews, participant-observation, unstructured and guided anthropological interviews, and structured, semi-structured and unstructured attitude interviews.[28] They were in an excellent position to evaluate and appraise types of data gathered by the use of one technique against other techniques. They wanted to know how to secure valid responses from informants. Whereas a great deal of work has been done on the problem of evaluating the validity of response in survey-type data, virtually none has been done in evaluating the quality of data secured from an informant in a wide variety of contexts and over a period of time.

The first source of misinformation that Vidich and Bensman list is 'Misinformation due to Purposeful Intent'. It includes slanted information, for example, from leaders concerned to give a favourable impression of the town, dramatized information to make the community seem less prosaic, over-information from those who want to reform and expose the community, blockages (the denial of the existence of problems), information distorted to serve personal ambition, and advanced preparation of responses based on rumours and other types of intercommunication about the research, leading to stylized and stereotyped responses. The second source of misinformation comes from the playing of the temporary role of 'respondent' – put at its simplest this results from the fact that all respondents attempt to form an image of

[28] Arthur J. Vidich and Joseph Bensman, 'The Validity of Field Data', *Human Organiaztion*, 1954. Reprinted in 2nd edition of *Small Town in Mass Society*, 1968.

the fieldworker and the organization that he represents and to form a basis of response with respect to the interviewer. So respondents, frequently with the best of intentions, provide information which they hope will enable the researcher to solve his particular problem. There can also be involuntary error 'not because they are unwilling or deceptive, but because they are not consciously able to respond to the demands' of the fieldworker 'due to blockages, inhibitions, or constraints'. All this implies that the community sociologist is in grave difficulties when supporting the validity of his data and the interpretations that he puts on them. He may feel more confident if he is working in a team. The necessity for, and the advantages of, team research in the community have already been elaborated. Team research will allow the same events to be viewed from more than one position. Yet it is likely that the research team will share the same values and the same hypothesis about the study. Whilst they can cover more ground and perhaps have different sets of informants it is by no means certain that they will necessarily produce more valid data. The third check on the validity of a community study is the re-study. It is axiomatic in the physical sciences that experiments are repeatable by different scientists and that they should get the same results. Yet in sociology and anthropology, especially in community studies, the social scientist is his own measuring instrument and so perhaps some wider variation in findings is to be expected.

The discrepancy, though, that has been found in re-studies by different authors is alarming. The most famous, Oscar Lewis' re-study of Robert Redfield's Tepoztlan, has profound implications for the validity of the community study method. The reports of fieldworkers in general and community sociologists in particular have to be accepted at their face value. Their reliability has to be judged in terms of the respect, for and confidence in, the author's integrity, the inner consistency of his work, and the extent to which it agrees with one's own preconceptions. It is as well to recognize, as Lewis says 'that the objective and value of re-studies is not to prove one man right and another man wrong. It is not a matter of listing another's errors, in itself a distasteful and painful task, *but rather of finding out what kind of errors tend to be made by what kind of people under what kind of conditions.*'[29] Lewis did, after all, dedicate his *Life in a Mexican Village* to Redfield.

Lewis distinguishes four types of re-studies.[30] Firstly, those re-studies in which a second or third investigator goes to a community with the express design of re-evaluating the work of his predecessor.

[29] Lewis, *op. cit.*, p. 112 (our emphasis).
[30] Oscar Lewis, 'Controls & Experiments in Fieldwork', in A. L. Kroeker *et. al.* (eds.), *Anthropology Today*, Chicago, Chicago U.P., 1953.

Lewis's own study of Tepoztlan comes closest to this type. Secondly, those in which the same or an independent investigator goes to a community studied earlier, this time to study change and uses the first report as a basis upon which to measure and evaluate change. The Lynds' *Middletown in Transition*, discussed in more detail in the next chapter, is an example of the same investigators going back to study change. Art Gallaher Jr's *Plainville Fifteen Years Later* is another example, in this case of another investigator going back. The second Banbury study was also set up with this aim. Thirdly, those in which an investigator returns to study some aspect of the community not studied earlier. Fourthly, those in which an investigator studies more intensively, and perhaps from a new point of view, some aspect of the community studied earlier. Of course, these are not mutually exclusive categories.

Much depends on the amount of quantitative data in the first report, for when there is a fair amount re-studies have a more solid base for comparison. It was easier to re-study Banbury because *Tradition and Change* is relatively highly quantified, at least in comparison to other British community studies. Lewis's findings are in many cases in marked contrast to those of Redfield and the questions that need to be answered are: to what extent and in what ways do the results obtained from the independent study by two anthropologists differ? What are the implications of such differences concerning the reliability and validity of reporting?

The impression given of Tepoztlan by Redfield has a Rousseauan quality: relatively homogeneous, isolated, smoothly functioning, well-integrated with contented, well-adjusted inhabitants. The emphasis throughout his study is on the co-operative and unifying factors. He glosses over evidence of violence, disruption, cruelty, disease, suffering and maladjustment, poverty, economic problems and political schisms. Lewis, on the other hand, emphasizes 'the underlying individualism of Tepoztlan institutions and character, the lack of co-operation, the tensions between villages within the *municipio*, the schisms within the village, the pervading quality of fear, envy, and distrust in interpersonal relations'.[31]

How can these differences be explained? A variety of reasons can be advanced, all of which are highly relevant to an appreciation of community study methodology. The first reason is the personal one, and Redfield has always tended to stress the element of art in social science. The second reason must lie with the fact that there were nearly twenty years between the two studies, between which time there must have been some changes in the community itself. Thirdly, the second study

[31] *Ibid.*, p. 123.

had all the advantages of being second, of having, as it were, a head start. Fourthly, Lewis had many more resources at his disposal, for not only had fieldwork techniques advanced in twenty years, but he also had the assistance of Mexican personnel. He also had double the amount of fieldwork time. In addition, there had been a change in anthropology in that much greater emphasis was put on economic analysis. Perhaps most crucially a careful reading of Redfield will bring to light that he relied upon about half-a-dozen informants, whereas Lewis's study was based on the testimony of well over 100 informants (out of population of 4,000, though). The fifth reason, however, is the most important.

This has already been introduced earlier in this chapter when the blinker-like nature of theory in fieldwork was discussed. Redfield's theoretical orientation influenced the selection and coverage of facts and the way in which these facts were organized. The concept of the folk culture and the folk-urban continuum was Redfield's organizing principle in the research. As Lewis says, 'this helps to explain his emphasis on the formal and ritualistic aspects of life rather than the everyday life of the people and their problems, on evidence of homogeneity rather than heterogeneity and the range of custom, on the weight of tradition rather than deviation and innovation, on unity and integration rather than tensions and conflict'.[32] Put like this it is possible to understand why two studies of the same community give such a different picture. Redfield was interested in the study of a single social process: the evolution from folk to urban, rather than a well-rounded ethnographic account. The questions that he asked of his data were quite different to those asked by Lewis. In Yucatan as a whole Redfield was looking for evidence that with increased urban influences there is greater disorganization, secularization and individualization. Lewis, in fact, doubts this thesis, to put it mildly. Redfields' thesis, though, located Tepoztlan at the folk end of his continuum and therefore he expected to find less disorganization, secularization and individualization there. Lewis disputes this and certainly seems to provide convincing contrary data on each of these points from Tepoztlan.

The place of ideal types stemming from the great dichotomies of the sociological tradition has been discussed in the previous chapter. The concern here is to point out their consequences in practice. The checking of a specific hypothesis, like Redfield's, in a community study is certainly worthwhile but the lesson to be learnt is the danger of the highly selective role of the hypothesis itself in directing the gathering of the data. As Lewis concludes: 'It may be that what is left out, because of the limiting needs of the hypothesis, is *all important* for an understanding

[32] *Ibid.*, p. 126.

of the total cultural situation.'[33] One final point, though, about Lewis's critique of Redfield that should be remembered is that he clearly believes that his predecessor in Tepoztlan started with a poor set of concepts and an incorrect, or at least improperly formulated, hypothesis. Lewis really is arguing that the folk-urban hypothesis is questionable or inadequate as an explanation of social change and that the concept of the folk culture itself is either invalid or, so far, very inadequately defined. So his critique cannot be used as more than a cautionary tale, the lessons of which are not conclusive. A good theory will have hypotheses that direct the fieldworker towards good and relevant data.

Later, Redfield himself tried to explain the discrepancies between his findings and those of Lewis. He confessed (his word) that he saw and suggested to his readers 'certain good things in Tepoztlan; a sense of conviction in the people as to what life is all about; and a richness of the expressive life of the community'.[34] But he rightly points out that if he brought his values to the community, so then did Lewis. Lewis wanted to improve life in communities like Tepoztlan. Improvement consisted of trying to make agriculture produce more and in substituting scientific for 'superstitious and primitive' understanding.[35]

A community study is not, despite what its critics say, just abstracted empiricism. Facts do not speak for themselves, they have no intrinsic meaning or value. They take their meaning from the way they are bound together with theory. That is, facts become meaningful as they are lifted from the level of the fortuitous and related to the more abstract. Facts, as empirically verifiable observations, are never gathered at random, they may be gathered in accordance with an unconscious preference, or they may be gathered in terms of some systematic scheme. For the scientist, facts are the meaningful products of efforts to relate them to a point of view. Science seeks to structure fact in some consistent fashion, so that an orderly relationship is established between and among them. This logical structure or systematic scheme is usually called a theory. Since it is impossible for anyone to observe or cope with all there is to see in any situation, theory functions to narrow the range of observation and define the things that are relevant. It becomes a set of directions to the researcher telling him what data he should be able to observe so that he can hope to organize and systematize his empirical findings. And by no means of least importance, theory makes specific for the reader the colour of the glasses through which the researcher was looking when he gathered his data.

[33] *Ibid.*, pp. 133–4 (emphasis in the original).
[34] Robert Redfield, *The Primitive World and Its Transformations*, Penguin Books, 1968, p. 158.
[35] Lewis (1951), *op. cit.*, p. 448.

Community study, as a social science tool, is also essentially a research *process*. If properly documented it can provide relevant and significant data about the community. The first two major stages of this process have already been discussed in some detail, those of entering and maintaining a position in the structure of social relations that will then permit the collection of data. This second stage is considerably extended and it is often surprising that so many community studies have such a timeless quality. This is not the same point as was made earlier about the 'historyless' anthropological tradition. It is that the resulting monograph is often very similar to a single snap shot despite the fact that the fieldworkers have sometimes spent several years in the community. The task of putting together a coherent account of the local social structure is, of course, not an easy or a simple one, but nevertheless it is surprising that changes within that period are so rarely described. It is very rare for the reader of a community study to know whether a reported observation took place at the beginning, middle or end of the fieldwork. It is as if it has all happened on the same day. Though the fieldworkers are only in the community for a relatively short period, it should be possible for them to glimpse some of the social changes that have taken place.

The third stage of the community study process is that of exit. This stage is taken to include more than just the getting out and the cutting off of some social relations, but also that of analysis and publication. In a community where the fieldworker has worked openly and with publicity, publication should be expected. This, of course, will not be the case when the data has been collected secretly. It is in the nature of literate societies that they read books, especially books about themselves. The community sociologist in an advanced society always has his community looking over his shoulder when he is back in his cloister or plate glass tower writing up his results. What criteria can be used to decide what should be published or not? One position would be what might be called the extreme academic one: the advancement of human knowledge, or at least our accumulation of social facts. This position is in fact modified quite extensively. It is a convention that individuals should not be recognizable and that anonymity and confidentiality should be respected. In practice this is very difficult to achieve, as individuals can be recognized by their structural position, e.g. a school principal in a village of 2,500 (in the case of *Small Town in Mass Society*). At this stage it is usual to create case studies, ideal types, composite characters. This kind of fictionalization is rampant in community studies and, although there are good and honourable reasons for it, it is nevertheless very hazardous. The creation of ideal-type characters, for example, the portraits of 'traditionalists' and 'non-traditionalists' in

Tradition and Change, whilst protecting individuals, may have made the analysis neater. This is all part of what Merton calls 'post factum sociological interpretation' and will be dealt with below. Another position, if not the opposite to the extreme academic one, is the general rule (or cardinal principle as Frankenberg has called it) of scholarship that no researcher has the right to make impossible the studies of those who will follow him. While this seems laudable and unexceptional, the very act of publication will almost certainly offend some members of a community. This is particularly the case when a sociologist has dwelt on the latent rather than the manifest functions of social action, and on status and on social class. And of course most community studies do just that.

It is not the purpose of this chapter to discuss the analysis of data in community studies – this will be done particularly in the next two chapters with specific studies. A great deal has been made in this chapter, though, of the consequences of having a theory before entering the field. The opposite weakness is equally the case, sometimes in the same studies. Interpretations have been developed after the observations were made and are not tests of prior hypotheses. So observations, findings, data are subject to retrospective selection, if not downright falsification. Memory is a hazardous instrument. A great deal must therefore be taken on trust, especially the integrity of the fieldworker. There are two ways to meet this criticism. Firstly, to write in detail a natural history of the research process in the community – of how the study was carried out, what observations took place when, of when ideas came, of how and when they were modified. In other words keep a detailed research diary as part of the intellectual craftsmanship so brilliantly described by C. Wright Mills in his *The Sociological Imagination*. Other models would be William Whyte's account of how he carried out his research into *Street Corner Society* and the other essays in Vidich and Bensman's *Reflections on Community Studies*. Hypotheses can be stated in advance and what will or will not be accepted as proof. One weakness of these accounts is that they, too, are usually written after the event.

The second defence against Merton's strictures, which in effect reiterates the old Jewish proverb, 'for example is no proof', is to meet it head on. In fact to say '. . . yes, but. . . .' Gans, concluding his *The Urban Villagers: Group and Class in the Life of Italian Americans*, could be speaking for many sociologists of the community when he writes: 'This, then, is not a scientific study, for it does not provide what Merton has called compelling evidence for a series of hypotheses. It is, rather, an attempt by a trained social scientist to describe and explain, using his methodological and theoretical training, to sift the observa-

COMMUNITY STUDY AS A METHOD　81

tions, and to report only those generalizations which are justified by the data. The validity of my findings thus rests ultimately on my judgements about the data, and of course, on my theoretical and personal biases in deciding what to study, what to see, what to ignore and how to analyse the products. Properly speaking the study is a *reconnaissance*, an exploration of a community to provide an overview, guided by the canons of sociological theory, and method, but not attempting to offer documentation for all the findings. I do not mean to cast doubt on the conclusions I reached (I stand behind them all) or on the methods I used. Participant-observation is the only method I know that enables the researcher to get close to the realities of social life. Its deficiencies in producing quantitative data are more than made up by its ability to minimize the distance between the researcher and his subject of study.'[36]

Whether this is justified or not really depends on the substantive findings. It is not possible to discuss, at least not very fruitfully, theory and method in isolation from each other or from the sociological problem to which they are being applied. In these two chapters we have felt some impatience to get on with discussing the consequences of this theory and that method. How the theories and methods of community studies have worked in practice form the rest of this book.

[36] H. J. Gans, *The Urban Villagers*, New York, Free Press, 1962, pp. 349–50 (London, Collier-Macmillan).

4

The American Community Studies

No pretence can be made that it is possible in a relatively short chapter comprehensively to survey and assess all American community studies. What can be done is to take some of the unquestionably most important studies and consider their contribution. Some of the themes raised in the two previous chapters will be seen again both in this chapter and in the next. The sociological purposes served by community studies can be broadly divided into two. First, they provide a basis for a general understanding of a society – though, as will be shown below, the extension of findings particular to one community to the whole of society is a besetting sin of American community studies. Second, community studies allow the exploration of the effects of the social setting on human behaviour, that is, treating the community as an independent variable. This again is a pervasive tendency of American community studies.

Middletown

Middletown is for the sociologist of the community what Durkheim's *Suicide* is for sociology as a whole. It represents a magnificent and imaginative leap forward. The Lynds' contribution is such that, just as *Suicide* has shaped the development of the whole discipline, *Middletown* has shaped the development of community studies. Both studies have provided a model for sociological analysis and many later achievements were only possible because of the innovations of both Durkheim and the Lynds. We are now on the shoulders of giants. Whereas it is all too easy, with hindsight, to belittle these achievements, especially in the light of later advances, their seminal contribution should be remembered. The Lynds set the style for future community studies. Their approach, techniques and analysis have been followed remarkably closely by many later sociologists of the community. The problems that they encountered and to which they posed solutions are the same, in many cases, as those faced by all community sociologists, only those who followed the Lynds into other communities had the benefit of the Lynds' monographs to guide them. This is by no means to suggest that they were always right (nor for that matter was Durkheim), but they were both first in the field and often right.

In a way the community study came about by accident. The Lynds originally had no intention of giving a total picture of the town of Muncie. In the early 1920s the Lynds – Robert and Helen, husband and wife – were working for a small institute of social and religious research which decided to survey religious provision and practices in a typical small American town. The Lynds sought a suitable frame of reference into which to put their study and were attracted by the then current work of Clark Wissler and W. H. R. Rivers, who both presented n-fold classifications under which the activities of any 'culture' (key term) could be classified. It was the latter's classification that was adopted and which provided the organisational framework for the Lynds' analysis. The classification is: Getting a living, Making a Home, Training the Young, Using Leisure, Engaging in Religious Practices, and Engaging in Community Activities. The Lynds found that just as a study of primitive religion requires an understanding of a primitive society in all its aspects, so the methods and approach of social anthropology can legitimately be applied to the study of American religion in its *total* setting. It did not prove possible to study one social institution in a locality – religion in this case – in isolation, but rather it proved necessary to examine its interrelations with other institutions. And so it might be said that the modern community study was born.

The Lynds described what they were doing as 'studying synchronously the interwoven trends that are the life of a small American city'. They go on to face the continually besetting problem of the *typicality* of any community. They claim that 'a typical city, strictly speaking does not exist' but add that Muncie 'was selected as having many features common to a wide group of communities'. One other point mentioned in their first paragraph has continued to be a matter of some contention, seen alternatively as the main strength or the chief weakness of the field of community studies: 'Neither fieldwork nor report has attempted to prove any thesis: the aim has been, rather, to *record* observed phenomena, thereby raising questions and suggesting fresh points of departure in the study of group behaviour.'[1] This is

[1] Robert S. Lynd and Helen M. Lynd, *Middletown: A study in Contemporary American Culture*, New York, Harcourt Brace, 1929, p. 3 (our emphasis) (London, Constable).

either to be attacked as smacking of some casual empricism, or praised as being unbiased and for letting the data speak for themselves. This duality of reception for community studies has, of course, continued, and was exemplified in the Introduction to this book.

The Lynds' books were extraordinarily successful by any standards – *Middletown* went through six printings in 1929 alone. Its achievement has been summed up by John Madge when he said that it was 'the first scientific and ostensibly uncritical, objective description of small-town life. Here for the first time, without reformist overtones and without dramatization was a mirror held up to the ordinary American.'[2] Their achievement is in fact even greater for they returned to Muncie almost a decade later, in 1935, to ascertain what had happened to the community during the Depression and produced an equally good, some would say better, community study, *Middletown in Transition*.

The second study, however, is markedly different in tone. For example, whilst in *Middletown* the Lynds had, it would seem almost instinctively, divided the community into two groups, the 'working class' and 'business class' they maintain a somewhat deadpan 'getting at the facts' approach. In *Middletown in Transition*, Robert Lynd adopted within a similar basic structure (the anthropological classification detailed above) what has been seen as a hard-hitting exposure of the sources of power in what he regarded as a typical American small town. Though it will be shown below[3] that some of his evidence is open to alternative explanations, he packed into *Middletown in Transition* all his militant and evangelical feelings about what was wrong with American society. The two Middletown monographs illustrate well that it is a relatively short step from the community study as empirical description to the community study as normative prescription.

The Lynds also set the style for future community research by going to live in their community. The fieldwork for *Middletown* took eighteen months and was completed by 1925. There is an appendix, 'Note on Method', describing their fieldwork techniques. They tried to be unobtrusive but not covert and said they had just come to 'study the growth of the city'. They had no general questionnaire, just the anthropological conceptual scheme around which they organized their data. This is prior to the days when sociologists sampled, and it is clear that they may well have been biased in those they talked to. Under the heading 'interviews' in their appendix, they write: 'These varied all the way from the most casual conversations with street-car conductors, janitors and barbers, to chance associates at luncheon or club meetings

[2] John Madge, *The origins of Scientific Sociology*, London, Tavistock, 1963. p. 128.
[3] See Chapter 7.

to carefully planned interviews with individuals especially qualified to give information on particular phases of the city's life.'[4] These included, for example, leading ministers and club secretaries. In order 'to test in individual families certain hypotheses as to trends observed in the behaviour of the community' they interviewed 124 'working class' families and 40 'business class' (called 'just good substantial folks') families. It is clear that these were not samples in the scientific sense (in that all families in Muncie stood an equal chance of being selected for study) – for example it is explicitly said that they would only interview those members of the business class who were willing to co-operate.

It is necessary to consider carefully how Muncie was chosen in the first place (this information is always vital for community studies and is frequently omitted from the published monograph). The Lynds say that they had no ulterior motive and they appear to have listed the characteristics a city should possess so as to be representative of contemporary America.[5] These characteristics were: a temperate climate, a rapid expansion rate so that the community should feel the stresses of social change, an industrial culture with a fair amount of modern high-speed machine production, it should *not* be a one-plant town (they were wrong in equating a single-plant town with a single-industry town – as will be seen below the whole of Muncie, not just its industry, was dominated by the activities of one family), a substantial and autonomous local artistic life and a location in the mid-West. It also had to be small enough to study – this criteria which is central to so many community studies has meant that we are forever being told that relatively small towns are typical even though the majority of the population in most industrialized societies live in large towns. Madge for one has been suspicious of the apparent complete rationality of their selection criteria. Lynd came from Indiana and so probably already knew something about the community.[6]

The Lynds, once they were established in Muncie and organizing their data under the six headings borrowed from anthropology, began to concentrate on two key dates, 1890 (when the population was 11,000) and 1924 (when the population was 35,000). They clearly aimed to describe and explain the differences that had taken place in Muncie between these dates. The dichotomous class classification used has been

---

[4] Lynds, *op. cit.*, p. 507.

[5] Compare Warners approach discussed below pp. 101-111.

[6] It is interesting to note that when in the early 1950s Katz and Lazarsfeld were looking for a locale for their study that became *Personal Influence* Muncie got onto their short list as being nearly average by some quite vigorous criteria and yet was rejected on the grounds of being a one-industry town. This factor must be remembered when the substance of the Lynds' findings are recounted below.

mentioned above, the working class were those who dealt with things, the business class were those who dealt with people. It is marvellously simple but totally atheoretical, and in detail empirically difficult to apply. The Lynds are the first community participant observers, accepting all invitations and going to all meetings. Unlike Lloyd Warner, they also made extensive use of locally produced documentary data, the census, court and school records, and the newspapers. They also used diaries, club minutes and scrapbooks. These data were of course especially valuable for the 1890s. By the standards of the time, the Lynds were scrupulous in describing the sources of their data in the body of their monographs.

It is to be expected that the anthropological classification adopted by the Lynds for anlysing the community would not fit in easily with their data. Yet there is no strain apparent when reading their monographs. The classification performed the function of letting the authors describe in a 'value-neutral' way a style of life acidly etched by Sinclair Lewis. At least in *Middletown* their objective, which by and large they attain, was systematic description and not external judgement. The chapter on 'The Organization of Leisure' (which is within the general section 'Using Leisure') points out, for example, that the family is declining as a unit of leisure time pursuits, and that friends are becoming more important. It was discovered that more working class women had 'no friends'.[7] There are many verbatim comments which give a richness to their analysis, but as in the more recent work of, for example, the Institute of Community Studies in Britain, it is not always possible to exactly attribute these quotations to an individual whose characteristics are known. The Lynds, like the much later writers on suburbia (see below), go on to discuss the effects of propinquity (what the Lynds call 'vicinage') on the pattern of social relationships. They Lynds point out the effects of informal groups, like the neighbourhood, on the one hand and formal groups, like the church on the other, in 'acquainting members of the community with each other'[8] – and how this varies by their two classes. They similarly discuss sex differences in friendship patterns. They contrast the number of parties reported in the local press in 1890 with 1924 (the population had increased three-and-a-half times and the parties over tenfold). 'Dropping-in' had decreased. They work their way through a large number of voluntary associations describing (but not quantifying) their activities and their membership, concluding that 'the unorganized social occasions of the neighbourhood in 1890 have given way increasingly to semi-organized dances and clubs'.[9] In fact

[7] Lynds, *op. cit.*, p. 272.
[8] *Ibid.*, p. 275.
[9] *Ibid.*, p. 283.

THE AMERICAN COMMUNITY STUDIES

they located 458 active clubs – one for every 80 people, whereas in 1890 there were 92 – one for every 125 people. They note, without comment, that there was a growing tendency for the business class to make club life serve other than recreational ends, notably those of getting a living,[10] and there is a particularly perceptive account of the activities of the Rotary Club. Their concluding sentence to this chapter, however, hints at what was to come in *Middletown in Transition*. 'In view of the tightening of social and economic lines in the growing city, it is not surprising that the type of leisure-time organization which dominates today tends in the main to erect barriers to keep others out.'[11] However, the Lynds' methods in *Middletown* are well illustrated by this chapter, for by and large they muster facts in order to convey impressions. What now appears so surprising is that these facts, or rather the accumulation of facts like these, over nearly thirty chapters were horrifying to cultured metropolitan America: *Moronia* in Mencken's memorable metaphor. The point remains, though, that for the modern sociologist, the Lynds handling of their data in *Middletown* is elementary and there is nothing approaching what Madge calls 'a well-ordered theoretical structure'.[12]

However, by the time Robert Lynd produced *Middletown in Transition*, he knew quite clearly what he was doing. The number of man-days of fieldwork was about one-tenth of that for the first study. Simplicity was their aim the second time, not elaboration. As Robert Lynd wrote, 'Here was an American city which had been the subject of eighteen months of close study in 1924–5. During the following decade the conditions of its existence had been unexpectedly altered in a way which affected every aspect of its life. Its growing population had been tossed from prosperity beyond any experienced prior to 1925 to an equally unprecedented depression. The opportunity thus presented to analyse its life under the stress of specific interrupting stimuli, whose course can be traced, offered something analogous to an experimental situation.'[13] This time precise questions were posed of Muncie: had the basic culture remained intact? Had the trust in self-help and belief in the future been maintained? Had too old faiths survived and were the young adopting them? Had the sense of community developed further or had the latent cleavages become 'sharper'?

The changes that are described in *Middletown in Transition* can be epitomized by the villains of that book, the 'X' family. They are not mentioned in *Middletown*. The Lynds say that they themselves were

[10] *Ibid.*, p. 286.
[11] *Ibid.*, p. 312.
[12] Madge, *op. cit.*, p. 147.
[13] Robert S. Lynd and Helen M. Lynd, *Middletown in Transition*, New York, Harcourt Brace, 1937, p. 4.

blind and that the 'X' family was invisible. But in 1935 'after ten years' absence from the city, one thing struck the returning observer again and again: the increasingly large public benefactions and the increasing pervasiveness of the power of this wealthy family of manufacturers, whose local position since 1925 is becoming hereditary with the emergence of a second generation of sons.'[14] Though from their own evidence when one of the brothers 'X' died in 1924 'the entire business of the city stopped during his funeral'.[15] In 1935 business ran *Middletown* and the 'X' family dominated business; in the words of one of the Lynds' informants: 'The one big point about this town . . . [is] that the 'X' dominate the whole town, *are* the town, in fact.'[16] Another Middletowner told Robert Lynd in 1935 that 'If I'm out of work I go to the X plant; if I need money I go to the X Bank, and if they don't like me I don't get it; my children go to the X college; when I get sick I go to the X hospital; I buy a building lot or house in an X subdivision; my wife goes down town to buy clothes at the X department store; if my dog strays away he is put in the X pound; I buy X milk; I drink X beer, vote for X political parties, and get help from X charities; my boy goes to the X YMCA and my girl to their YWCA; I listen to the word of God in X subsidized churches; if I'm a Mason, I go to the X Masonic Temple; I read the news from the X morning newspaper; and, if I am rich enough, I travel via the X airport.'[17] There is an interesting contrast in 'Government' between *Middletown* and *Middletown in Transition*. In the first book there is only a short twenty-page chapter, whereas in the second it is fifty-four pages, and much of the chapter on the 'X' family is devoted to government.[18] The Lynds concluded that the lines of leadership and related controls were highly concentrated and were more concentrated than in 1925. However, it is also shown that at many points this control was unconscious and when conscious, well-meaning or 'public-spirited'. But so long as the owners of such vast personal resources as the 'X' family exhibited a public-spirited willingness to help with local problems, leadership and control would be forced upon them by circumstances and their patterns would tend to become the guiding patterns, or so runs Lynd's analysis.

There is, of course, much more to *Middletown in Transition* than the 'X' family, and the changing patterns of social activity of the rest of

[14] Lynds (1937), *op. cit.*, pp. 74–5.
[15] *Ibid.*, p. 75.
[16] *Ibid.*, p. 77.
[17] *Ibid.*, p. 74.
[18] The chapter that most increased in length between the two studies was 'Caring for the Unable'. This was clearly an area of major institutional re-organization, since most working-class and some middle-class families had suddenly found themselves involuntarily thrust into the 'unable' category.

the population are examined, though not in as much detail as in the earlier volume. The last chapter, however, requires special attention as it was an ambitious attempt to sum up the ideology of *Middletown*. The chapter is called 'The Middletown Spirit'. The technique of exposition used by Lynd is first to list what Middletown was *for*, and then what it was *against*. Middletown was for being honest, kind, friendly, loyal, successful, average, simple, sound, traditional and courageous. It valued 'character' above 'brains'. It believed in progress, but not too much too quickly, in individualism, and that one got what one deserved. It was convinced American ways were best and that American business was the core of society; the family was the fundamental institution and schools should stick to teaching the facts. Leisure was great but work came first. American democracy was the ultimate and ideal form of government and Christianity was the final form of religion. To give charity was good, to receive bad. Middletown was against the opposite of this list and also divergent personalities, innovations in ideas, art, literature, government, religion, education, the family. It was against Washington, or more exactly centralized government and planning that curtailed the making of money. It was against foreigners, minorities, deviants, frills and the weak.

As Robert Lynd points out, this complex of beliefs naturally favoured the contribution of the businessman in the community. 'As . . . the chief contributor to the community's welfare, the successful businessman in Middletown elicits from his fellow citizens whole-hearted praise, as well as envy and emulation. Since Middletown's values are regarded as leading to "success", it follows easily that those who are successful must obviously have these values to have become successful. So by this subtle and largely unconscious process, Middletown imprints to the successful businessman the possession . . . of the qualities of . . . the city's other values.'[19] The greatest achievement of this ideology lay in its ability to reconcile the apparent contradictory qualities of ruthlessness on the one hand and consideration for others on the other. The successful businessman was licensed to be harshly enterprising in his strictly business relations in order that he might enjoy the luxury of friendliness out of business hours.

Between the time of the two studies tolerance increased in some directions, for instance religion, but decreased in others, particularly with regard to political and economic affairs. This was especially true in relation to Middletown's attitude to organized labour. The Middletown spirit was the businessmen's ideology and it dominated Middletown – for example it was repeatedly claimed that there were no class differences in Middletown. This was a denial by both the business and

19 *Ibid.*, p. 422.

the working class, because the latter adopted the former as a reference group. The conclusion of the Lynds was 'that the line between the working class and business class, though vague and blurred still, is more apparent than it was ten years before'.[20] However, the Lynds did not develop a satisfactory tool to analyse social class, and their contemporary in the field, Lloyd Warner, tried much harder. Unlike him, though, the Lynds do not make much use of their class distinctions for analytical purposes. Nevertheless their usage of class is based on objective measures whereas Warner's is based on subjective.

The Lynds conclusion is that despite the shock of the Great Depression the basic texture of Middletown's culture had not changed between 1925 and 1935. The Depression was viewed as an 'interruption' to be 'waited out'. In 1935 the community was still living by the same values. Robert Lynd hardly bothers to conceal his regret that Middletown had as he puts it 'learned nothing'. The paradox is that Muncie was better off than neighbouring communities, largely through the activities of the 'X' family. He was of course writing against a background of Fascism in Europe, and whereas the return of Roosevelt in 1936 secured the New Deal, he concluded with a deeply pessimistic sentence that this did not preclude the possibility 'of a seizure of power carefully engineered as *by* the business class and *for* the business class and publicized in the name of Americanism and prosperity'.[21] This last sentence shows the strengths and weaknesses of *Middletown* and *Middletown in Transition* in particular and community studies in general. At best the Lynds' contribution was to write meaningfully on significant issues, and they do so against a detail of vividly reported empirical fact. And yet their political interpretation of the community and their far-reaching forecasts have not only been overtaken but seem out of place.

The 'Lynds in transition' demonstrate the path that community sociologists have often found it necessary to follow. They started work in a condition of almost total theoretical naiveté, and having set out to collect the facts adopted a current anthropological framework into which to fit them. It must be stressed that they did indeed collect these facts with a rare rigour. It is also to their credit that they came to recognize a need for a theory – Lynd admits to reading Marx between the two studies. They adopted a 'stratification' model of the community, though without Lloyd Warner's insistent use of it as almost the only analytical variable in analysis. And they became interested in what two decades later would have been called 'community power'. They remained to the end, though, better fieldworkers than theoreticians, for

[20] *Ibid.*, p. 451.
[21] *Ibid.*, p. 510.

as Polsby has shown[22] they collected data that allowed their own model of the community to be shown as in some ways mistaken if not false. Their first volume does, however, contain the main conceptions necessary for interpreting the effects of industrialization on American communities, and their second for interpreting the effects of the Depression. However, unlike so many community sociologists, Warner for instance, they were reluctant to make sweeping generalizations from Middletown to America. This first major community study is distinguished by the fullness with which the social structure before industrialization is described, indeed it has a historical grasp rarely equalled in many later community studies.[23]

The Chicago School

The theoretical ideas behind the 'human ecologists' of the Chicago school of community sociologists were discussed in Chapter 2. The concern here is to discuss both their methods and their substantive contributions through their empirical monographs. Don Martindale has called the Chicago school 'urbanism incorporated'.[24] The founder of the firm was Robert Park and his associates were Ernest Burgess, Niels Anderson, Frederick Thrasher, Roderick McKensie, Harvey Zorbaugh, Paul Cressey, Clifford Shaw, Walter Reckless and Louis Wirth. Their products were not only a marvellous series of monographs but they also had a distinctive style and approach to the community. The titles of their books are peculiarly evocative: *The Hobo: the Sociology of the Homeless Man* (1923), *The Gang* (1927), *The Gold Coast and the Slum* (1929), *The Taxi Dance Hall* (1932), *The Jack-Roller: A Delinquent Boy's Own Story* (1930), *Six Boys in Trouble* (1929) and *The Ghetto* (1929). The author of the last was also the author of arguably the single most famous paper ever written in sociology: 'Urbanism as a Way of Life'.[25]

In toto the production from Chicago in less than a decade is very impressive. No other city has ever been studied in such detail. The methods used in each monograph prove on inspection to be diverse: participant observation in the case of Anderson who became a hobo

[22] See the detailed discussion in Chapter 7, pp. 232-233.
[23] In writing about the Lynds' work we are only too aware of the wealth of detail that has been left out, and clearly it must not be thought for one moment that the above account is a substitute for reading the originals. This point will not be frequently reiterated but applies to most of the community studies discussed in this book.
[24] p. 28 of his 'Prefatory Remarks' to his translation of Max Weber's *The City*, New York, Free Press, 1958.
[25] Originally published in the *American Journal of Sociology*, 1938.

(though both his fieldwork and that of Zorbaugh seem shallow in the light of William Whyte's *Street Corner Society*), the collection of life histories in the case of Shaw studying the 'Jack-Roller', official statistics in the case of Reckless or organized vice. They are unified not so much by their methods, though they all tended at some stage to tramp the streets, as by the general ecological model of the city, first formulated by Park and elaborated by Burgess and by their field of interest: Chicago. This is both the schools greatest strength, for their data is wonderfully rich, and its greatest weakness for all their data is on one city at one time. Despite their historical investigations like many other American community studies they can be charged with 'localism', with having a curious local ethnocentricity notwithstanding the fact that they were the most cosmopolitan and worldly-wise of men. They failed to work out the relations between the special conditions existing in Chicago during the first thirty years of this century and other possible patterns of urbanisation during that time and after.

Whilst much of the work of the Chicago School is primarily descriptive (how else can Thrasher's location of 1,313 gangs be justified?) it has the advantage of being written from within a common framework. The techniques of the school can be approached from this auto-biographical remark of Park's, 'I expect that I have actually covered more ground, tramping about cities in different parts of the world, than any other living man. Out of all this I gained, among other things, a conception of the city, the community, and the region, not as a geo-graphical phenomenon merely, but as a kind of social organization.'[26] Soon after Park went to Chicago, he published an article in 1916 in the *American Journal of Sociology* called, 'The City: Suggestions for the Investigation of Human Behaviour in the Urban Environment'.[27] This was the manifesto and programme of what was to become the Chicago school. It is a long article, of forty-six pages and contains the origins of many of the ideas which saw empirical fruition in the later monographs. He relates what he calls 'local organization' to the city plan and intro-duces the term 'natural areas' for areas of 'population segregation'. These 'natural areas' became the locale for specific studies, e.g. 'The Gold Coast' or the 'Ghetto'. He quotes with approval the old German adage that 'city air makes men free' (*Stadt Luft macht frei*). Here is a central paradox in the formulations of the Chicago school: they stress the freedom that results from living in large, dense, socially hetero-geneous and anonymous cities (the elements of urbanism as a way of life) and yet also posit a rather narrow determinism that is too crude for

[26] R. E. Park, *Human Communities: the city and human ecology*, New York, Free Press, 1952, p. 5 (London, Collier-Macmillan).

[27] Reprinted in Park, *ibid*.

geographers let alone sociologists. They most certainly relate types of social behaviour in communities to a precise and specific ecology – hence the Chicago monographs are spattered with maps of this or that activity against the 'concentric ring' pattern of Chicago (see diagram).

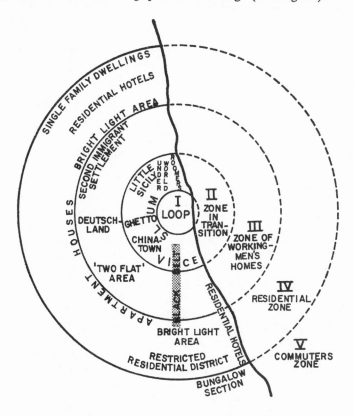

Park puts it like this: 'Because of the opportunity it offers, particularly to the exceptional and abnormal types of man, a great city tends to spread out and lay bare to the public view in a massive manner all the human characters and traits which are ordinarily obscured and suppressed in smaller communities. The city, in short, shows the good and evil in human nature in excess. It is this fact, perhaps, more than any other, which justifies the view that would make the city a laboratory or clinic in which human nature and social processes may be conveniently and profitably studied.'[28] Clearly Park believed that he could study the

[28] *Ibid.*, p. 51.

city as an object and the methods he favoured were the 'same patient methods of observation that anthropologists like Franz Boas and R. H. Lowrie had expended on the life and manners of the North American Indian'. He also began the collection of statistical data, i.e. relating to the city, and began the trend that culminates in the 'neo-ecologists', Shevky and Bell, Leo Schnore and Otis Dudley Duncan. Park was not free from community being used as normative prescription for he clearly cherished a vision of a developed science of the community which could chart patterns of change so that men might finally fashion their social environments to conform more closely with their ideals. Park wanted to preserve unity in the face of diversity, instead of the custom-bound homogeneity of rural life.

Burgess's famous diagram (adapted above) represents an elaboration of Park's formulation of the ecological idea on which the Chicago studies are based. The key point is that it is what would now be called a 'dynamic model' and the central concept is that of *succession*. Succession is used to describe the fact that these concentric rings, built up one after another historically as a city grows, are also invaded successively from the inside: for example, when an area which has been occupied by wealthy families begins to run down the homes are taken over as rooming houses, while the wealthy former residents move to a more suburban locality. They leave behind the now familiarly titled 'twilight zone'. Until Rex and Moore's[29] work in Birmingham, though, the approach of pursuing ecological studies of the community in conjunction with detailed fieldwork seemed almost to stop after the early 1930s. Perhaps by this time Chicago has been overstudied. It will now be seen that it is no longer sufficient to identify a community as, say, located in the zone of transition or in suburbia. Common location in the physical structure of a community may be a starting place for an investigation, though few modern sociologists would now treat this factor as a sole, or at least as a very important independent variable, or for that matter as an independent variable at all.

The actual social experience of Chicago was not that of every other city – it increased in population by half a million in each of the first three decades of this century and many of the newcomers were immigrants from Eastern and Southern Europe. To a quite remarkable extent Chicago was also the creation of the railway: towns that developed either earlier or later, Boston and Los Angeles to take two American examples, have an ecological structure markedly different to that of Chicago. So, like many community sociologists, those who worked in Chicago became bound by the peculiarities of their community and assumed that the rest of the world was similar if not identical. When

[29] See below pp. 204-208.

a Chicago sociologist writes generally about the 'community' or the 'city', he means Chicago. There was little concern for comparing Chicago with any other city to see differences as well as similarities in their adaptations to population influxes.

What precisely was the urban community? It 'turns out, upon closer scrutiny, to be a mosaic of minor communities, many of them strikingly different one from another, but all more or less typical. *Every City* has its central business district; the focal point of the whole urban complex. *Every City*, every great city, has its more or less exclusive residential areas of suburbs; its areas of light and of heavy industry, satellite cities, and casual labour mart, where men recruited for rough work on distant frontiers, in the mines and the forests, in the building of railways or the borings and excavations for the vast structures of our modern cities. *Every American City* has its slums; its ghettos, its immigrant colonies, regions which maintain more or less alien and exotic culture. Nearly every large city has its bohemias and bohemians, where life is freer, more adventurous and lonely than it is elsewhere. These are the so-called natural areas of the city.'[30]

Such natural areas were studied by Zorbaugh in *The Gold Coast and the Slum*. Not only is this one of the finest of the many good Chicago monographs but it also raises, in particular, interesting and crucial questions about the whole school's approach to and view of the community.

The Gold Coast and Little Sicily (the slum) have few common customs and 'there is certainly no common view which holds the cosmopolitan population of this region together in any common purpose . . . the laws which prevail are not a communal product, and there is no organized public opinion which supports and contributes to their enforcement'.[31] So Zorbaugh doubts whether 'in any proper sense of the word' the 'Lower North Side' can be called a community at all. 'It is a region . . . an area of transition, the character of its populations and the problems which it presents are at once a reflection and a consequence of the conditions which this period of transition imposes.'[32] The test for this book, indeed of the Chicago school, might well be 'everywhere the old order passeth, but the new order hath yet to come'. Underlying this is a very Durkheimian view of society which appreciated that the old forms of mechanical solidarity had broken down and that organic solidarity is ever precarious.

The area that interested Zorbaugh was one of extremes, not just of

---

[30] Park, *op. cit.*, p. 196 (our emphasis).
[31] Harvey W. Zorbaugh, *The Gold Coast and the Slum*, Chicago, University of Chicago Press, 1929, p. vii (London, Chicago U.P., 1929).
[32] *Ibid.*, pp. vii–viii.

contrasts. The Gold Coast 'has the highest residential land values in the city, and among the lowest are to be found near by . . . the Lower North Side has more professional men, more politicians, more suicides, more persons in *Who's Who*, than in any "community" in Chicago'.[33] The Gold Coast was on the lake side, the blocks behind were rooming houses – Anderson's 'hobohemia' was located here, and still further inland, but in most cases only a couple of dozen blocks away from the Gold Coast, were 'Little Italy' and 'Little Sicily' – the slums. In common with the other Chicago monographs Zorbaugh begins with a detailed physical description of the locality, for example of Lake Shore Dive, 'the Mayfair of the Gold Coast . . . rise the imposing stone mansions, with their green lawns and wrought-iron-grilled doorways, of Chicago's wealthy aristocracy and her industrial and financial Kings'.[34] In contrast, 'The slum is a bleak area of segregation of the sediment of society; an area of extreme poverty, tenants, ramshackle buildings, of evictions and evaded rents; an area of working mothers and children, of high rates of birth, infant mortality, illegitimacy, and death; an area of Pawnshops and second-hand stores, of gangs, of "flops" where every bed is a vote,'[35] and 'it harbours many sorts of people: the criminal, the radical, the bohemian, the migratory worker, the immigrant, the unsuccessful, the queer and the unadjusted'.[36] Everywhere there is movement – the strength of the Chicago school is their feeling for describing urban processes: Zorbaugh noted for example that 'the Negro, too, is moving into this area and pushing on into "Little Hell" (the core of "Little Italy")'.[37] Within the slum, but not of it, was 'Towertown', a considerable colony of artists and would-be artists.

Zorbaugh's methods are indicated by the number of paragraphs that begin 'As one walks' – for example, 'One has but to walk the streets of the Near North Side to sense the cultural isolation beneath these contrasts.'[38] Some of the individuals that once lived in the slum 'have succeeded in climbing' but for the rest 'the district east of State Street exists only in the newspapers'.[39] Similarly the 'Gold Coaster' knows little except through sensational newspaper reports of what happens in the slums. In a key passage Zorbaugh sums up his impressions: 'The *isolation* of the populations crowded together within these few hundred blocks, the *superficiality* and *externality* of their contacts the *social distances* that separate them their absorption in the affairs of their *own little worlds* – these and not mere size and numbers, constitute the problems of the inner city. The community, represented by the town or

[33] *Ibid.*, p. 6. [34] *Ibid.*, p. 7.
[35] *Ibid.*, p. 9. [36] *Ibid.*, p. 11.
[37] *Ibid.*, p. 11–12. [38] *Ibid.*, p. 12.
[39] *Ibid.*, p. 13.

peasant village where everyone knows everyone else clear down to the ground, is gone. Over large areas of the city "community" is little more than a geographical expression. Yet the old traditions of control persist despite changed conditions of life. The inevitable result is cultural disorganization.'[40] There is, of course, a posture of nostalgia here for the rural community, but integration may be possible on another basis than *Gemeinschaft*. Chicago in the 1920s appears, though, to be classical *Gesellschaft*.

The greater part of Zorbaugh's book is devoted to a detailed examination and description of each area in the Near North Side. He begins with the Gold Coast itself, but first makes a detailed historical examination of the changes that had occurred in the area over the previous century. The Chicago school were always aware that they were observing the latest stage, that could only be understood in relation to the past growth of the city. The Gold Coast was 'society' but membership, unlike in the recent past and in smaller communities like Newburyport,[41] was no longer based entirely on birth. Wealth rather than hereditary social position was the criterion. Zorbaugh collected a document from a female member of one of Chicago's 'oldest and most aristocratic families' in which she wrote, 'The society of today is topsy-turvey. No doubt it is due to the growth of the city. Great fortunes and great wealth have led to ostentation and display. The city is so large that society can no longer hold together.'[42] And as Zorbaugh describes: 'One no longer is born to social position; one achieves social position by playing "the social game".'[43] This game is described in some detail – for example the techniques of breaking into *The Social Register*. Zorbaugh demonstrates that the Gold Coast families were not one group but were internally differentiated into cliques.

'Back of the ostentatious apartments, hotels, and homes of the Lake Shore Drive, and the quiet, shady streets of the Gold Coast lies an area of streets that have a painful sameness, with their old, soot-begrimed stone houses, their none-too-clean alleys, their shabby air of respectability.'[44] This is the next area that Zorbaugh describes: the world of furnished rooms. Demographically this area is interesting: 52 per cent were single men, 10 per cent were single women, while the remaining 38 per cent were married 'without benefit of clergy'. It was also a childless area.[45] The whole population turned over every four months.[46] In this social situation Zorbaugh argues that 'there can be no community

[40] *Ibid.*, p. 16.
[41] See below, pp. 101-111.
[42] Zorbaugh, *op. cit.*, p. 48.
[43] *Ibid.*, p. 49.   [44] *Ibid.*, p. 69.
[45] *Ibid.*, p. 71.   [46] *Ibid.*, p. 72.

tradition or common definition of the situation, no public opinion, no informal social control'.[47] The exaggerated mobility and astonishing anonymity 'are the direct antithesis of all we are accustomed to think of as normal in society'. It should be noted that the stereotype 'community' has been taken to be 'normal'. One typical weakness of the Chicago school is exhibited here: their concentration on 'natural areas' prevented them always from viewing the city as a whole. If they had stepped back a bit, as it were, it might have been possible for them to consider where those who were living in the rooming house district had come from and where they were moving to. It is then conceivable that the sheer temporality of their stay should have suggested that this district was meeting temporary needs, in many cases reflecting a particular stage in the life cycle. They had come from and would return to a community thought of by Zorbaugh as 'normal in society'. The Chicago school's contribution to our knowledge of urban processes is surer on 'inter-generation' mobility processes: 'children' moving 'out' and 'up' from Little Sicilies, than on 'intra-generational' processes: leaving home to live in a rooming house, or flat or bedsitter, and later moving to suburbia after marriage to have and rear children.

The bohemia of 'Towertown' is described next, demonstrating that many who lived there were seeking an escape from the 'repressive conventions' of the smaller community. This is at the same time as the 'X' family in Middletown are preventing 'modern' literature and 'modern' art being found in the public libraries and galleries. He then moves to discuss what he calls 'The Rialto of the Half World' – the world of bright lights, restaurants and jazz. Here are hobos, squawkers (pedlars and street salesmen) and the 'Wobbly' headquarters, cabaret and brothels, tea-rooms and homosexuals. That most large cities have areas such as this is indisputable (one thinks of the juxtaposition of radical publishing houses and stripclubs in Soho), but few people live there: it is a 'service' area for the wider community.

Behind these bright lights were the slums and 'one alien group after another had claimed this area. The Irish, the Germans, the Swedish, the Sicilians have occupied it in turn. Now it is being invaded by a migration of the Negro from the south.'[48] The Negroes have come from communities like those described in a later section. Here the immigrant to the city 'meets with sympathy, understanding and encouragement . . . (and) . . . finds his fellow-countrymen who under-stand his habits and his standards and share his life-experience and viewpoint. In the colony he has a status, plays a role in a group. In the life of the colony's streets and cafés, in its churches and benevolent

[47] *Ibid.*, p. 82.
[48] *Ibid.*, p. 127.

societies, he finds response and security. In the colony he finds that he can live, be somebody, satisfy his wishes – all of which are impossible in the strange world outside.'[49] This looks extraordinarily like the usual view of the traditional community, for indeed these are what Herbert Gans later was to call 'urban villages'.[50] Zorbaugh located twenty-eight district nationalities in the Near North Side Slum. He wants to call the specific areas 'ghettos' and like the medieval Jewish ghetto they form a more of less independent community with their own customs and laws. It was out of 'Little Sicily' that the Mafia emerged – they had mostly come from around Palermo. It seems that in 'Little Sicily' it was possible for many Sicilians to remain *encapsulated* – to use Mayer's term[51] – in Chicago: they continued in almost every respect the mores, especially those relating to sexual relations, of the village areas from which they had migrated. And the Mafia continued the fierce and persistent feuding between families.

So the contrasts within the area described by Zorbaugh are tremendous and yet there was a common theme in the very great difficulty found by all groups in maintaining or reconstructing any *sense* or *feeling* of community. The Gold Coasters, we are told, had no sense of community apart from sharing a good address; the rooming-house people as described by Zorbaugh were completely detached from society and the hobos by definition were isolates and wanderers. The only place where there was any rootedness was in Little Sicily, but they would be displaced by the next wave of immigrants.

The one important ingredient in all the Chicago monographs is the concept of ecology and the practice of relating (if not determining) community structure to geographical and spatial realities. Otherwise their theoretical advances were slight: they provided a truly impressive amount of factual detail on Chicago, but little else. Take for example Zorbaugh's theoretical chapter, 'The City and the Community', and it will be seen that this adds little to the theory of community. True, he rejects idealized notions of community and stresses 'that the life of a local area has a natural organization which must be taken into account',[52] but this is little more than a plea for yet more empirical work 'to discover how the community acts, how it sets up standards, defines aims and ends, gets things done; and to analyse what has been the effect of the growth of the city upon the life of local areas, what changes have

[49] *Ibid.*, p. 141.

[50] H. J. Gans, *The Urban Villagers*, New York, Free Press, 1962 (London, Collier-Macmillan, 1962).

[51] P. Mayer, 'Migrancy and the Study of Africans in Towns', *American Anthropologist*, 1962.

[52] Zorbaugh, *op. cit.*, p. 221.

come with the industrial city'. The village still represents the example *par excellence* of the community and he writes that in the city 'an area becomes a community only through the common experiences of the people who live in it, resulting in their becoming a cultural group, with traditions, sentiments and attitudes and memories in common – a focus of belief, feeling and action. A community, then, is a local area over which people are using the same language, conforming to the same mores, feeling more or less the same sentiments, and acting upon the same attitudes.'[53] However, he clearly feels that though this may have existed in European peasant villages or early American towns, communities like this are not found in the modern city '. . . as a glimpse of the life (this may be the true contribution of many Chicago monographs) of the Gold Coast, of Little Hill, of Towertown, or the world of the furnished rooms so vividly shows, local areas of the city are vastly different from the village and over great areas of the city the last vestiges of the community are disappearing'.[54] This would seem to be denied by his own data, especially on the migrant colonies. He goes on to use Burgess's concentric zone typology of urban growth and repeats Burgess's claim that these are displayed (only modified by physical features) in every city. Within each zone of these broader zones 'competition, economic and cultural, segregates the population'.[55] The local consequence of this competition, a reflection of the division of labour, is an exaggeration of social distance in the residential locality. In the constantly idealized village practically everybody has some economic and cultural relationship with everybody else. In the city, however, such relationships no longer occur in the local community and social distance consequently increases. There is in the city, he argues, a replacement of face-to-face and intimate relationships by casual, transitory, disinterested contacts and as there is 'no common body of experience and tradition, no unanimity of interest, sentiment and attitude which can serve as a basis for collective action, local groups do not act. They cannot act, local life breaks down.'[56]

The Chicago school in general, and Zorbaugh in particular, fail to take account of the general tendency in industrial societies towards individuation and the extent to which people positively *choose* city life for what it can offer. If the sociologists approach the study of community with an ideal typical community in mind, it can but only be always disintegrating. If the Chicago school were presiding over the total eclipse of some past rural community, then later sociologists have presided over the collapse of city communities into suburbia (see below). It is not helpful to identify a particular way of life with a particular

[53] *Ibid.*, pp. 222–3.   [54] *Ibid.*, p. 228.
[55] *Ibid.*, p. 232.   [56] *Ibid.*, p. 251.

ecological space. Yet what ecology can do is to give some indication of the spatial *constraints* within which choices are made. The particular contribution of the Chicago school was an appreciation of *how* cities changed. Their dynamic model of successions and areas of change has very wide applicability, and not just to large cities. As will be shown in the next section Lloyd Warner's assumption about the stability of 'Yankee City' seriously misled him about that community's past. A careful reading of Zorbaugh's *The Gold Coast and the Slum*, which had been published six years before Warner entered the field, would have sensitized him to urban processes and perhaps allowed a more realistic analysis of 'Yankee City'.

Yankee City

The Yankee City project must rank as the most intensive, exhaustive and expensive single study ever made of a small American community, or anywhere else for that matter.[57] The first of the five volumes that reports the findings of Lloyd Warner and his colleagues lists a research staff of thirty: four were writers, analysts and fieldworkers, nine were analysts and fieldworkers, five were just fieldworkers and twelve were just analysts, i.e. eighteen people, at least had done fieldwork in Newburyport, the small New England town for which Yankee City is the pseudonym (the use of pseudonyms are a verbal manifestation of his assumptions of the broader generalization of his study). The project was conceived as part of a research programme conducted from Harvard, and it was originally aimed to examine the 'non-work' aspect of the lives of the workers being studied by Elton Mayo at Western Electric (the famous Hawthorne experiments). Warner found this prospect impossible. He had just returned from three years fieldwork among Australian aborigines and wanted to apply the same techniques used there to the study of American communities. Unfortunately 'Cicero and Hawthorne (the location of the Western Electric factory) and other industrial sub-communities in Chicago . . . seemed to be disorganized; they had a social organization which was highly disfunctional if not in partial disintegration. If we were to compare easily the other societies of the world with one of our own civilization, and if we were readily to

[57] W. Lloyd Warner and Paul S. Lunt, *The Social Life of a Modern Community* (Yankee City Series, 1), New Haven, Yale University Press, 1941; *The Status System of a Modern Community*, 1942; Warner and Leo Srole, *The Social Systems of American Ethnic Groups*, 1945; Warner and J. O. Low, *The Social System of a Modern Factory*, 1947; Warner, *The Living and the Dead*, 1959. These five volumes will be referred to respectively as Yankee City I (YCI), YCII, YCIII, YCIV and YCV. Students may like to know that Warner has abridged the series into one volume published in 1963 (New Haven, Yale University Press).

accommodate our techniques, developed by the study of primitive society, to modern groups, *it seemed wise to choose a community with a social organization which had developed over a long period of time under the domination of a single group with a coherent tradition.*'[58]

New England and the Deep South seemed likely locations for such a community. Warner's fatal error was that his anthropological orientation and techniques misled him into believing Yankee City was, in fact, like that. It has been shown that he had serious misconceptions, particularly about the communities history, that his ahistorical functionalist conceptual framework and methods never allowed him to realize. Warner's strength was his lack of ethnocentricity which certainly allowed him to see and report phenomena long ignored in American Society, for example, stratification and yet he was blind to other aspects of the community. Warner wrote that 'to be sure we were not ethnocentrically biased in our judgements, we decided to use no previous summaries of data collected by anyone else (maps, handbooks, histories etc.) until we had formed our own opinion of the community'.[59] In the fifth volume, *The Living and the Dead: the symbolic life of a community* Warner, commenting on the 'history' portrayed in Yankee City pageants, said that it 'was what community leaders now *wished* it were and what they *wished* it were not. They ignored this or that difficult period of time or unpleasant occurrence and embarrassing group of men and women; they left out awkward political passions; they selected small items out of large time contexts, sizing them up to express today's values.'[60] It is unfortunately true that Warner's own words quoted above can be used as a similar indictment against his work in Yankee City as a whole. His unwillingness to consult the historical record and his complete dependence on materials susceptible to traditional anthropological analysis, i.e. the acts and opinions of living members of the community, served to obliterate the distinction between the actual past and current myths about the past. This is particularly ironic, as the determination of the Yankee City investigators to escape the ethnocentric biases of culture-bound history led them to accept uncritically the community's legends about itself. This is, as Stephen Thernstom Yankee City's historian, has remarked, 'surely the most ethnocentric of all possible views'.[61]

Warner's view of the community is explicitly and rather crudely

[58] YCI, p. 4 (our emphasis).

[59] *Ibid.*, p. 40.

[60] YCV, p. 110.

[61] Stephen Thernstrom, *Poverty and Progress: Social Mobility in a Nineteenth-century City*, Cambridge, Mass., Harvard U.P., 1964, p. 230 (London, Harvard U.P.–Oxford U.P., 1965).

functionalist, for he admits that 'the analogy of the organism was in our thinking when we looked at the total community of Yankee City and the various parts of its internal structure'.[62] Elsewhere the community is called a 'working whole in which each part had definite *functions* which *had* to be performed or substitutes acquired, if the whole society were to maintain itself'.[63] His functionalism is of an evolutionary variety and he refers to 'higher' and 'lower' cultures. The community was defined as 'a body of people having a common organization or common interests and living in the same place under the same laws and regulations'.[64] The ordered social relations of this locally bound group he calls the social structure and 'all local groups differ sufficiently everywhere for the individuals in them to be aware of belonging to one group and not to another, even though the other may be but little different from their own'.[65] This would seem to belie the geographical mobility of Americans. Warner had a two dimensional geometrical view of the community: social space was seen as having two dimensions, the vertical which is a hierarchical order in which people occupy higher and lower positions, and the horizontal which is the social differentiation at any given level.

The community is variously called a 'convenient microcosm for field study' and a 'laboratory' by Warner. 'In my research', he wrote, 'the local community was made to serve as a microscopic whole representing the total American community.'[66] It is therefore particularly important to know how Yankee City was chosen. Twenty-two variables were used to categorize many communities and Newburyport was chosen because it was the one that 'most nearly approached the ideal-typical expression' of the central tendencies of American society. These 'tendencies' are expressed rather vaguely when Warner wrote ' . . . we know America is a large industrial nation, founded on a vast agricultural base, that it constantly assimilates and fails to assimilate large numbers of immigrants from different European cultures, that its religious life is largely Protestant, but that it has a strong Catholic minority, that it has powerful political and economic hierarchies, that its associational and civic enterprises are deeply pervasive, and that there is a considerable distance from the bottom to the top levels of the socio-economic heap.'[67] He uses the community study both as a 'sampling device', i.e. a method to get at these tendencies (which we should note

[62] YCI, p. 12.
[63] *Ibid.*, p. 14 (our emphasis).
[64] *Ibid.*, p. 16.
[65] *Ibid.*, p. 17.
[66] W. Lloyd Warner, *Structure of American Life*, Edinburgh, Edinburgh U.P., 1952, p. 33.
[67] *Ibid.*, p. 34.

are assumed, not proven), as empirical description, and as an object, for he refers to varieties and sorts of communities.

So above all 'we sought a well integrated community',[68] but he had already commented on the lack of integration in Chicago – did that city *not* represent the central tendencies of American society? But they 'did not want a community where the ordinary daily relations of the inhabitants were in confusion or conflict'. They did, however, want a community 'where the social organization had become firmly organized and the relations of the various members of the society [are] exactly placed and known by the individuals who made up the group'. And what is more, that is what they found, or appeared to find. Warner also specified that the community should have a few industries and several factories because 'we wished to see how the factory and the workers were geared into the life of the larger community'.[69] It should be autonomous and not a metropolitan satellite, which implied that the anthropologist in Warner was yearning for 'isolated wholes'. It is questionable whether this is a reasonable approach to communities in advanced industrial societies. The community also had to be small 'since, if [it] were too large, our detailed methods of observation could not be applied'. 'Such a community, we believed would manifest much of the complexities of modern life but would be beyond the possibilities of detailed examination.' The final condition that the community had to meet makes one wonder whether the other conditions were so many *post facto* legitimations, ' . . . the community had to be near enough to Cambridge (Mass) so that [we] could go back and forth without difficulty or loss of time'.[70]

Their techniques were in the first place to do 'a Robert Park': they walked round the town and produced a map of the physical nature of the community. They introduced themselves to prominent individuals who introduced them to their friends, 'which shortly spread our sources of information from the top to the bottom of the community'. This is diametrically opposed to Warner's main substantive conclusion on 'social classes' in Yankee City which by (his) definition are discrete and bounded friendship groups. If early informants could in fact introduce Warner to friends from the top to the bottom of the community, this is important data in its own right and contradicts his main conclusions on stratification in the community. In any case they used the local stratification system to enter and one frequently voiced criticism is that Warner was in fact captured by his key informants, the Lower Uppers and Upper Middles, as he calls them. Certainly right from the start of the project there appears to be no attempt to ensure and demonstrate that informants covered the whole social range in Yankee City. The

[68] YCI, p. 38.　　　[69] *Ibid.*, p. 39.　　　[70] *Ibid.*, p. 43.

investigators appeared to have had no real entry problems and 'assumed that everyone would have the good sense to know that what we were doing was important and deserving of confidence'.[71] They appear, though, to have made no attempt to really explain their aims, but then you probably would not to Australian aborigines either. They let Yankee City define their role and give them a place in the social structure: as social historians and economists and genealogists and 'to the members of the varied ethnic groups were we fair-minded gentlemen interested in seeing that their groups received their rightful place in the economic and historical study we were making'.

Their techniques were eclectic: observation (as has been shown in the previous chapter, this is not a single technique), interview, documents, newspapers and even an aerial survey. They felt the need to use many and varied techniques for ' . . . the general objective of our research was to determine the *complete* set of social relations which constituted Yankee City society'.[72] Their first task was to 'place' (their term) the person being interviewed and in a very revealing remark Warner says that this was not difficult as 'common knowledge provides a good rough general framework within which a given individual can be placed'.[73] So not only did Lloyd Warner make insupportable assumptions about what sort of community Newburyport was, but he also made initially rather cavalier assumptions about its internal structure, or maybe he believed that his early informants had told him all there was to know. The community was both very thoroughly and somewhat eccentrically covered by any standard – they 'had an observer to complete a list of those who bought magazines and papers to find out what journals were purchased', and they sampled traffic to get those just passing through! The health office told them who had venereal disease in the community.[74] Warner rejects the sample survey as a research tool – in the great Boothian tradition he wanted to know all the facts, though the survey's main advantage of obtaining systematic facts appertaining to individuals would surely have allowed Warner to defend himself against some of his critics.

All these data were collated on what must be seen as the centre of Warner's research – the Social Personality Cards. There was one card for each adult in the community. On them were recorded, name, residence, age, sex, social status, occupation, maiden name of wife, names of children, membership of cliques and associations, church affiliation, type of house, newspapers and magazines taken, movies attended, his doctor and undertaker and summary budget data (which *was* apparently from some sort of sample, the details of which we are

[71] *Ibid.*, p. 48.   [72] *Ibid.*, p. 48 (our emphasis).
[73] *Ibid.*, p. 48.   [74] *Ibid.*, p. 63.

not told). Also any information from public welfare and police records relating to each individual was added. These data were punched on to machine-readable cards and described statistically, though precious little of it is reported in the five Yankee City volumes. These data were collected over the four years from 1930–4 and so it is not a *real* population study for the 16,785 individuals do not correspond to the population of Yankee City at any one time.[75] Warner appreciates that the key problem about his Social Personality Cards is that they are 'data . . . centred on individuals'. So whilst they lend 'themselves readily to statistical compilation and correlation of attributes and relational characteristics of individuals . . . difficulties arose, however, when it became necessary to compare one relation between individuals with another'.[76]

The Yankee City volumes are well known for their characterization of the population of Newburyport into six distinctively named classes. Warner claims that he started with a general economic interpretation of human behaviour. He does not say that it was a marxist orientation but it would seem to have been very similar. Yet while in Yankee City he discovered that some people were ranked low even when they had higher incomes than people ranked above them, and that others with low incomes were ranked high. People with the same jobs were ranked differently, for instance doctors, and this was *not* related to how good a physician he was. The famous Warner definition of social class is 'two or more orders of people who are believed to be and are accordingly ranked by the members of the community in socially superior and inferior positions'.[77] This had consequences for the physical structure of Yankee City as different areas had a different status: Hill Street was top, Side Street in the middle, and Riverbrooker low. These 'class' differences are reflected in Yankee City cliques, clubs and associations. The titles of the 'classes' and their sizes are shown below:

	Per cent	Per cent in full employment
Upper Upper	1·44	90·00
Lower Upper	1·56	94·44
Upper Middle	10·22	83·14
Lower Middle	28·12	62·26
Upper Lower	36·60	41·48
Lower Lower	25·22	27·57
Don't Know	0·84	

[75] See the remarks in Chapter 3 about the 'timelessness' of community studies.
[76] *Ibid.*, p. 73.   [77] *Ibid.*, p. 82.

It is relevant to point out that in 1933, Newburyport had an unemployment rate of nearly 19 per cent: the proportion in full employment of each 'class' is shown in the second column of the table. Lloyd Warner's procedure for 'classing' a community will be discussed in more detail in Chapter 6. He, himself, sums it up like this: 'All the types of social structure and each of the thousands of families, thousands of cliques and hundreds of associations were, member by member, interrelated in our research. With the use of all structural participation, and with the aid of such additional testimony as the area lived in, the type of house, kind of education, manners and other symbols of class (*sic*), it was possible to determine very quickly the approximate place of any individual in society. In the final analysis, however, individuals were placed by the evaluations of the members of Yankee City itself, by such explicit statements as "she does not belong" or "they do not belong".'[78] Imagine trying to use this technique in a city! Warner clearly believes that a community has a social structure with 'classes' as 'real entities' (not categories) into which *all* the inhabitants can unambiguously be placed, that people use their local community as a reference group and that people agree on their criteria of ranking and can classify each other by them. This definition of class led to an extraordinary outburst from other social scientists that will be considered in the later chapter on local stratification. All that should be noted here is that, in the words of C. Wright Mills, 'Warner's insistence upon merely one vertical dimension led to the consequent absorbing of three analytically separable dimensions [economic, status and power] into one "sponge" word "class".'[79] Mills adds that most of the confusions and inadequacies of Warner's study flow from this fact. Warner has threaded *all* the many coloured beads on one vertical string.

Having said what he means by class and categorized the population, Warner then adopts the technique of drawing up what he calls 'profiles'. Though compulsive reading if one has a taste for Thirties American prose (' . . . on that autumn evening Mrs Henry Adams Bredkenridge . . .') – should they really be confused with social science? They are admittedly fictionalized and indeed they could have been written by Sinclair Lewis. Warner even makes one of his characters refer to *Babbitt* (Chapter XV) with reference to the class system in Zenith. 'No one actual individual or family in Yankee City is depicted, rather the lives of several individuals are compressed into that of one *fictive* person'[80] and similarly 'the persons and situations in some of the

---

[78] *Ibid.*, p. 90.
[79] C. Wright Mills, review of YCI in *American Sociological Review*, 7, 1942, reprinted in his collected essays edited by I. L. Horowitz, *People, Politics and Power*, London, Oxford U.P., 1965.   [80] YCI, p. 127 (our emphasis).

sketches are entirely imaginary'. The central damning limitation of these
'profiles' is that they were all constructed without regard for the
scientific canons of verifiability and in a manner which allowed the biases
of the authors to operate unchecked. We have no idea how typical they
are, and so stylistically similar are they to Sinclair Lewis that we
could be forgiven for thinking them fiction. After the profiles, however,
'the remainder of the volume is concerned solely with this quantitative
problem of how many, etc'.

All data on Yankee City are presented 'by class'. Class is the major
analytic variable and so there are chapters on 'sex and age, birthplace,
ethnic minorities, ecology, all 'by class', i.e. the six status groups
enumerated by Warner and listed above. The confusion between class
and status is everywhere evident, for example, we are told that in
'Yankee City houses are (thus) symbols of *status*, in the society. The
cultural differences in the family life of the several *classes* are reflected
in house type and symbolized by it. The house is, moreover, the
paramount symbol of the unequal distribution of the valued things of
life among the several *classes*'[81] and 'age of marriage is in direct relation
to *the status* [to be consistent he should have written class] of an
individual, the upper class marry late, the lower class marry
young'.[82]

He continues his analysis 'by class' of the economic life of the community, the control of property, and how individuals spend their money.
The approach of the principal investigator and the general style of the
volumes are well depicted in this passage: 'When an individual in Yankee
City spent money for articles which could be purchased, he was acting
in accordance with his system of values and thereby satisfying certain
of his desires. The desires of all those who spent money for the things
they wanted were basically physical, but the values which dominated
the expression of their wants were social. All men and women in Yankee
City as physical organisms needed food and shelter, but the values
which dictated their choice of a house or of food for a meal were
socially determined and also expressed the demands, needs and
limitations of their social personalities in a status [*sic*] system.'[83] Here
the community, through its status system (or as Warner usually calls
it, class system) is seen as an independent variable affecting individual
behaviour. Treating the 'association' as one of the foremost mechanisms
of integration of Yankee City society, Warner presents an analysis 'by
class', similarly with church and school, the political structure and
reading.

[81] *Ibid.*, p. 215 (our emphasis).
[82] *Ibid.*, p. 252.
[83] *Ibid.*, p. 287.

THE AMERICAN COMMUNITY STUDIES

Volume II of the Yankee City series, *The Status System of a Modern Community*, is a descriptive statistical extravaganza. There is a concern to tabulate nineteen varieties of 'class types of associational membership' against the six classes. This gives fifty-four 'positions' to which are added varieties of family and clique membership giving eighty-nine 'positions'. The eighty-nine 'positions' are described separately and contain 71,149 memberships which are tabulated (the famous Table 18 lasts for eighty-six pages!). We are almost completely baffled by this volume, especially as its authors admit they cannot say anything about the strength or intensity of the relationship involved.[84] Volume III, *The Social Systems of American ethnic groups* relates in more detail their position in the social structure of Yankee City. The social history of each ethnic group is traced from its arrival up to the 1930s. This volume, together with Volume IV, *The Social System of the Modern Factory*[85] contains Warner's important statements on the 'blocked mobility hypotheses'.[86] Warner computes the 'social position' (average occupational status) of the Irish for 1850, 1864, 1873, 1883 and 1893 and goes straight on to talk about their 'moderate and slight mobility'. Thernstrom, in a magnificent piece of historical research into nineteenth century Newburyport has shown though that (1) the Irish were not an 'entity' in that 'to compute overall occcupational status indices for all Irish names in the community in 1864 and 1883 was of dubious value, because in fact a majority of the Irishmen living in Newburyport in 1864 had left the community by 1883 and the bulk of the 1883 group consisted of newcomers to the city'[87] and (2) manual Irish immigrants who stayed in the community, though they begat manual sons, also bought property and so certainly should have been seen as socially mobile. Warner's techniques do not allow him to differentiate between different dimensions of social mobility (nor do most other techniques for that matter). Thernstrom shows that paradoxically Yankee City may in fact have been a 'sample' of the main trends of American society, though Warner was wrong about what they were. A host of critics have attacked the assumption that seemingly small and static communities like Newburyport and Morris (Jonesville)[88] are adequate laboratories for observing American social life. Thernstrom has shown that Newburyport was far less deviant than Warner made it out to be.

---

[84] YCII., p. 200.
[85] Note in passing the use of the definite rather than the indefinite article.
[86] YCIV, pp. 87–9, 182–5.
[87] Thernstrom, *op. cit.*, p. 238.
[88] Studied by Warner and his colleagues and reported in the community study, *Democracy in Jonesville*, New York, Harper Row, 1949 (London, Harper Torchbooks).

Newburyport was not the dormant, self-contained, predominantly old American *Gemeinschaft* village portrayed in the Yankee City volumes.[89]

In the abridged version of *Yankee City* it is interesting to note that what was Volume IV is now called 'the transition'. It is from this volume that Maurice Stein pulls his message about the destructive effect of bureaucratization on the community.[90] It is the study of a strike which broke the 'open shop' and led to unionization. The extension 'upwards' out of the Yankee City of the factory hierarchy (i.e. absentee ownership), and 'outwards' through manufacturing associations and unions increased the breakdown of communication between management and labour. This, and the breakdown of the old skill hierarchy with modern methods of mass production, replaced by task anonymity, were the underlying causes of the strike. This was interpreted by Warner as an attempt on the part of the workers to gain a new and different sense of status through unionization. As the old mobility of workers up the factory skill hierarchy was blocked this, and the acquisition of the factory by New York Jews, removed the social constraints against striking. Lipset and Bendix, though, argue that the strike sentiments were an expression of anti-semitic attitudes on the part of a large part of the population. Jews with high economic position and low status were, they argue, a threat to the whole value system of the community.[91] The fifth and final volume, *The Living and the Dead*, is about the symbolic life of Yankee City, about political myths and 'dead heroes'.

There have been so many criticisms of Warner that it might well be time to call for a moratorium on them. Never in the history of community studies has so much effort been expended by so many people with such wrongheaded assumptions and with such inappropriate concepts and techniques. Yet Lloyd Warner did break the academic taboo and open up the debate about stratification in the United States. Occasionally he was just silly: 'Jonesville is in all Americans and all Americans are in Jonesville, for he that dwelleth in America dwelleth in Jonesville, and Jonesville in him',[92] and his work suffers throughout from the basic delusions that the ahistorical, functionalist

[89] Warner describes the Upper Uppers as having lived in Yankee City for generations but in fact a close examination of his data shows that less than 60 per cent had been born in or near Newburyport and almost a quarter had been born outside New England (YCI, p. 209).

[90] Stein, *op. cit.*, Chapter 3.

[91] S. M. Lipset and R. Bendix, 'Social Status and Social Structure: a reexamination of the data and interpretations', *British Journal of Sociology*, Vol. I, 1951, p. 232.

[92] *Jonesville*, p. xv.

assumptions of the old equilibrium school of social anthropology provided an adequate framework for studying a complex modern community in an industrial society. The details of Warner's study can be used to document the changes occurring in some American communities in the Thirties, for example, it is difficult not to conclude that 'the transition' and the strike described in Volume IV shows a breaking down of the old status hierarchies – through they may not have been so old, as Thernstrom has shown – and the rise to some considerable power of the working class. What Warner calls the 'classes' of Yankee City, which are described in Volume I as joint participants in a common community system, increasingly confront each other as embodiments of collectivities under the control of remote power centres which determine their relationships to each other far more than factors arising in the local community. The 'Warner approach' to community studies has also been used in other communities, one of which will be discussed next.

Communities in the Deep South

The first chapter of Davis and the Gardners' *Deep South* was written by Lloyd Warner, and their whole research project was directed by him. It will be remembered from the previous section that the deep South of the United States had, it was argued by Warner, some similar characteristics to New England in general and Yankee City in particular. The techniques and approaches to the community of Natchez in Mississippi – 'Old City', the community reported on in *Deep South* – are almost identical to those used in Yankee City and so need not be discussed further. Except for one point: Natchez was deeply and, it would seem, inevitably divided on the basis of 'race', between black and white. The fieldwork difficulties that this poses were briefly mentioned in Chapter 3: they were solved by having two husband and wife teams of different colour. The Gardners and the Davises, in fact, could not meet in Natchez but had to go to the neighbouring 'Big City' to discuss their research. The aims were straightforward: 'To understand the social structure and customs of the Negroes and whites of Old city [Natchez] which their fellow-anthropologists have used when they have told of the natives of New Guinea, the Indians of the Amazon or the aborigines of Australia.'[93] The population of the town was just over 10,000 and was 50 per cent Negro, the surrounding rural district was 80 per cent Negro. This was cotton country based on the plantation system and one might be forgiven for thinking that little had happened

[93] Allison Davis and B. B. Gardner and M. R. Gardner, *Deep South*, Chicago, University of Chicago Press, 1944. Abridged edition, 1965, p. 3.

to the social structure since the abolition of slavery, in name. This would, of course, be wrong.

The type of social structure found in this sort of local social system, and popularized by *Deep South*, was that of a 'colour-caste'.[94] This is markedly different to the view of race relations that emerges from, say, the Chicago school discussed above. It will be remembered that they did not use the term caste, but tended rather 'to view specific "communities" as areas in which ethnic groups were involved in continuous competition and conflict, resulting in a hierarchy persisting through time, with now one, and again another, ethnic group at the bottom as previous new comers moved "up".'[95] Each ethnic group developed its own stratification system within it and as individuals acquired better jobs, more education and an ability with the English language, they and their families often detached themselves from immigrant colonies (located in specific parts of the urban structure) and sometimes from all ethnic institutions as well. This is the essence of the Chicago school's view of communities as being in 'competition' with 'successions' and mobility. There is, of course, a strong suggestion that as these ethnic groups moved 'up' they became assimilated into the middle class and 'disappeared'. This was the end of what had been called 'hyphenated Americans'. Large metropolitan communities had been viewed then as 'open', relatively so even for Black Americans. The consequences of Negroes remaining 'visible' and not being able to 'pass' in white society is, of course, a significant flaw in this argument and in the Chicago school's approach, but it cannot be developed here. Communities in the deep South were, however, closed, both in the sense of their being no mobility across the colour-caste line and in the sense that one planter meant when he told the fieldworkers, 'You have to have a passport to come in here from the United States'.[96] He meant it was a closed society.

The view of race relations developed in *Deep South* is of a system of social relations organized by a colour-caste system that shaped economic and political relations as well as family and kinship structures, and which was reinforced by the legal system (this was, of course, before the historic Supreme Court decisions of the 1950s). Within each of the two castes (superordinate white and superordinate black) social classes – Warner's 'social classes' existed, status being based upon possession

[94] We are using the term 'caste' as it is used in *Deep South*. There has, though, been an acrimonious debate with Indianists over Warner's use of the term.

[95] St Clair Drake, 'The Social and Economic Status of the Negro in the United States, *Daedalus*, Vol. 94, No. 4, 1965, p. 771.

[96] Davis and Gardners, *op. cit.*, p. 343.

THE AMERICAN COMMUNITY STUDIES

of money, education and family background as reflected in distinctive styles of behaviour. 'Exploitation' in the marxist sense was present within this caste-class system, but also much more, for an entire socio-cultural system, not just an economic order, functioned to distribute power and prestige unevenly between whites and Negroes and to punish any individual who questioned the system by word or behaviour.

The caste system in Natchez was based on endogamy and taboos upon sexual relations between white women and Negro men, but permitting sexual relations between white men and Negro women. It is organized around the control of sex. It is reflected in the ecology of the community and there is a marked spatial segregation of the two castes. It is possible with Stein to view 'Southern community life as a gigantic conspiracy through which Negroes are kept from turning against their white masters by a network of control mechanisms ranging from deference patterns to lynch violence'.[97] The two castes have also developed their own internal differentiation. This is demonstrated through the analysis of clique and associational membership by the same techniques as those used in Yankee City. Class for example is defined as 'the largest group of people whose members have intimate access to one another [this is more than a little ingenuous as white men have intimate access to Negro women!]. A class is composed of families and social cliques. The interrelationships between these families and cliques, in such informed activities as visiting, dances, receptions, teas and larger informal affairs constitute the structure of a social class. A person is a member of that social class with which most of his participations, of this intimate kind, occur.'[98]

The contrast with Chicago was mentioned above. There are also important differences within the deep South. The long quotation that follows is a very good indication of the differences between communities that emerge based on size and stability: 'The whole pattern of caste behaviour and controls is also significantly affected by the differences between rural and urban situations. It is commonly recognized for instance, that the rural Negro is more subordinated in his behaviour than the urban Negro. In fact, the rural Negro frequently follows the formal pattern of caste etiquette exactly. . . . The urban Negroes often crowd whites in the stores, ignore them on the streets and sidewalks, and frequently are accused by whites of 'seeing how far they can go'. The whites are well aware of this difference in behaviour and often speak with wistful approbation of the politeness and good-manners of the country Negroes, as compared to those in the city. The whites in a

[97] Stein, op.cit., p. 154.
[98] Davis and Gardners, op. cit., p. 59.

neighbouring county frequently complained that the whites in Old City are too lenient with the Negroes and "don't keep them in their places".[99]

A community study that is the essential complement to *Deep South* is John Dollard's book, *Caste and Class in a Southern Town*. Dollard, a social psychologist, not an anthropologist, shows that the forces sustaining the local social system are very deep. He never presents a detailed description of the social structure of the community in which he worked but focuses on aspects of social control hardly touched by Davis and the Gardners. He describes in detail his biases, and he realizes that by listing them he has not necessarily avoided them. However, the reader of his monograph is in a better position to judge his research findings after reading this chapter, than he would be without it. He thought it would be as well to do this after persistent enquiries as to what 'this Yankee sociologist was doing here studying niggers'.[100] He realized that he was reacting like a Northerner and with recommendable honesty reports that at that time he had written in his field notes: 'These people down here are very charming and really exert themselves to do friendly things once you are accepted, but they seem very much like the psychotics one sometimes meets in a mental hospital. They are sane and charming except on one point and on this point they are quite unreliable. One has exactly the sense of a whole society with a psychotic spot, an irrational, heavily protected sore through which all manner of venomous hatreds and irrational lists may pour, and – you are eternally striking against this spot.' Dollard was working, then, as a Northern, white, middle-class male: it was difficult, before he got an office in an anonymous down-town block, to persuade Negroes to talk to him. Altogether he spent only five months in Southern Town. His principle research tools for the Negroes were the social-psychological techniques of the depth interview and the life-history – how the latter were collected is described in an appendix. He was less systematic with the whites, apparently relying on ordinary participant observation with special emphasis on everyday expressions of the unconscious, like jokes and slips of the tongue.

Dollard's achievement is the detail he provides on the coercive aspects of Southern community life. It was clear from *Deep South* that Negroes despise and fear intimidation by Whites, yet the ramifying effects of these fears and hatreds are never treated. Similarly, the emotional responses of the whites to this latent hostility are revealed in quotations in *Deep South*, but never actually analysed in detail. However, Dollard

[99] *Ibid.*, p. 54.
[100] John Dollard, *Caste and Class in a Southern Town*, New York, Doubleday, 1957, p. 36. Originally published 1937, Yale University Press.

collected a different kind of data. For example, while both community studies describe the circumstances under which white men have privileged access to Negro women, their observations as well as their interpretations of this pattern differ. In *Deep South* it is dealt with in a section on endogamy and the authors analyse the various possible structural interconnections to which relationships can give rise.[101]

In *Caste and Class in a Southern Town*, Dollard deals with the same problem of inter-caste relations but his interpretations are different to those of Davis and the Gardners. It is dealt with in a chapter called 'The Sexual Gain': he presents a very subtle picture of the web of unconscious attractions and fears that underlie sexual relations between the castes and within each caste. He exposes what he calls the 'sickness' of the South – the warped sexual identities that are forced on Whites and Negroes alike by the caste system. White females are almost forced into frigidity by their husbands who get sexual satisfaction from Negro females without having to acknowledge their social existence. Negro males are forced to watch their females being exploited by White males without intervening and thereby suffer blows to their own masculine self-esteem while the Negro female cannot heal the wound since she is the unwilling, or perhaps even willing, participant in the process. Not only are the sexual 'gains' those of the whites (by and large the males) but also the economic and prestige 'gains'. Dollard brilliantly explores 'the emotional forces which drive and support social action' in the community and devotes four chapters to describing and analysing the patterns of aggression management adopted by each caste. Some of his explanations are exceedingly complex and sophisticated, particularly his interpretation of the multiple functions of the white belief that Negro men invariably desire white women.[102]

What is clear from both these community studies is that despite the apparently autonomous internal organization of both castes, they are not in anyway separate 'communities'. The *whole* community social structure, which is based on one caste exploiting the other invariably affects the white exploiters as well as the exploited Negroes.[103] Stein has maintained that: 'White Southerners are displacing aggression so that attention is diverted from real inadequacies in the communities in which they live onto the Negroes.'[104] Their caste superiority gives them a minimum of self-esteem but, as Dollard has shown, at a high price. *Deep South* demonstrates that there are communities organized around

[101] *Ibid.*, p. 33.
[102] *Ibid.*, pp. 382–3.
[103] *Ibid.*, pp. 445–6.
[104] Stein, *op. cit.*, p. 172.

race which create overwhelming problems for social control and *Caste and Class in a Southern Town* shows the importance of analysing covert emotional life in a community. Dollard's talents are unlikely to be found in most sociologists for he has used his knowledge of psychoanalytic processes to show how persons with different characters are forced to adapt to the role playing alternatives confronting them in the community. His successor in this style of community analysis is, of course, Erving Goffman, but Dollard's analysis was unequalled until *The Presentation of Self in Everyday Life*.

Small Town in Mass Society

There are three reasons why Vidich and Bensman's *Small Town in Mass Society: Class, Power and Religion in a Rural Community* is necessary reading for all students of community studies. First for its substance, for its findings, second for its methodology and thirdly because its publication was a *cause célèbre* in American sociology.

The central message of this community study is contained in its title, and the question which is answered in the monograph is, what is the place of a small town (in fact in rural upstate New York with a population of 2,500) in mass society? One important conclusion is that it was not possible to talk about 'Springdale' (the pseudonym for their community) as a whole in relation to mass society but only about the relationship of particular groups. Since the work of Vidich and Bensman it has been increasingly impossible to conceptualize communities as 'isolates', for they showed that it was only possible to make sociological sense of what was going on in Springdale by viewing the community within the framework of large-scale bureaucratic mass society rather than as the polar opposite of urban society. *Small Town in Mass Society* makes it less possible than ever to talk realistically about a rural urban dichotomy or even a continuum. The general approach of the authors is very similar to that of Stein discussed in Chapter 2, in that they see industrialization, urbanization, and bureaucratization as the central processes in the community and hence in society. The authors wrote: 'Our central concern was with the processes by which the small town (and indirectly all segments of American society) are continuously and increasingly drawn into the central machinery, processes and dynamics of the total society.'[105] They make no claims to have studied the whole community, but rather have viewed

[105] Arthur J. Bensman and Joseph Vidich, *Small Town in Mass Society: Class Power and Religion in a Rural Community*, Princeton, University Press, 1958. Revised edition 1968, p. xi.

the community as a limited and finite universe in which they can examine some major issues. '(Their) study is an attempt to explore the foundations of social life in a community which lacks the power to control the institutions that regulate and determine its existence. It is in this sense that the community is viewed as a stage on which major issues and problems typical of the society are played out.'[106]

It is highly relevant to the major themes of this book that Vidich and Bensman did not go to the community with highly developed hypotheses: originally they aimed to trace in detail the relationships between the rural community and the various agencies and institutions of American society that affect rural life. That is to say, though, they were always concerned with what might be called the communities 'external relations'. Out of data collected with this in mind they came to the conclusion that they needed to analyse the local class structure and far more wide ranging connections to economic, political and social institutions. For internal class and political arrangements in Springdale are both partly determined by outside forces and act as a 'screen and funnel' for 'the very forces which determine them'. This led the authors to perceive that the community contained sharp contradictions and that 'the public enactment of community life and public statements of community values seemed to have little relationship to the communities operating institutions and the private lives of its members'.[107] They were therefore led to ask new questions of their data, particularly, what are the integrating psychological and institutional factors that make the community's social life possible? What are the major cultural systems which make it possible for the members of a community to function as individuals in spite of the demonstrated negation of their basic beliefs by their immediate social environment? And what techniques of personal and social adjustment enable the community members to live constructive and meaningful lives in the face of an environment which is hostile to their values, aspirations and illusions? Vidich and Bensman claim that their community study is 'only a description and social analysis . . . not a prescription of a prognosis'.[108] They do not offer solutions.

They begin with a detailed analysis of the social, economic and historical setting of their community from 1793 and this is followed by a socio-economic description of the present population. Though there is a wide range of incomes Springdalers do not like to think of their community and themselves in it as too broadly differentiated in economic terms. Similarly whilst only 25 per cent of the population

[106] *Ibid.*, p. xviii.
[107] *Ibid.*, p. xviii.
[108] *Ibid.*, p. xiv.

were actually born in the community, they like to think of their community as predominantly made-up of a stable native population. Economically the village now is really a farm trading and service centre, for example, its school is often referred to as its biggest industry. The place of work of the community's inhabitants can be equally divided into three, those who work in the village, the surrounding rural areas and those who commute to neighbouring towns and cities. And the Springdaler works hard. Social organizations in the community, as elsewhere, bring together the socially similar and the like-minded and yet 'it is a feature of Springdale that such social distinctions are rarely noticed and never verbalized'.[109] There are in fact over two hundred formally constituted organizations.

The chapter 'Springdale's Image of Itself' is the only rival in community study literature to Robert Lynd's account of 'the Middletown spirit', which it stylistically resembles. Springdalers think of themselves as 'just plain folks' – this excludes 'city people' but includes everyone in the community. 'To be one of the folks requires neither money, status, family background, learning, nor refined manners.'[110] It includes a whole set of moral values: honesty, fairplay, trustworthiness, good-neighbourliness, helpfulness, sobriety and clean living. 'To the Springdaler it suggests a wholesome family life, a man whose spoken word is as good as a written contract, a community of religious-minded people and a place where "everybody knows everybody" and "where you can say hello to anybody".'[111] They are in fact, as Vidich and Bensman show, clinging to an image of their community as a stronghold of opposition to urbanism. Cities are seen as corrupt and devoid of human values. In Springdale, in contrast to the 'big city' 'personal relations are face-to-face and social gatherings are intimate, church going retains the quality of a family affair, the merchant is known as a person and you can experience the "thrill of watching nature and the growth of your garden".'[112] 'Shack-people' are of course excluded because they fail to fulfil the image of good friend and neighbour, though 'in everyday social intercourse it is a social *faux pas* to act as if economic inequalities make a difference'.[113] Social control is through gossip. The dominant ideology can be summed up like this: equality, industriousness, improvement and optimism, all of which gain meaning and substance through the pursuit of hard work.

However, Vidich and Bensman found that Springdale did contain a set of socio-economic classes which exhibit entirely different styles of life, both from each other and from the publicly dominant ideology

[109] *Ibid.*, p. 23.   [110] *Ibid.*, p. 30.
[111] *Ibid.*, p. 30.   [112] *Ibid.*, pp. 32–3.
[113] *Ibid.*, p. 40.

elaborated above. They develop what might be called a 'Keynesian' view of social class and the distinctions between the groups in Springdale are based on differences in:

Investment	+	—	—	—
Hoarding (savings)	—	+	—	—
Consumption	—	—	+	+
Work	(+)	+	—	+
which gives:	Expanding Farmers	Non-Expanding Farmers	Shack people	professionals

They write that: 'The basic class dimensions of the community . . . can be described in terms of different emphasis on hoarding, investment and consumption'.[114] Vidich and Bensman argue that Keynes was also describing basic psychological orientations to the disposition of income and that those psychological orientations can be the basis of classes. Vidich and Bensman go on to document how, despite the dominant ideology, judgements of personal worth were based almost entirely on economic success. Also in contrast to the local belief system they claim that 'an historically indigenous local culture does not seem to exist,'[115] and what there is has been brought by immigrants to the community, expecially the professionals who they describe as 'gatekeepers to the mass society' for the community. The community was also dependent economically on outside industry, and as so many were employed outside the community even in this relatively 'simple' rural community there is no single standard for social stratification. 'The reason why a single standard of stratification cannot be used is that it presupposes knowledge which makes assessments possible.'[116] If this was true of Springdale how much more was this likely to be true of 'Yankee City'?

The 'political surrender to mass society' is documented. Everybody talks politics in Springdale we are told. Despite the ethos of democracy and open decisions openly reached, there was what Vidich and Bensman call an 'invisible government'. They show the community to be run by a single leader who used three associates to control all of the elected political offices and who made all important policy decisions. Here again was a great disparity between the public imagery and the social reality as revealed by the community sociologist. Like the local class system and the dominance of mass culture, the local political machines were

114 *Ibid.*, p. 76.
115 *Ibid.*, p. 86.
116 *Ibid.*, p. 95.

not only unrecognized but when attention was called to them, their existence was vigorously denied. The existence of this 'invisible government' could constitute a threat to social integration if its workings were recognized and seen to make a mockery of their assumptions about 'grass-roots democracy'. This is prevented from happening by what Vidich and Bensman call 'particularization', which consists of seeing events and processes in isolation so that generalizations cannot be drawn. Springdalers are able to encounter any number of specific facts proving the existence of the 'invisible government', class, or the towns dependence on mass society without ever recognizing that these encounters indicate the existence of important regularities. The very hard work and constant pressure towards activities of all kinds also prevents introspection, they argue. Vidich and Bensman conclude strongly that 'the people of Springdale are unwilling to recognize the defeat of their values, their personal importance in the face of larger events and any failure in their way of life . . . (but) . . . because they do not recognize their defeat, they are not defeated'.[117]

Some of their fieldwork methods were mentioned in Chapter 3 and the methodological papers associated with this project are some of the most important ever produced from community studies – particularly on participant observation, the validity of field data and the role of theory in field work.[118] Small Town and Mass Society was also a scandal and the student is fortunate in that it is fully documented. In discussing the methodology of community studies it was suggested that the final stage of 'exit' should include the post-publication relationships of community sociologists to their community. In Small Town and Mass Society not only are individuals clearly recognizable by their structural positions, for instance the school principal in a community of 2,500 but, as will have been gathered from the exposition above, it made explicit many things that were implicit in the community. The community's reactions have, in fact, been recorded by Vidich and Bensman. This and their earlier relations with the academic body from which the study was conducted (unofficially it should be noted) have been soundly criticized and defended. They have certainly made future fieldwork in the community almost impossible. The reader must judge for himself from the references cited whether the behaviour and procedures were

[117] *Ibid.*, p. 314.
[118] 'Participant Observation and the Collection and Interpretation of Data', *American Journal of Sociology*, Vol. 60, No. 4, January 1955; 'The Validity of Field Data', *Human Organisation*, Vol. 13, No. 1, 1954; 'Social Theory in Field Research', *American Journal of Sociology*, Vol. 65, No. 6, May 1960. All three of these papers are reprinted in the revised edition of *Small Town in Mass Society*, 1968.

justified in the light of the contribution this provacative study makes to sociology.[119]

North American Suburban Communities

A suburb would seem, by definition, to be less than urban and less than a community. Indeed if communities are viewed as types along a continuum then suburbs are always at the opposite extreme to *real* communities, folk villages or what have you. They are seen as the apothesis of *Gesellschaft* and nothing called 'community' should be found there. As will be seen below there are community studies that show this to be grossly inaccurate. Suburbs, as local social systems, have until recently been but poorly analysed by sociologists. However, there are now several community studies that have taken suburbia as their locale and there can be no excuse for the crudities of 'the myth of suburbia'. This section will first analyse *Crestwood Heights*, a community study of a wealthy suburb of Toronto, Canada and then show how certain aspects of middle-class suburbs have been exaggerated, and given wide currency through *The Organization Man*, into a mistaken and sociologically implausible view of suburbia and will conclude with an analysis of the 'birth' of a suburban community: Levittown, which has been studied by Herbert Gans.

Seeley, Sim and Loosley follow a largely ethnographic model for their field report on Crestwood Heights: chapters on time, space and architecture, on the family and on the life cycle, on ceremonial and associational life and on belief systems. Unlike most ethnographic accounts of primitive tribes, the crucial problem is where to bound the study: true Crestwood Heights was an administrative unit, adjoining metropolitan Toronto, but the men did not work there, few had been born there and few expected to stay. As David Reisman has commented, it is difficult 'to know where Crestwood Heights ends and where Big City [Toronto], or Canada, or North America, or the Jewish subculture, or the Western world begins'.[120] The authors of this community study appreciate that their locale will be familiar to most of their readers 'for some community like it is to be seen in and around almost

[119] See the editorial of *Human Organization*, Vol. 17, 1958–9 and Vidich and Bensman's reply. There are further comments in Vol. 18 and further replies in Vol. 19. See also Vidich and Bensman's 'The Springdale Case: Academic Bureaucrats and Sensitive Townspeople' in Arthur J. Vidich, Joseph Bensman and Maurice Stein (eds), *Reflections on Community Studies, op. cit.*, All of the above are also reprinted in the revised edition of *Small Town and Mass Society*, 1968.

[120] J. R. Seeley, R. A. Sim and E. W. Loosley, *Crestwood Heights*, New York, Wiley, 1963, p. xiii (originally New York, Basic Books, 1956) (London, Wiley).

any great city on this continent'.[121] They are prepared to call Crestwood Heights a community because of the relationships that exist between people – 'relationships revealed in the functioning of the institutions which they have created: family school, church, community centre, club, association, summer-camp'.[122] Not all these groups to which the inhabitants belong are actually to be found within the geographical boundaries of Crestwood Heights. However, there is clearly a local social system: institutions are interrelated locally and what is more this complex net of human relationships which is the community exists from the viewpoint of the participants for a definite purpose (i.e. the community is viewed by the authors of this particular monograph as a purposive organization). This purpose is child rearing.

The name 'Crestwood Heights' suggests, as it is clearly meant to, the sylvan, the natural, and the romantic, the lofty and the serene, the distant but not withdrawn; the suburb that looks out upon, and over the city, not in it or of it, but at its border and on its crest. Though there is little strong local identification, being in Crestwood Heights is a source of pride: it represents one temporary goal achieved; yet Crestwooders are highly individualistic, they will move on and up the bureaucratic hierarchy in which the men are employed. Peoples' backgrounds are not 'known' in this community, there are few ties of locality of kinship and so 'a man is judged largely by the number and the quality of the things he owns'[123] – but possessions (mostly material and social status) are not pursued in Crestwood Heights for the direct and sole satisfaction of the competitors, but for one's children. The community has only a brief history, therefore family name has little weight (compare Warner's view of Yankee City), since almost all are strangers to each other. Prestige depends on wealth and occupation, not lineage.

As a community, no matter how much it tries to keep itself aloof from Toronto, it is clearly dependent in some respects on it: Crestwood Heights has no industry, no hospitals, no large stores, no sewage disposal plant – and virtually no slums. It has a population of 17,000 (almost the same as Newburyport). The highly organized industrial and commercial civilization, of which Crestwood is a part, needs highly trained and highly specialized people. Their importance is reflected in what they earn: 'These are the people who can afford the exclusive environment of Crestwood Heights, who, in the very truth, *must* be able to afford it as part of their careers.'[124] So the wage-earner departs each morning to the city and at the same time services come to Crestwood Heights from the city: cleaning women, deliveries, repairmen and

[121] *Ibid.*, p. 3. [122] *Ibid.*, p. 4.
[123] *Ibid.*, p. 7. [124] *Ibid.*, pp. 10–11.

so on. Employment and, Seeley and his colleagues add, 'golf clubs, symphonies, and like activities' are all extra-community. This has had the effect of both deepening and specializing those social relations which are left exclusively local. 'These ties are institutionalized primarily in the family, secondarily in the school and its affiliated activities, and less powerfully, in the municipal services. The institutions of Crestwood Heights therefore converge upon the family, existing as they do to regulate the life of *a purely residential community devoted to* child rearing.[125] Crestwood Heights is built literally around the school. It was chosen for study for strategic and scientific reasons – the authors wanted to use the community as a field for testing hypotheses about social pathology which previously had only been examined in areas where it was dramatically obvious, or socially, economically or politically inconvenient. This was a community which lacked neither time, money, nor professional highly-trained people and so if pathology was found there, this would raise questions as to the then current hypothesis about social pathology. This point and their findings and conclusions cannot be developed here.

There was another reason for choosing Crestwood that, as shall be seen below, was questionable: the authors wrote 'We sense that [Crestwood Heights] represents what life is *coming to be* more and more like in North America – at least in the middle class. If this is true, the community *is* normative, or "typical", not in the sense of the average of an aggregate of such communities, but in the sense of representing the norm to which middle-class community life tends now to move.'[126] It is frequently forgotten that they were describing a very wealthy upper-middle-class suburb: at the point at which they were writing virtually no serious sociological investigation had been carried out in ordinary working-class suburbs. One small empirical fact: the Crestwood Heights project lasted five years: in that time there had been a massive turn-over in population – the 'object' moved. This is very different to the situation discussed below for Levittown. The Crestwooder had achieved, *for the time being*, a place to live. This phrase, the authors claim, pervades much of the lives of the people they studied and 'reflects the migratory habits and transitory values of a people: some, in a new land: most in a new community; many, occupying new roles in a rapidly changing society'.[127]

The house, in Crestwood Heights is more than a repository for an exceedingly wide range of objects: it is the 'ship in which persons related by blood and marriage make their voyage together through

[125] *Ibid.*, p. 11 (our emphasis).
[126] *Ibid.*, p. 20.
[127] *Ibid.*, p. 39.

time'.[128] The important triad is the house, its occupants and the movable things – out of which 'home' develops. If at the other end of the folk-urban continuum, in a relatively undifferentiated pre-industrial society, the house would also be a centre of production, at the Crestwood Heights end, the house is a centre of consumption. It is the stage upon which certain productions are played: especially hospitality, for 'in a changing, unstable society, there is, for those who are its most mobile members, a continuing need to revalidate the material objects with which the house has been "dressed".'[129] Crestwooders take it for granted that they will occupy a succession of houses. The rationale and reference point of this mobility is the man's career: it is this rather than the local community that provides a focus for their lives. This is similar to Webbers' formulation discussed in the Introduction. This is not entirely satisfactory for it provides a feeling of rootedness in only one role, whereas spatial rootedness cuts across all roles. This mobility implies a certain personal flexibility, adaptability, and ease in making new social relations. It will be necessary to drop and leave behind neighbours, friends, old colleagues and perhaps kin as well: by implication the husband-wife bond is therefore very important. There is no space here to develop the authors perceptive account of the role of women in Crestwood Heights: suffice to say that in comparison to the men their social relations were frequently more locality bound.

The greater part of the Crestwood Heights monograph is about child rearing: the central paradox being 'that highly individualistic, success-oriented persons, such as the Crestwood Heights family tends to produce, may be eminently suited to the business world but [are] of limited usefulness beyond'. The central voluntary association is the Home and School Association, but there are many others built around *specific* rather than *diffuse* activities. Of course, whatever their manifest functions there will also be latent functions of status conferred and Seeley, *et al*, describe the rigorous inclusion-exclusion mechanisms that clubs and associations use to safeguard their 'status-capital'. *Crestwood Heights* presents a picture of the social system in which 'experts' (marriage guidance councillors, psychotherapists, aptitude testers, child guidance experts) and their clients are enmeshed. It elaborates both the dysfunctions and functions of the highly individualistic and mobile orientations of its inhabitants. Clearly there are local social relations which can be fruitfully studied. *Crestwood Heights* shows well that it is false to believe that if *all* social relations, or even the most important (significant to the actor?) are not locality bound then there is nothing to study.

[128] *Ibid.*, p. 43.
[129] *Ibid.*, p. 52.

William Whyte's *The Organization Man*[130] has been responsible for many people's images of suburbia. His section on 'Organization Man at Home' is near-sociology but should not be confused with the real thing. In that section he analyses Park Forest: this is where Organization Man, far from being rootless, has put down his new and shallow roots. They are 'transients' in Whyte's term. Park Forest can be seen as a 'stopover' community for upwardly mobile young business executives (certainly they were several rungs below those living in Crestwood Heights); 35 per cent of Park Forest left in the year Whyte studied it. To use the favourite term of his informants they were 'all in the same boat' which, put in sociological terms, meant they were all in the child rearing stage of the family life cycle and in the relatively early stages of a bureaucratically organized career. Whyte clearly concentrates on their homogeneity. This is undoubtedly the reason for his finding that the 'micro-ecology', the physical layout of the community had such a strong causal influence on neighbouring patterns. He sought other explanations for the pattern of local social relations but the cause of this pattern of the web of friendship was, like his informant said, the layout. Despite the range of actual occupations (again virtually nobody worked *in* this suburb) they do not differ, Whyte argues, in any important respects. All Park Foresters must focus their attention on gaining approval from their superiors and all accomplish this by demonstrating their 'flexibility and capacity to adjust'. The whole social life of their community becomes a training ground for 'adjustment'. Propinquity determines neighbouring relationships. Participation in group life is socially necessary. Anybody living next door can become as good a friend as anyone else, spatial patterns determine friendship patterns. Everybody is equal and therefore equally suitable for friendship. Whyte appears to show that religion, common interests, common background are suspended in favour of proximity and adaptability. Whyte's thesis of the pervasiveness of the organization man's ethic, extended to suburbia, is an important element in what Bennett Berger has called 'the myth of Suburbia'.[131]

'Suburbia', however, in the sociological and quasi-sociological literature has confused ecology ('the growth of the suburbs'), with a 'way of life' – some aspects of which have been discussed above, with reference to Crestwood Heights and Park Forest. It has been a short step from noting the ecological shift in the location of residence of urban populations to saying that the facts of suburban residence *caused* what has become viewed as a 'suburban way of life'. What is

130 Penguin Book edition, 1963 (originally published 1956).
131 Bennett Berger in his *Working Class Suburb*, University of California Press, 1960 (London, Cambridge U.P., 1969).

worse, as Berger shows, is that much of what was the received wisdom on suburbs was largely mythical. The elements of this myth may be arrived at by taking certain facts from the Crestwood Heights and Park Forest studies, exaggerating them and claiming they apply to all suburbs. If this were true, there would be little alternative but to suggest that suburban residence engendered a particular style of life, for suburbs in fact have little else in common when examined closely. The elements of the myth are as follows: there is a common physical prospect (Pete Seeger's 'Little Boxes') of similar houses in which temporarily reside a 'new middle class' of upwardly mobile executives who are, together with their wives, college educated. There is a hyperactive social life both at the neighbouring and organizational level, encouraged by the absence of older people who would normally be leaders. This rich social life is fostered by the homogeneity of the suburbanites. As Berger says, 'They have a maximum of similar interests and preoccupations which promote their solidarity.'[132] In the familiar pattern of community studies there is a rapid shift from his empirically variable proposition to claiming that this caused 'conformity': this is the shift from community as empirical description to community as normative prescription. Suburbs are given over to child rearing (based on Spock and Gesell rather than grandma). Suburbanites are all commuters: this last is a very important element in the myth.

Berger then goes on to ask one of the key sociological questions about suburban communities. Why should a group of tract houses, mass produced and quickly thrown up on the outskirts of a large city, apparently generate so uniform a way of life? What is the logic that links tract living with 'suburbanism as a way of life'? Ecologically, as the prices of houses reflect, suburbs are far from similarly located. House prices can be likened to the size of a mesh of sieve through which families with the appropriate income fall to their appropriate place in the urban structure. We should therefore expect that differences between suburbs would be based on social class differences. This implies differences in income, occupation, journey to work patterns, education and so on. Indeed it might be more truthful to concentrate on the differences between suburban communities rather than their similarities. Class and stage in family cycle differences could be the starting place for such an analysis. Berger's *Working Class Suburb* has shown that large numbers of unquestionably working-class people will be migrating to the suburbs – to suburbs that look from the *outside* to be middle class. It is sociologically naïve in the extreme to believe that this move *alone* engenders a suburban way of life derived from

[132] Berger, *op. cit.*

exaggerating *some* tendencies found to be present in the upper middle and middle class suburbs of Crestwood Heights and Park Forest.

It was dissatisfaction with the formulations of the suburban myth that led Herbert Gans to produce his second community study, *The Levittowners*. Some of the techniques he used to study this New Jersey suburb have been discussed in Chapter 3. It is a 'bedroom' community for working and lower-middle-class people and was developed by a single builder: Levit & Sons. Gans had sixteen years earlier worked on Park Forest and he was disturbed by the extent to which Whyte's findings had become both exaggerated and generalized. Gans' observations had persuaded him that people were not changed when they moved to suburban communities and if there were any changes they were not traceable to the new environment, especially the physical environment. Levits planned to build 12,000 houses in ten neighbourhoods. Gans bought a house and moved in.

The Levittowners must be seen as a thorough-going critique of 'the myth of suburbia' outlined above. His techniques were those of participant-observation and he had the advantage of being in at the birth of the community. Levittowners were primarily young families who came to raise their children (over 80 per cent of men were under forty) and nearly half said they had come to settle permanently (compare this to the 35 per cent annual turnover at Park Forest). They were considered by Gans to be 'lower middle class culturally speaking',[133] (26 per cent were manual workers, 56 per cent lower white collar and 18 per cent lower professional). He distinguished three separate 'class' cultures (working, lower middle and upper middle) by their 'styles of life'. There were marked differences for example in child-rearing patterns and associated membership patterns between them. Levittown, then, was in no sense the totally homogeneous community of the suburban myth. They had come to Levittown, for 'house related reasons' in the main, not for 'job related reasons' as the myth suggests. Gans discovered that 'they wanted more comfortable and modern surroundings, but that they did not want to change their old way of life or to make a new one in the community'.[134] The aspirations of these suburbanites were for their family life – they were prepared to leave what Gans calls the 'organization of the community' to others. In fact, the pattern of social relations in the community, developed after 'the initial nest-making period'.[135] And they made friends on the basis of *shared interests* not propinquity. 'Propinquity may initiate intimate social contacts but it did not determine friendship.'[136] After friendship groups based on common values and interests developed, the third

[133] Gans, *op. cit.*, p. 23. [134] *Ibid.*, p. 38.
[135] *Ibid.*, p. 45. [136] *Ibid.*

stage was the sorting of community into informal clubs and cliques – what Gans calls the community stratification.[137] Formal clubs and associations were founded still later. Working-class associations were primarily social whereas the more middle-class associations were 'activity-specific' and frequently 'community service' orientated. Gans notes that 'the organizations were primarily *sorting* groups which divided and segregated people by their interests and ultimately, of course, by socio-economic, educational and religious differences'.[138] Internally each organization was relatively socially homogeneous. Gans analyses the founding of churches, the setting-up of the new school system and the political parties, all of which can be used to demonstrate the cultural *diversity* rather than the *homogeneity* of the community.

So Levittown followed a developmental pattern in its community organization – from neighbours on the same block through those 'in the same boat' to class and religion differentiated organizations. This class difference in the community was overlain and cross-cut by the distinction between those who were locals or cosmopolitans in their orientation. This clearly is another sociologically relevant variable that can be used to good effect in analysing the suburban or any other community. The inhabitants of Levittown, as would be the case in any other new community, did not know each other before they shared their common residence. Gans found that occupation and education were the most reliable indicators of class and that Levittowners only initially used 'status signs' to differentiate each other. However, he found what he calls a 'multinucleated' class structure 'consisting of fairly separate working-class, lower middle-class and upper middle-class sectors, each of which will consider itself to be of most worth, if perhaps not of highest status, in the community, and each of which will award top prestige to its own organizational, political and social leaders'.[139] This multinucleated class structure was subdivided by religion. Levittown as an employment-less community was more likely, Gans argues, to have its power structure determined by the local class hierarchy. It is a pity, therefore, that his methods did not allow him to collect the voting behaviour of the community systematically. However, Gans feels that because of the existence of a catholic Democratic working-class bloc, Levittown has a 'somewhat more monolithic local power structure, less varied from issue to issue than in most American communities'.[140] In a later chapter the problem of 'community power' will be discussed in more detail. It would seem that Gans, somewhat against his pluralist predictions, adopted the 'stratificationist' position on Levittown (see below, Chapter 7).

[137] *Ibid.*, p. 49.   [138] *Ibid.*, p. 61.
[139] *Ibid.*, pp. 132–3.   [140] *Ibid.*, p. 135.

Gans is quite prepared to call Levittown a community. What brought it into being 'was not the pre-occupancy aspirations of the residents, but rather a complex process of external initiative and subsequent internal transformation that produced organizations and institutions which reflected the backgrounds and interests of the majority of the population'.[141] Levittowners went into and shaped organizations on the basis of needs that had developed in the situation in which they found themselves. This situation was the presence of the kinds of people with whom they lived, for insofar as Levittowners used organizations for sorting purposes and sorted themselves as they did 'they were reacting to the population mix that had come about in Levittown'.[142] By traditional criteria Levittown was not a community: it was not an economic nor a social nor even a symbolic unit. Levittowners were not dependent on each other for their livelihood, there was no reason for them to relate to each other on any recurring basis and there was no 'sense of community'. However, Gans says: 'If Levittown was a community, and of course it was, it could best be defined as an administrative-political unit plus an aggregate of community-wide associations within a space that had been legally established by William Penn and his associates some three hundred years before.'[143] Levittown provided residents with a variety of services and required them to act in a limited number of community roles (voters, taxpayers and organizational participants), but these roles divided rather than united Levittowners.

The women of Levittown reported an increase of neighbouring on moving, but it was hardly the frenetic activity of the suburban myth. And they visited what Gans calls their 'compatible' neighbours,[144] not necessarily their nearest. This is not surprising as there were marked differences between the class cultures about child rearing that exhibited themselves over things like discipline. If there was not social hyperactivity, nor were friendships shallow and superficial. Many Levittowners had developed close friends in the community that they were not prepared to drop. Nor could Gans find much evidence of overt 'conformity' or deliberately *changed* behaviour to be more like perceived behaviour of neighbours. Of course the class cultures were internally similar, but that is what by definition distinguishes them from each other, and there were three in Levittown. The lack of 'high culture' and political concern discerned to be present in all suburbia by the commentators, what is 'seen as blandness and apathy is really a result of the invisibility and homecentredness of lower middle class culture'.[145] Earlier the distinction between cosmopolitans (those interested in

[141] *Ibid.*, p. 141.
[143] *Ibid.*, p. 145.
[145] *Ibid.*, p. 186.
[142] *Ibid.*, p. 141.
[144] *Ibid.*, p. 159.

national society) and locals (those interested in the community) was mentioned. Gans thinks that many Levittowners would 'be better described as *sub locals* for they are home orientated rather than community oriented'.[146] For most Levittowners, their own home was the centre of the community and that determined its social structure. This may, of course, be a function of their present stage in the family cycle.

Levittowners do not want to be transients, they are not organization men. Yet they do not have one characteristic beloved of traditional writers on the community: 'integration rootedness'. This will be increasingly rare in industrial society for it requires the kind of economic stability (or stagnancy) characteristic of only the most backward areas. The romanticizing of this type of rootedness, at the core of prescriptive notions of community ignores the fact that for many people it blocked progress, especially for those at the bottom of the social heap who were permanently labelled in their home community, in which they were 'known', as 'shiftless' and 'good for nothing'. Levittown, like many suburban communities, was planned for families with young children, for breeding. These young children, for whom it was home, will move away to work, to marry and have children of their own. Any satisfactory theory of community must take account of the mobility (without overstressing it) of modern society. Gans has provided a model for the analysis of one emerging community and it is through sociological analysis of this kind that our knowledge and understanding of society will grow, not through the armchair bound condemnations of suburban living by sensitive intellectuals. Few changes could be traced to the suburban qualities of Levittown. The crucial differences between communities is that they are home for different kinds of people. Such concepts as 'rural', 'urban' and 'suburban' add little by themselves to our knowledge.

[146] *Ibid.*, p. 189.

5

The European Studies

AT the beginning of the previous chapter we remarked that it was impossible to survey comprehensively and assess all of the American community studies. This applies *a fortiori* to those studies that have been undertaken in Europe. One result is that we have been forced to be even more arbitrary in our choice of examples than we were in the previous chapter. We have, therefore, eliminated from consideration all studies that are not available in English and have concentrated on perceived clusters – in either a theoretical or geographical sense – while including a few studies which fall outside both groups, but which we feel are of sufficient importance in the field as a whole to warrant their inclusion.[1]

Community in Southern Ireland

In the previous chapter we noted that Lloyd Warner came to study Yankee City after having completed an anthropological study of Australian aborigines. Warner felt sufficiently encouraged by the success of applying similar techniques to such apparently diverse communities to embark on the construction of a scheme of classification of all societies. At the same time the Department of Anthropology at Harvard University was beginning a study of Ireland, concerning archaeology and physical anthropology in addition to social anthropology. Warner, having been appointed Director of the work of the social anthropologists, seized the opportunity 'to place rural Southern Ireland on the roster'.[2] In the summer of 1931 Warner made a preliminary survey

---

[1] For Britain alone, the field – up to the early 1960s – has been dealt with by Ronald Frankenberg in his *Communities in Britain*, part one.

[2] C. A. Arensberg and S. T. Kimball, *Family and Community in Ireland*, Cambridge, Mass, Harvard U. P., p. xxv. All references here are to the second edition, published in 1968. (Also London, Oxford U.P., 1968).

of the twenty-six counties of Eire and chose County Clare as the most likely to fulfill his needs. With Conrad Arensberg, one of his former students who had worked with him on the Yankee City project, Warner settled in Clare in the summer of 1932 and began the task of collecting data. Warner returned to Harvard at the end of the summer and was later replaced by Solon Kimball, another protégée from the Yankee City study. Together, Arensberg and Kimball continued their fieldwork for a period of almost two years in the rural areas of County Clare before transferring to the town of Ennis. The original intention was to publish two monographs which would compare and contrast town and country life in the area. Unfortunately war intervened, and all that was available until recently was the rural study, published in 1940, and entitled *Family and Community in Ireland*.[3]

This background is an important point to bear in mind in considering what is frequently – and perhaps rather mistakenly – regarded as a pioneering work. For example, it accounts for their strong insistence on the classical functionalist theory of Malinowski and Radcliffe-Brown: 'Experience in Yankee City in New England had led the authors to the point of view which is the central hypothesis of functional anthropology. The more they worked, the more it grew certain to them that to a certain approximation it is useful to regard *society as an integrated system of mutually interrelated and functionally interdependent parts. A study in Ireland, then, should be a study to test this hypothesis.*'[4] Arensberg and Kimball, therefore, brought their theory to the data and, as we shall see in Chapter 7, such a procedure is not without its difficulties. Their theory not only determined to some extent what they would see, it also governed where they would see it. In choosing to examine the lightly-populated rural areas of County Clare, they were in no way choosing an apparently disconfirming instance in order to test their hypothesis. Far from being a pioneering work, Arensberg and Kimball were merely adapting well-tried and trusted anthropological techniques to the study of yet one more relatively small homogeneous population living in a limited and isolated area. Such small-scale subsistence-economy enter-prizes as were to be found in County Clare were as likely to be receptive to functionalist techniques there as in the Trobriand or Andaman Islands. This is one reason why it was unfortunate that the urban half of the study had to be discontinued – though Ennis (pop. 5,518) would hardly be regarded as urban elsewhere.

Having, then, chosen a locality which, on the basis of existing anthropological theory, was unlikely to disconfirm their hypothesis, Arensberg

[3] Published in England in 1949. The second edition includes six additional chapters utilizing data from the abortive study of Ennis.

[4] *Ibid.*, p. xxx (our emphasis).

and Kimball compound this by choosing *one* group within the locality to test a hypothesis about 'society'. They acknowledge that 'Censuses have laid bare the existence of two widely different types of agricultural activity in the Irish countryside. There are two widely different groups of persons whom we can tentatively designate as large and small farmers. Indeed the statistics, if used correctly, give factual base to the divisions the Irish themselves reckon in the countryside. They remind one continually that the large and small farmers are different beings and belong to ways of life which are quite opposed. . . . Large farmers differ from small farmers in their techniques, in their products, in their use of the soil and the land. They differ in the way in which members derive support from their farms. They differ significantly in the organization of labour upon these farms and presumably in consequence in the relations with other elements of the community. Family labour characterizes the small man, hired labour the big fellow.'[5] Yet in spite of this deep division in the community, Arensberg and Kimball deal with only one side of it – that of the small farmer. The small farmers are, indeed, in the majority in Clare, but there are areas of Ireland where this is not so, and the trend has been towards larger farms. Thus Arensberg and Kimball are dealing with subsistence farmers in the rural areas of Western Ireland and not with 'society' or even Irish society as a whole.

Having pointed out the limitations of their study, however, it needs to be said that within their framework they provide an outstanding analysis of 'the relationships between the institutional arrangements and the behaviour and values of those participating in them . . . in answer to the question of how and why human beings come to act upon one another in certain ways'.[6] They provide an impressive array of quantitative and qualitative data that makes the statistical paucity of some later studies inexcusable. They amply succeed in 'getting to grips with the social and psychological facts in the raw' and the fact that their study remains widely read today is a tribute to this. What one does not know, however, is how representative Arensberg and Kimball's attempt to 'place rural Southern Ireland on the roster' is. Has their essentially static view in which 'the forces operative within the structure are of such a nature as to allow the society of which they are a part to continue to function in essentially similar fashion through the welter of economic, political and other events' been borne out by later events?[7] In many ways County Clare is an area which cries out for a re-study.[8]

[5] *Ibid.*, pp. 3–4.   [6] *Ibid.*, pp. ix, xxxii.
[7] *Ibid.*, p. 150.
[8] We have recently learned that it has indeed been re-studied – by Art Gallaher Jr.

Arensberg and Kimball do not deal with a single settlement, but with an area, a locality. Indeed, their purpose is 'not as much to characterize the communities described as it is to examine the behaviour of the persons living in them'.[9] Though they range back and forth across the countryside, there is a marked concentration on two particular settlements, Luogh and Rynamona. Both communities consist of families of small farmers inhabiting the holdings from which they make their livelihood. Consequently the farmhouse is comparatively isolated, standing on its own ground and forming an integral part of the holding. The typical community is thus scattered (though Rynamona is somewhat nucleated) but this does not mean that the farmhouses are *socially* isolated. 'We observe of a farmer of Luogh, for example, that he coors largely in Luogh townland. But he has kinsmen scattered around about as far as Mount Elva, four miles to the north, and Liseannor, three miles to the south. He attends the parish church of Killilagh, a two-mile walk from his house, but sends his children to school at Ballycotton, only a mile off. He does most of his shopping in Roadford, a crossroad settlement two miles away. Yet he takes his larger produce for sale and his larger needs of purchase to the market town of Ennistymon, some eight miles off, or the smaller one of Lisdoonvarna, some five miles off. He votes and pays his taxes as a member of a certain electoral district which overlaps exactly none of these regions. He associates himself in tradition with Clare and Munster as a North Clare man, rather than with Galway and Connaught. . . . The small farmer of Luogh has allegiances to all these communities. . . . Each one of these allegiances has a geographical base, though in the last analysis each one of these is built up out of his personal experience of human relations.'[10]

Outside the immediate household the most pressing allegiance is to the family's kin. In the Irish countryside kinsmen are referred to as 'friends', particularly if they occupy one's own generation. Economic endeavour on the farms is assisted by a complex series of rights and obligations concerning one's 'friends'. It enables co-operation between farms – which is essential at certain times of the year such as the hay harvest – to take place within the kinship system and reinforces the identification of the family with their particular plot of land. The daily activity of the farm family is, indeed, totally centred upon the house and the surrounding few acres. 'In it the farm family group spends its entire life, sleeping, eating, giving birth and dying there, and sallying forth every day for work upon the fields.'[11] The holding is thus closely identified with the family and the family place great store on 'keeping the

[9] *Ibid.*, p. xxix.
[10] *Ibid.*, pp. 273–4.
[11] *Ibid.*, p. 31.

name on the land' – a value crucial to an understanding of the institutional arrangements of the locality.

Keeping the name on the land is thus the over-riding value, or goal. Arensberg and Kimball draw out the institutional implications of this with regard to the family and kinship network. In the first place the very action of the life-cycle provides a problem for the continuance of the family's connections with their farm. Birth and marriage involve the introduction of new members of the family unit; death concerns their departure. All must be catered for in such a way that the system can continue undisturbed. One arrangement that deals with the problem of inheritance is the patrilinearity of the kinship system – the land is passed from father to son; the kinship system is also patrilocal so the father has absolute authority over the dispersal of the farm, concerning both the timing and the inheritor. Late marriage and a high incidence of bachelorhood in rural Ireland are associated with the reluctance of the father to renounce his authority and leadership, and with the necessity of acquiring sufficient means to apportion to non-inheriting children in recompense for not receiving the farm. Because the identification of the nuclear family with the individual farm prevents the setting up of more than one new family group on the holding, the family must be given time to disperse before it is possible to create a new one. There are, at this point, therefore, three related problems – the dispersal of the non-inheriting progeny, the marriage of the inheritor and the production of children following on the marriage in order to ensure a further successor to the land.

Emigration provides a socially acceptable mechanism for dispersing the surplus children who cannot inherit the land or be married to a prospective inheritor. 'Viewed in this light, the decline of population becomes interpretable not as a flight from intolerable conditions, though economic distress had a powerful effect, not as a political gesture, though political disturbance took its toll, but rather as a movement arising from the effect of all these causes upon a family system whose very nature predisposed it to disperse population and which could, therefore, accommodate itself to this dispersal when it occurred. Emigration . . . derives much of its character, such as assisted passages and remittances, from the social forces at work in the family. It can become a traditional movement like the movement from country to town without destroying the family structure or the rural culture whose members it takes away.'[12]

Arensberg and Kimball show that marriage and inheritance together provide a much greater threat to the stability of the social system on the small farms than emigration. A mechanism must exist to restore the

[12] *Ibid.*, p. 150.

equilibrium that the problems associated with marriage and inheritance disturb. Marriage and inheritance involve the introduction of new members to the family group and the loss of old ones. Some institution must be created to obviate the difficulties that they pose to keeping the name on the land and to the transfer of the farmer's authority over his family and farm. Such an institution is the 'match' and Arensberg and Kimball concern themselves with its operation in some detail. The 'match' is a marriage contract arranged by the two fathers over the heads of the bride and groom. The father of the bride agrees to pay the father of the groom a sum of money as a dowry, the size of which increases in relation to the prosperity and worthiness of the other party's farm (and, therefore, family). The groom's father uses the dowry either as an income for old-age, to apportion to his non-inheriting children by buying them their own farm elsewhere, as a dowry for their match, or to assist their emigration. Marriage is also a badge of adulthood. At marriage either the ownership or the control of the land, or both, are transferred to the son – otherwise bachelors remain 'boys' even when they are over forty years old. The new bride moves into the house with her husband and the husband's parents retire to the 'west room' a symbolic withdrawal from the centre of the family unit. The match thus brings a re-formation of the family, involving a dispersal of former members and the introduction of a new set of component individuals – the bride and her kin – into the relationships between land and labour. Once installed in the house, however, it is imperative for the son's wife to produce children, and particularly male children to continue the family line. 'The old couple appraise their daughter-in-law accordingly. The first year of the girl's new position is a time of apprenticeship. Work is light. Pregnancy is her major duty.... To have no children is a source of shame to [her husband] and a terrible disappointment in his desire to continue his line upon the farm.'[13]

Arensberg and Kimball sum up by stating that: 'The sociology of Irish rural life and small-farm subsistence is largely a matter of the anatomy of two institutions of characteristic form. These are the family and the rural community.'[14] These form 'a master system articulating five major subsidiary systems'[15] which they list as:

1. The relationships of the familistic order.
2. The relationships of age-grading, or generation.
3. The relationships of sex organization.
4. The relationships of the local division of labour.
5. The relationships of economic exchange and distribution.[16]

[13] *Ibid.*, pp. 131–2.   [14] *Ibid.*, p. 301.
[15] *Ibid.*   [16] *Ibid.*, pp. 302–3.

These, then, comprise 'the framework of social life in the countryside'. No event, they argue, can be understood without reference to them.[17] The weakness of such grandiose claims has already been pointed out, but this form of structural-functional analysis was to be extremely influential on later studies, which were to continue this view of the countryside as essentially unchanging. This led to some serious misinterpretations, as we shall see later in the chapter.

Life in the Welsh Countryside

At the time that Arensberg and Kimball were completing their study of County Clare, Alwyn Rees was embarking upon a study of the Welsh parish of Llanfihangel yng Ngwynfa in northern Montgomeryshire. Rees' study was much more of a pioneering work than that of Arensberg and Kimball in the sense that Rees was starting almost completely from scratch with little or no *a priori* theoretical perspective to provide a framework for his data. The founding of what was to be a rather overlooked school of Welsh anthropology was, in fact, something of a historical accident. Rees was a member of the Department of Geography and Anthropology at the University College of Wales, Aberystwyth, and an extra-mural tutor in Montgomeryshire. In 1938 it was suggested to him by the College Principal, Ifor Evans, that he should undertake a study of this relatively secluded and entirely Welsh-speaking area. The motives are not entirely clear, but one suspects that an attempt was being made to record the dying Welsh culture before it succumbed to encroaching English influences. The original intention was to do a series of such studies of selected communities in various parts of Wales, but, as in Ireland, war intervened and the project was only continued some years later. Rees, however, was able to conduct the basic fieldwork for his own study in 1939 and 1940 and was able to maintain contact with the parish by frequent visits during the remainder of the war. The resulting monograph, *Life in a Welsh Countryside*, was published in 1950.

In many respects Llanfihangel bears a striking resemblance to Luogh and Rynamona. The five hundred inhabitants of the community live in scattered farms and there is no nucleated settlement that would pass for a village in lowland England or Wales. As in County Clare these farms are family farms involved in the rearing of cattle. The family is not only the primary social unit, but also the primary economic unit. Eighty per cent of all work on the farms is carried out by the farmers, their families and relatives.[18] Ideally the occupational unit consists

[17] *Ibid.*, p. 303.
[18] A. Rees, *Life in a Welsh Countryside*, Cardiff, University of Wales Press, 1950, p. 60.

of the father, mother and one or two unmarried sons in their youth or early manhood and perhaps a daughter. There is a rigid division of labour, but the respective roles are complementary. At certain stages of the life-cycle when family labour is short – when children are being born and reared and when they have married and left home – surplus sons of other farmers will be hired to perform labour on the farm, living in with the family. The sons return to their fathers' farms when the latter decide to retire, for sons cannot inherit until their mother dies and their father retires. Thus, as in Ireland, marriage is delayed, a custom that 'can be understood only in the light of filial duty and the custom whereby the paternal holding and stock are inherited'. And, as in Luogh and Rynamona, middle-aged sons can still be 'boys' if they are serving their long apprenticeship. On marriage non-inheriting sons are 'set up' with a farm of their own jointly by their family of origin and their spouse's family.

Thus kinship plays a major part in the local social structure, a situation exacerbated by the fact that 85 per cent of the inhabitants were born in the area. Rees claims that in many parts of the parish every household is bound to every other by kinship ties – 'they are woven together like a pig's entrails'. Those households not joined by kinship ties within Llanfihangel were so joined to neighbouring parishes. Rees evokes aspects of community life to explain why the farmers of Llanfihangel have not migrated like so many of their neighbours (the population has almost halved in a hundred years): the solidarity of the family, the bonds of kinship, the connection with a chapel or a church and the individual's status among his neighbours 'all tie him to his locality and make life incomplete elsewhere'.[19] Thus kinship binds the individual to the locality, but it also constrains the behaviour of the individual while he is there. Kinship becomes an agency of social control, for an individual's actions reflect not only on himself, but also on the reputation of his relatives. Thus not only is a member of the kinship group constrained by a non-member, but must also consider the consequences of alienating a body of neighbours with whom he must continue to live. The particular agents of conformity are not only ostracism, but the actions of the youth group who are licensed enforcers of community norms.[20]

Class distinction is comparatively weak in Llanfihangel and it fails to interfere with the free social intercourse between individuals and families. As in Ireland, there is a fine network of reciprocal obligations between neighbouring farms, and the varied social activities of the parish reflect a system of values which attaches some importance to

[19] *Ibid.*, p. 31.
[20] *Ibid.*, pp. 83–4.

non-economic accomplishments. The hearth, not the village hall, is the scene of recreation and the houses gain reputations for their theological argument, or their card playing, their poetry or their music, rather than their wealth. This emphasis on non-economic determinants of status, however, should not obscure the effect of the ecology of the area. The amount of capital required to start farming on an upland farm is far smaller than elsewhere. The 'agricultural ladder' is thus able to operate and a third of the farming families in Rees' study 'may have belonged to the wage-earning class two generations ago'.[21] One class thus merges imperceptibly into another. But Rees is aware that economic changes are undermining this situation: 'These pre-industrial standards are, however, being rapidly replaced by modern ones, and the change has been accelerated by the two Great Wars. During these periods of scarcity money could be made so easily and quickly that it became worth seeking it to the exclusion of all other values. . . . Notwithstanding the free social contact between families, there remains a considerable distinction between the independent farmer of, let us say, a hundred acre farm and a wage earner who supplements his earnings from a smallholding.'[22]

Rees is pessimistic about the future of Llanfihangel: urban (and therefore English) influences will disrupt, if not destroy, the community. So far, Rees acknowledges, Llanfihangel has not suffered as much as some other rural communities from what he calls 'the modern system [that] uproots the ablest members of the community, educates them and scatters them indiscriminately into official positions up and down the country. They are birds of passage and their interest in their adopted localities is not, generally speaking, as great as it might have been in their native localities among their own kith and kin.'[23] This is because in Wales, while its 'aristocracy' are certainly exported, they are replaced in each generation by a new élite promoted from among the people themselves and so the standards of the leaders have been essentially those cherished by the community in general. However, Rees points out that the planners of housing estates, 'anxious to confer urban amenities', fail to appreciate that the whole pattern of social relationships in a diffuse society becomes meaningless when settlement is concentrated: 'There is no need to offer hospitality to the man who lives next door.'[24] A further point of contrast with other communities is that the traditional activities of the parish, like the Eisteddfodau, were for the *whole* community. This is one reason why Rees stresses 'the completeness of the traditional rural society – involving the cohesion of family, kindred and neighbours – and its capacity to give the individual

[21] *Ibid.*, p. 142.   [22] *Ibid.*, p. 145.
[23] *Ibid.*, p. 165.   [24] *Ibid.*, p. 168.

a sense of belonging'.[25] In addition, Rees adopts a somewhat extreme view of the urban world, which he views as failing 'to give its inhabitants status and significance in a functioning society and their consequent disintegration into formless masses of rootless non-entities'.[26] Here, Rees' anti-urban (and anti-English?) attitudes appear to have run away with him. This seems more like community as normative prescription than empirical description.

Nevertheless, Rees, rather than Arensberg and Kimball, can be considered the founding father of the British community study – over the next fifteen years the prefaces of most studies acknowledge a debt to him and the University of Wales remains the centre of British community study. Rees' direct influence, however, is most evident in the comparative Welsh study of which his was a precursor. This was published in 1960 as *Welsh Rural Communities* edited by Rees and Elwyn Davies. There have been more Welsh studies, notably Ronald Frankenberg's *Village on the Border*, about the village of Glynceiriog in Denbighshire and Isabel Emmett's *A North Wales Village*, on the village of 'Llan' in Merionethshire. Any attempt to give some unity to the Welsh studies, however, is prevented by that bane of community studies, non-comparability of data. It is clear that whilst these studies may be intrinsically satisfying in their own terms, it is by no means possible to synthesize them into something more. Though part of the same *genre*, they share no common framework or theoretical position. Indeed, most of them lack any explicit theoretical position and even basic descriptive information. For instance, *Village on the Border* is full of insights into what Frankenberg calls the politics of recreation, but is almost totally lacking in sociographic data, even an accurate figure for the population of Glyndeiriog.[27]

The Sociology of an English Village

W. M. Williams was a student of Rees, but his study of Gosforth in Cumberland, carried out from 1949 to 1951, owes as much to Lloyd Warner as to the Welsh study. Gosforth is larger than Llanfihangel

[25] *Ibid.*, p. 170. It should be noted that these are all ascriptive roles.

[26] *Ibid.*, p. 170.

[27] Pentrediwaith (Frankenberg's pseudonym for Glynceiriog) is given a population of 'about 600' (p. 35). This non-comparability hinders Frankenberg's otherwise meritorious attempt to give some unity to the British studies as a whole in *Communities in Britain*. He also takes no account of the differences in time – there is a span of over twenty years – at which the studies took place. One of the contentions of this chapter is that these studies have no unity in the sense that Frankenberg attributes to them. Each has something to contribute to sociology yet, as it turns out, they contribute little to each other.

with 723 inhabitants and, unlike Llanfihangel, has a recognizable village, though the farms are scattered. Gosforth is somewhat less isolated than Luogh or Llanfihangel and this is reflected in the greater encroachment of outside influences, symbolized by the introduction of the tractor and the arrival of the baker's van with the consequent abandonment of home baking.[28] Gosforth, however, is in another upland zone and the economic and social organization of the farms is similar to that in County Clare and Wales.

Thus the basic economic and social unit in Gosforth is the family. In 1950, 73 per cent of the male labour on farms in Gosforth was provided by farmers, their families and relatives and 95 per cent of the female labour by farmers' wives, daughters and other relatives.[29] Once again we meet the strong patrilinearity and patrilocality of County Clare and Llanfihangel; sons and daughters remain in a state of complete dependence on their parents until they marry or their father dies; the peak age of marriage is about five years later than the national average. As in County Clare, marriage is vitally important in this area of family farming since it is the 'structural hinge' which ensures the continuity of the system. Marriage is closely linked to methods of inheritance and, whilst in Gosforth there is no rigid rule of primogeniture, 'in the majority of cases, where the eldest son inherits, he remains at home unmarried until his parents retire. He then assumes control and is free to marry, and the limited information available suggests that marriage follows inheritance within a very short period. The remaining sons are free to marry more or less when they choose, subject to the labour requirements of the holding. Where there is a superfluity of man-power, the parents attempt to establish one or two sons as freeholders or tenants in their own right when they marry. . . . Whatever the variations in practice, the underlying principle is the maintenance of the family group as a relatively self-sufficient economic unit and the retention of the holding within the family.'[30] All these aspects are familiar from our consideration of County Clare and Llanfihangel.

These farm families are in marked contrast to the village families whose family organization 'reflects the absence of the fundamental principles' described above.[31] This is because in the village, as elsewhere in Britain, the family is not a productive unit. However, in both the village and the outlying farms, the absence of rapid means of

[28] W. M. Williams, *The Sociology of an English Village*, London, Routledge and Kegan Paul, 1956, pp. 20-1.
[29] *Ibid.*, p. 57.
[30] *Ibid.*, p. 50.
[31] *Ibid.*, p. 55.

communication and the lack of immigration implies that the inhabitants of Gosforth are placed within a complex social network in which kinship is very important. This kinship system is, in Williams' words, 'a framework of reference points which help the individual to identify other people. It explains the stability of the community by linking its present members with those of the past.'[32] It is the presence of kin, the inevitable consequence of population stability that, more than any other factor, gives the inhabitants of the village the feeling of community.

The kinship network is a communication network and people are known and placed by their personal ties. This, and the stability of Gosforth, is the underlying basis to the local stratification system as Williams conceives it. Williams' methods can be compared with those of Lloyd Warner in Yankee City[33]. He divides Gosforth into seven social 'classes' (status groups) 'since the same people were always mentioned in connection with a particular class and never as belonging to another class'.[34] Each 'class' is thought by members of the other 'classes' to have special attributes and modes of behaviour. Locally these status groups are believed to have definite limits. In Gosforth, stratification is a *system* and it is an *interactional system*. The local names for the 'classes' are shown in the table.

(i) *Upper-Upper class:*

Upper-Upper class	'Our social level.' 'Better class.'
Lower-Upper class	'Social climbers.' 'Not quite our class.' 'He *tries* to behave like a gentleman, but . . .'
Intermediate	'Neither here nor there. More intelligent than the normal run of people around here.' 'Quite well educated and very handy when you have about a dozen village organizations to see to.'
Upper-medial	'Social climbers in the village.'
Medial and Lower-Medial	'Villagers and farmers.' 'Decent lower class people.' 'The country people.'
Lower class	'The immoral element in the village.' 'The worst kind of countryman.' 'The worst of the lower orders.'

[32] *Ibid.*, p. 76.
[33] See Chapters 4 and 6.
[34] W. M. Williams, *op. cit.*, p. 86.

(ii) *Lower-Upper class:*

Upper-Upper	'The Upper Ten.' 'The people who have more breeding than sense.' 'They have no money, but because they talk like a BBC announcer and their great-grand-father was a tuppen-ha'penny baronet, they think they own the place.'
Lower-Upper	'Ambitious people.' 'Go-ahead people.'
Intermediate	'In between.'
Upper-Medial	'The village aristocracy. They try their best to get ahead, but everything is against them.'
Medial	'Farmers and small professionals.' 'Farmers and village tradesmen.'
Lower-Medial	'The village.'
Lower class	'Dirty people. I can't understand them. Some of them are quite well off, but you'd never think it to look at them.'

(iii) *Intermediate class:*

Upper-Upper	'The nibs.' 'The usual well-off people you find in the countryside these days. Mostly retired people; very few of them are old established.'
Lower-Upper	'The money-maker class. They have ambitions of climbing, but they don't seem to have much luck.'
Intermediate	'We are in a class of our own.' 'Our position is not a very easy one to understand.'
Upper-Medial	'The kind of people who don't mix with their neighbours. Usually they are social climbers.'
Medial	'The majority of ordinary people with good jobs – including farmers, of course.'
Lower-Medial	'The average villager.'
Lower class	'An unfortunate minority. You can tell them by the way they live. Most of them are dirty.'

(iv) *Upper-Medial class:*

Upper-Upper	'The sort of people you can really look up to.' 'The proper gentry.' 'The better class people.'
Lower-Upper	'They are not Upper Ten but they like to think they are. They are not all that different from us, except for their money.'
Intermediate	'School teachers and that sort.' 'I think folks make far too much fuss about them.'
Upper-Medial	'People who keep themselves to themselves.' 'Decent people who try to get on.' 'The sort of people who try to improve themselves a bit.'
Medial	'Farmers and such.'
Lower-Medial	'Village people.' 'The ordinary working class people.'
Lower class	'People who don't try to lift themselves.' Dirty people who have no self-respect.'

(v) *Medial and Lower-Medial:*

Upper-Upper	'People who are higher than we are.'
Lower-Upper	'Folks like X who have plenty of money and plenty of cheek. They want to get on in t'world.'
Intermediate	'In between because of education.'
Upper-Medial	'Snobs.' 'Stuck-up folk.'
Medial and Lower-Medial	'Ordinary Gosfer' folk.'
Lower class	'Folk who don't care what they look like.'

(vi) *Lower class*

Upper-Upper	'Them posh folks living in the big houses won't acknowledge you and the way some of them behaves you'd think you was some mak o' animal.'
Lower-Upper	'The folk with brass who acts like they was big nobs.' 'Bloody snobs.'

Intermediate	'Don't know much about them. A lot o' bloody barrack room lawyers if tha ask me.'
Upper-Medial	'A lot o' ***** ***** ***** snobs.'
Medial and Lower-Medial	'Village folks like us, but some on 'em is very high and mighty.'
Lower-Class	'Decent folk.' 'Folks that like to do what they wants to.'

(From *Gosforth*, pp. 107–9.)

That it is an interactional rather than an attributional stratification system is shown by the personalization of the labels applied to each social group. Such judgements are able to be made because of the close relationships resulting from kinship and the fact that Gosforth is a face-to-face community – the inhabitants not only live close together, but see a great deal of each other. However, Williams does point out that the building of the nearby Windscale nuclear power station is bringing people to Gosforth who do not 'fit in' and who have urban values.[35]

The social status divisions of the community affect behaviour in the local voluntary associations, and their Presidents are drawn from the 'upper-upper' class, though the community has no organizations which are confined in membership to one social 'class'. However, 'offices are given to people with high status and this enhances and confirms their status. Also, the giving of offices to people of high status enhances the prestige – and therefore the attraction – of offices.'[36] In Gosforth, however, ties of neighbourliness and kinship still cut across class and status divisions in what might be called the daily round, though there is a contrast between village and farm. Prestige in the former does seem to be more related to possessions than in the latter where prestige derives from co-operation.

Gosforth, then, is a community of close-knit social relations; it is cohesive and has well-defined territorial units. However, Williams does see urban influences as increasing. He writes in his concluding paragraph that 'Every development that has taken place in parish affairs in recent years has emphasized and reflected an urban way of life in various ways. . . . If the present change continues to its logical conclusion, then the sociologist of fifty years hence may well find it difficult to distinguish Gosforth from any other rural parish in England.'[37] This is obviously a

[35] *Ibid.*, pp. 31–2.
[36] *Ibid.*, p. 126.
[37] *Ibid.*, p. 202.

matter of some regret to Williams, and the conclusion to his monograph is reminiscent of that of Rees, especially as there are comparisons to be drawn between Cumberland and Wales.[38] The picture presented is of a static but decaying way of life, fighting a rearguard action against threatening urban values: 'Gosforth has changed more in the past two or three decades than it did in the two previous centuries, largely as a result of the increasing influence of urban culture. . . . Against this the traditional way of life is static and can offer nothing to replace the loss in community feeling which is a result of these developments.'[39] Apart from the implied normative prescription, such a view of rural life is also derived from the structural-functional anthropological method, which Williams adopts. As with Arensberg and Kimball, this can lead to the assertion that these rural communities *are* static social systems, rather than merely treating them as such for the heuristic benefits of such a model. With such an approach values and methodology become so intertwined that, as Williams was later to realize,[40] serious mis-interpretations can result.

Village in the Vaucluse

This viewpoint of rural communities is not limited simply to the British Isles, however, nor to structural-functionalism. As was pointed out in Chapter 2, it is a pervasive trait of much of Western European culture and its traces can be found in a great deal of early sociological thought. From the vast literature of European community studies we can, therefore, call forth a few more brief examples. One that is frequently referred to, but which will be dealt with only in passing here, is Lawrence Wylie's *Village in the Vaucluse*, a description of life between 1949 and 1951 in the community of Peyrane, a village in the foothills of the Vaucluse mountains just over thirty-five miles east of Avignon in Southern France. Peyrane is a community of small farms, though holdings are scattered and not in compact plots as in County Clare or Llanfihangel. Sixty per cent of the farms are worked by the families owning them, but the social distinctions between owner-occupiers and tenants are extremely blurred.[41] The phrase which repeatedly crops up in Wylie's study is, 'C'est comme ça'. It denotes the resignation, or even apathy, of the French peasants, while establishing Peyrane as an

[38] *Ibid.*, pp. 201–2.
[39] *Ibid.*, pp. 202–3.
[40] See above Chapter 3 and W. M. Williams, *A West Country Village: Ashworthy*, London, Routledge and Kegan Paul, 1963, pp. xiv, xviii.
[41] L. Wylie, *Village in the Vaucluse*, Cambridge, Mass,. Harvard U.P.; second edition, 1961, p. 22 (Also London, Oxford U.P., 1957).

essentially unchanging community indissolubly linked to the cycle of birth, life and death: 'One can only go on living from day to day, from year to year. Besides, the problems and pleasures involved in raising a family are so pressing that one need not think much about "all that". Wars come and bring disaster. Régimes change. Governments fail. But there is always the family.'[42] Much the same sentiments could be echoed in Luogh, Llanfihangel or Gosforth. Wylie's study is descriptive and personalized in the extreme – so much so that comparability with other studies, in France and elsewhere, is impossible.[43] It is important to point out that Wylie himself is neither a sociologist nor an anthropologist, but a Professor of French Civilization. His description, therefore, has no theoretical perspective, nor is it in any way systematized. It is a point he acknowledges in the preface to the second edition of *Village in the Vaucluse.* He writes that, 'For the sake of anthropologists and sociologists I should like to have been able to give a more complete description of social structure, genealogy, land tenure.'[44] This is not to say that Wylie's study of Peyrane does not contain information of interest to the sociologist, but it would be inappropriate to consider it as sociology. It's nearest equivalent in England would be Ronald Blythe's *Akenfield.*

The Deeply Rooted

The husband-and-wife team of John and Dorothy Keur studied the small agrarian community of Anderen in the Netherlands from September 1951 to June 1952. Anderen is a village of 'approximately 280 persons',[45] situated in the province of Drente in north-east Holland, not far from the German border. Dorothy Keur is an anthropologist, John Keur a biologist; it is thus not surprising to learn that their study, *The Deeply Rooted,* has a strong ecological flavour: 'The basic interest of the authors lay in the interrelation of natural environment and cultural development.'[46] The ecology of the area and the geological and economic history are related in some detail. Agriculture is the predominant activity of Anderen, fifty-three of the sixty buildings in the village being farmhouses.[47] Anderen is an example of an *es* village, the term *es* referring to the area of agricultural land in the neighbourhood of the

[42] *Ibid.,* p. 34.
[43] Yet *Village in the Vaucluse* was originally intended as a comparative work with a village in Northern France. See p. xiii.
[44] *Ibid.,* p. ix.
[45] D. Keur and J. Keur, *The Deeply Rooted,* Washington, Seattle, University of Seattle Press, 1955, p. 19.
[46] *Ibid.,* p.13.
[47] *Ibid.,* p. 54.

settlement. This area is sub-divided into 'parcels' belonging to the various farmers of the village. Since the settlement is nucleated the 'parcels' may be some distance from the farmhouse and widely scattered across the *marke* (civil parish). The area of agricultural land within the *marke* of Anderen is approximately 1,200 acres, subdivided into almost 1,000 separate 'parcels'. The average-sized farm is one of 40 acres, composed of 20–30 'parcels' of land, two-thirds of which are arable and one-third permanent pasture.[48] 'Mixed' agriculture is thus the norm with an emphasis on dairying. The widely-scattered 'parcels' are a serious obstacle to the efficient utilization of the land and mechanization has been slow. Though the legal machinery exists for the consolidation of the scattered parcels into compact holdings, there is a good deal of resistance to it; not only do the small farmers fear they will be 'squeezed out' but there is the tradition of 'keeping the name on the land'.[49]

Anderen, like Gosforth, is beginning to feel the encroaching influences of the outside world. Until 1900 it was a 'compactly self-contained economic unit',[50] but there has been a decline of village crafts and the old barter system has given way to a money economy. Bread is still baked in the village, but the greengrocer and fishmonger arrive by motor vehicle from outside the village. The most important change, however, has been from village-made goods to an ever-increasing reliance on the mass-produced goods of modern Dutch industry.

The life of the village is largely organized around the life-cycle of the nuclear family and the yearly cycle of the agricultural economy. As in the British communities described above, the strength of the family as a social unit is reinforced by its economic unity and there is the familiar extended network of kin. There is also the rigid division of labour between spouses: 'The woman occupies a position of considerable importance and influence in the family. Moreover, and this is of primary significance, she holds the purse strings. . . .'[51] Only at extremely busy periods – haying or harvest – will she perform labour in the fields, however, for 'the farmer has his own province'.[52] There is a general feeling that the man of the family has the final authority, but it is not unknown for a strongly aggressive woman to possess overall power. On the whole, though, generation rather than sex determines dominance, and in three-generational households, either grandfather, grandmother, or both together will hold the position of authority. It is still largely the practice for the newly-married couple to live with the

[48] *Ibid.*, p. 71.　　　　[49] *Ibid.*, p. 72.
[50] *Ibid.*　　　　[51] *Ibid.*, pp. 110–11.
[52] *Ibid.*, p. 111.

parents of one of them, though which one seems to depend on specific circumstances, and the bride by no means always moves into her husband's household. Childlessness is looked upon as 'a great pity and as somehow "not right" ',[53] but whether this is concerned with keeping the name on the land is not elaborated. The age of marriage, however, is unusually high, though again the Keurs overlook any connection with land tenure and attribute the fact to 'the social pattern of the family group in which the reins of authority, the power of decision and finances, rest with the parents, if not grandparents'.[54] We do learn, however, that in the Drents village, 'it is still fairly exceptional for the children to be sent even to the schools of advanced elementary education. The well-to-do old farm families with the most land almost never allow their children any "academic" education because they are expected to take over the farm. . . . The future of children presents a real and pressing problem [in Anderen] since there are too many for the available land. . . . Hence, more children must be trained for other than farm work. A trend in this direction is now apparent.'[55]

Social stratification in Anderen is based upon a combination of occupation and property. Those resident in the village, with non-agricultural occupations – mainly professional people such as teachers, doctors, lawyers, and so on – are given a high status and referred to as 'notables'. Their attachment, however, is primarily to social networks outside the village and they are therefore looked upon as a group apart: 'They are *not* Drents. Even though they have resided for twenty years in the same village and have actively served the community, they do not *belong*.'[56] Concerning the remainder, 'the village group', the Keurs assert that: 'Despite frequent boasting in Anderen that no social differentiations are made among rich freeholder, poor or "small" farmers, renters and farm-workers or labourers, certain attitudes indicate that this is not the case.'[57] Though the distinctions are much less rigidly adhered to than formerly, wealth – and hence prestige and status – are still judged by the number of cows in the barn. Rich freeholders are still referred to as 'rich' or 'fat' while 'small' farmers are termed 'rent-farmers'. Both of these groups are set apart from hired labourers. Thus, 'both renters and farm-workers are conscious of their status, even while they say, "We are all alike here in Anderen".'[58] Marriage tends to occur within, and not between, status groups.

Thus the social organization of Anderen is similar in many ways to that of those communities of the Celtic fringe considered above. The Keurs, moreover, come to similar conclusions concerning the rate of

[53] *Ibid.*, p. 108.
[54] *Ibid.*, p. 100.
[55] *Ibid.*, pp. 89–9, 100.
[56] *Ibid.*, p. 148 (emphasis in the original).
[57] *Ibid.*
[58] *Ibid.*, p. 149.

change in Anderen. 'Life here is emphatically cyclic. . . . In Anderen, however, repetitive patterning is extended almost to every phase of social life. . . . Thus the little cultural "plant" of Anderen, growing out of its sandy soil, its heath, meadow and forest, in relative isolation for centuries, displays a persistant toughness in the face of the twentieth century. While bending to the winds and storms of both minor and cataclysmic changes in nature and culture, it has, so the authors believe, the hardihood to survive for long years to come.'[59] This conclusion is certainly more optimistic than that of Rees or Williams, yet we may note the similarity of the imagery. The small strong, un-changing community is resisting the influences of the stormy, turbulent, ever-changing world, around it. Such a view of Anderen, however, belies much of the Keurs' own evidence. We have already noted the breakdown of the community as a self-supporting socio-economic unit and the relaxation of status differentials. In fact, change pervades the whole of the study, and, had the Keurs wished to, one feels that they could have written a study of an agrarian community on the threshold of large scale social change, resulting mainly from external influences. On consulting their book, the reader may care to note the number of times important sections contain such phrases as, 'formerly', 'during the past ten years, however', 'until about fifty years ago . . .', 'as short a time as fifty years ago . . .', 'in former times . . .', 'the modern world has broken the hard core of Drents tradition . . .' and so on.[60] Such a view, however, is not derived from any functionalist viewpoint, but from the Keurs' rather rigid brand of ecological determinism. Because a 'sub-stantial part' of Anderen's social life is 'unquestionably due to the soil and climate in which it is rooted',[61] it cannot change rapidly because the area's ecology cannot change rapidly. Their evidence, however, is not a convincing justification of such a view.

The Southern Italian Studies

Southern Italy is an area which has been the subject of a good deal of controversy, particularly with regard to issues which underlie the problems of social stability and social change. The *Mezzogiorno* has been a popular area for community study because it is generally considered one of the most 'backward', and therefore stable, areas of Western Europe, an area which has refused to come to terms with the trends of twentieth-century industrialized society. The basis of a

[59] *Ibid.*, pp. 170–1.
[60] See, for instance, pp. 55, 57, 72, 82, 91, 119, 148, 152 for some of the most important changes. There are many more examples too numerous to mention.
[61] *Ibid.*, p. 14.

consideration of this area is Edward Banfield's *The Moral Basis of a Backward Society*, a monograph resulting from the study of the village of Montegrano for nine months in 1954 and 1955. Banfield is concerned with the extreme poverty and backwardness of Southern Italy (of which he takes Montegrano to be typical), which he believes can be explained largely, though not entirely, by the 'inability of the villagers to act together for their common good or, indeed, for any end transcending the immediate, material interest of the nuclear family'.[62] Such an ethos he terms 'amoral familism'.

Montegrano has a population of 3,400, mostly poor farmers and labourers. It consists of a town and twenty-seven square miles of surrounding fields and forest and is situated in the province of Potenza, south-east of Naples, 'Montegrano is as poor as any place in the Western world.'[63] One-third of the inhabitants live on small scattered farms at the base of the mountain on which Montegrano stands and in the valley around it. About 80 per cent of the farms are in holdings of less than fifteen acres. The land is stony, steep and poorly watered, supporting a 'few light strands' of wheat, sparse natural pasture, olive and fig trees and forests of oak. 'Poor and small as they are, the fields and forests are Montegrano's principal source of income. There is no mining or manufacture of importance anywhere in the region.'[64] The farms are purely subsistence enterprises, producing little or nothing for sale.

Banfield perceives seven occupational classes – labourers, farmers, artisans, merchants, office workers, professionals and landed proprietors. The only voluntary association in Montegrano is a 'circle' of twenty-five upper-class men who 'maintain a clubroom where members play cards and chat'.[65] Though the gentry are generally sympathetic to the plight of the peasantry, they are not led by their sympathy to try to change society. Political parties are of little importance in Montegrano and Banfield notes that the variability in voting behaviour is 'striking'.[66] The school in Montegrano is poor and irregularly attended; although the Italian constitution guarantees that every child will receive schooling until the age of fourteen, in Montegrano only five grades are taught and children leave at the age of eleven or twelve. Any continued education must be undertaken outside the village, and only the rich are able to afford this. The nearest hospital is five hours away by car. Why, Banfield asks, is nothing done about these pressing local problems? Why are the political parties so unconcerned with local issues? Why, in fact,

---

[62] E. C. Banfield, *The Moral Basis of a Backward Society*, Glencoe, Ill., The Free Press, 1956, p. 10 (London, Collier-Macmillan, 1967).

[63] *Ibid.*, p. 43.   [64] *Ibid.*

[65] *Ibid.*, p. 16.   [66] *Ibid.*, p. 27.

is there no community action at all in Montegrano? Banfield's book attempts to answer these questions.

Banfield begins by offering some 'common sense' explanations that he is not going to accept.[67] These are:

1. The people of Montegrano are so desperately poor that all their exertions are concerned with merely staying alive.
2. Ignorance is so great that 'people so ignorant can have no notion of what it is possible to accomplish politically and they cannot make meaningful choices among parties and candidates'.[68]
3. Collaboration between the gentry and the peasantry is impossible due to class antagonisms based on the exploitation of the peasantry. Nothing, however, can be achieved without this collaboration.
4. The oppressed are split among themselves between the workers who own a plot of land and who wish to maintain the status quo, and the landless labourers who are communists.
5. Distrust of the state and all authority is pathological following centuries of oppression.
6. The Southern Italian is a resigned fatalist and believes the situation to be hopeless.

'There is an element of truth in each of the theories', writes Banfield, 'but none of them is fully consistent with the facts that have to be taken into account, and one could not on the basis of any of them – or all of them together – predict how the people of Montegrano would behave in a concrete situation.'[69] Thus, while it is acknowledged that each explanation possesses some *prima facie* validity, Banfield proceeds to demolish each of them so that his own theory may, as one observer has put it, 'shine even more brightly when contrasted with all the darkness'.[70]

Banfield first argues that pleas of poverty are used as an excuse by the peasant 'for not doing what he would not do anyway. . . . There is hardly a man in Montegrano who could not contribute a third of his time to some community project without loss of income.'[71] This observation is used to discard the poverty hypothesis. The ignorance argument is dispensed with by showing that the peasant does indeed possess political knowledge: 'Most of the opinions were reasonable. . . . Some were very thoughtful.'[72] Class and status antagonisms do not

[67] Most of these explanations are, in fact, taken from Carlo Levi's novel, *Christ Stopped at Eboli.*

[68] E. C. Banfield, *op. cit.*, p. 33.

[69] *Ibid.*, p. 35.

[70] J. Galtung, *Members of Two Worlds*, New York, Columbia U.P., forthcoming (page references here refer to typescript edition), p. 57.

[71] Banfield, *op. cit.*, pp. 35–6.

[72] *Ibid.*, p. 36.

explain Montegrano's political behaviour either. 'If it did, one might expect to find the peasants inciting action *against* the upper class. But there is no such action, nor is there likely to be. Class and status do, however, influence the situation profoundly in ways that are diffuse, indirect, and hard to identify. Like poverty and ignorance they are general conditions which, so to speak, form the causal background.'[73] Banfield also shows that the inhabitants of Montegrano, far from harbouring a pathological distrust of the state, frequently engage its help on suitable occasions. Finally, if all these factors explain too little, fatalism explains too much – it explains why the Montegranos do *not* act, rather than the choices they make when they *do* act. Moreover, Banfield, by alluding to their contraceptive practices, shows that the Southern Italians' pessimism exists where social rather than individualistic action is called for. However, there is a high Communist vote in the area, which might be construed as a call for collective action on the part of the peasantry. This presents Banfield with a problem which he removes by refuting any structural causes of a high Communist vote. Banfield includes a table showing left-wing voting, male illiteracy, density of population and the proportion of labourers, based on data from eleven communities in the Montegrano district. Banfield thus refutes what he believes: 'It is often said' – that the Communist vote is heaviest where poverty is most severe and widespread, where lack of education is greatest and where the proportion of landless labourers to proprietors is greatest.[74] The Communist vote cannot, therefore be seen as some kind of capacity for collective action in the underprivileged strata, nor do any of the above theories account for the unpredictably wild fluctuations in voting behaviour.[75]

We shall return to this demolition of 'common sense' explanations later, but Banfield has a more positive contribution to make. According to Banfield, 'A very simple hypothesis will make intelligible all of the behaviour about which questions have been raised and will enable an observer to predict how the Montegranesi will act in concrete circumstances. The hypothesis is that the Montegranesi act as if they were

[73] *Ibid.*, pp. 37–8 (emphasis in the original).
[74] *Ibid.*, p. 40.
[75] Galtung (*op. cit.*, pp.60–1) has used Banfield's table to show that there is in fact a strong negative correlation ($r = -0.81$) between left-wing voting and illiteracy which is overlooked by Banfield. Galtung perceives value judgements in this: 'For Banfield uses his data to discard the hypothesis that illiteracy is positively linked to Communist voting . . . but does not explore the much more interesting finding that it is negatively related. Again this seems to be attributable to the value-bias mentioned above: if Communism is regarded as a threat or at least as negative it is better to have it as a concomitant of a non-desirable condition such as illiteracy than of a desirable one such as education.' (p. 61).

following this rule: maximize the material, short-run advantage of the nuclear family; assume that all others will do likewise. One whose behaviour is consistent with this rule will be called an "amoral familist".[76] The remainder of the book is an elaboration of this principle and an enquiry into the genesis and operation of it. It is amoral familism that is the moral basis of the backward society according to Banfield.

Banfield analyses how the principle of amoral familism can be utilized to explain the lack of collective action on the part of the peasantry. If the interests of one's family are deemed greater than those of the village, the individual will grasp every opportunity to secure short-term advantages for the family, even at the expense of the community as a whole. Politics becomes enmeshed in this process: a vote is given to anyone who can secure such advantages while it is withdrawn from those who have failed to do so. This occurs irrespective of the fortunes of the community as a whole, and it thus accounts for the fluctuations in voting behaviour as well as the lack of community action. What the amoral familist really desires is an increase in his family's standard of living relative to that of other families in the community. To raise the standard of living of the whole village is thus regarded as something rather peripheral to the individual's main concerns and is capable of raising only limited enthusiasm. Banfield 'fills in' this outline of his theory with a large number of illustrative stories and quotations, and with data gained by means of the application of thematic aptitude tests, when the respondent is asked to choose 'which is better' out of a list of several traits. While one may wish to quibble over individual items, the cumulative effect of Banfield's data is to present a powerful collection of evidence in support of his theory.

This has not prevented Banfield's work from being subject to some considerable criticism, however, notably by John Davis,[77] and Johan Galtung.[78] Not all of their arguments can be considered in detail here and should the reader be interested in the controversy he is advised to consult the references for himself. However, we may consider a few of the arguments where they impinge on some of the wider themes of community study; this is in any case more appropriate, for Banfield's data are not seriously disputed – it is his interpretations of them which controversy surrounds. Banfield's book is an attempt to produce an explanation of why people do not associate, holding this to be the crucial variable in the development of a modern capitalist economy. Thus, as

[76] Banfield, *op. cit.*, p. 85.
[77] John Davis, 'Morals and Backwardness', *Comparative Studies in Sociology and History*, Vol. 12, No. 3, July 1970.
[78] J. Galtung, *op. cit.*, pp. 56–71, 229–48.

Galtung has pointed out, 'he concentrates the problem of stability (in the first page of his book) down to why there is almost no concerted action – comparing Montegrano with a small US town of the same size, in Utah. The book is permeated by the idea that *organization at the grass-roots level* is among the most important vehicles of progress.'[79] This leads Banfield to consider amoral *familism* as the impediment to social change because it generates loyalties which are contrary to those he believes essential to the emergence of new institutions – loyalties to the *community*. This, however, is an empirical point which Banfield never explores. He suffers here, not so much (*pace* Davis) from an ethnocentricism as a 'communocentricism', which may also explain Banfield's apparent acceptance of some indigenous explanations of the social situation in the community.[80] From further studies there is evidence to show, as Galtung puts it, 'that even in the *Mezzogiorno* the days of the village as the level of modernized economic activity and basic socio-political change are past, and that some sense of at least regional loyalty is needed to create and maintain patterns of exchange on a level better adjusted to the complexities of the socio-economic relations of modern, not to mention neo-modern society'.[81] Thus one could consider not loyalties to the *family* as impediments to change, but 'amoral egotism', 'amoral village'ism' or even 'amoral rationalism'. Banfield mistakenly appears to believe, as some other community sociologists have done, that the community holds the key to the explanation of a problem concerning wider society without considering if this is an appropriate level of analysis.

Galtung also chides Banfield for an altogether too cavalier dismissal of the six 'common-sense' explanations. We may concern ourselves here with one of them (which Davis also takes up) – that of class antagonisms.[82] As Davis points out, Banfield underestimates what class antagonisms can achieve: 'It takes an Englishman, with rather different prejudices, some time to realize the full import of using St George, Utah, as a model of politically progressive society, as Banfield does. There, where the Business and Professional Women's Club, the Red Cross, the Future Farmers of America and the Chamber of Commerce are all working together for the good of the community, the appearance of anything so sectional as class-consciousness must indeed appear a retrograde tendency.'[83] Banfield regards class antagonism as something

---

[79] *Ibid.*, p. 57 (emphasis in the original).
[80] See J. A. Davis, *op. cit.*, pp. 344–5.
[81] J. Galtung, *op. cit.*, p. 64.
[82] For the complete discussion of these explanations, see *Ibid.*, pp. 56–62.
[83] J. A. Davis, *op. cit.*, p. 344. Banfield does not in fact use St George, Utah, as a 'model', but the point holds nevertheless.

which may hinder rather than promote political progress. Yet this hindrance may be derived from one particular class who have the power to impose their viewpoint on all. Galtung writes that, 'a distinction should probably be made between co-operating *for* something to be done and co-operation for something *not* to be done. Given the general reason the upper classes in traditional societies have for resisting almost any change, and given the general asymmetry between preservation and innovation, the upper classes have a tremendous advantage. The innovators can rarely command so much consensus because innovation implies a choice between alternative *kinds* of innovation, whereas preservation involves only an answer to the much more fundamental question: shall we have any innovation at all? The broad and consensual *no* is at the root of much of the organized activity by the Sicilian Mafia, and it would be strange if Montegrano upper classes should not also be favoured by this differential in organizational capacity, dependent on whether it is actively in favour of or against something new.'[84] This point carries more weight when one considers the history of Southern Italy, something which Banfield signally fails to do.

Banfield's ignorance of the lengthy history of 'the southern question' results in his being 'too quick to still his etiology on what are in reality the results or symptoms of a much more complex and deep-rooted set of facts'.[85] Lopreato, in his book *Peasants No More*, recounts the lengthy history of the exploitation of the Southern Italian peasantry. He shows that the lack of co-operation between Italian peasants is due to the precariousness of their economic livelihood rather than 'amoral familism', and that this precariousness is due to class exploitation. 'The peasantry has traditionally been the most exploited and persecuted class in Southern Italy. While the gentry have for centuries institutionalized the sweet life of leisure as the chief pastime of their life [86] . . . the peasant has shed blood and sweat to wrench from a hostile soil enough for his minimal needs and much more for the luxuries of his gentry.'[87] Yet the peasant's life contains a limited number of 'good things' of which there is no way directly or indirectly of increasing the available quantities: 'The pie is constant in size.' 'Consequently, while the past evokes memories of painful hardship, and the present is a tense and uncertain struggle for survival, the future constitutes for many a threat of hunger, sickness, humiliations, and futile toil. Under these circumstances the peasant becomes a wolf preying on his fellow men. He is constantly on guard against possible infringements on his meagre share

[84] J. Galtung, *op. cit.*, p. 59 (emphasis in the original).
[85] J. Lopreato, *Peasants No More*, San Francisco, Chandler, 1967, p. 246.
[86] See p. 151 above.
[87] J. Lopreato, *op. cit.*, p. 67.

of the local 'economic pie'. . . . Change of any type never affects the members of a population in precisely the same way and to exactly the same extent. The destitute peasant must surely know that probability favours the more privileged and the more powerful – whether other peasants or gentry – when the economic pie is altered.[88] Thus, according to Lopreato, Banfield's lack of historical perspective has caused him to posit the causal connection in the wrong direction – rather than amoral familism causing economic backwardness, economic backwardness has caused amoral familism. This point is echoed by Davis: 'It is a man's role in the larger society that determines his family relationships, rather than the other way round.'[89] Like Lopreato, Davis sees the key factor as patron-client relationships, which engender, however transitorily, a vertical solidarity, whereas intra-class relationships are competitive due to the scarcity of resources.

Before leaving Southern Italy we may review the substantive contributions of Galtung and Lopreato, both of which help to modify the rather static, unchanging picture of Southern Italy drawn by Banfield. Galtung's study, *Members of Two Worlds* is of three villages in western Sicily in the autumn of 1960. The three villages are given pseudonyms reflecting their ecological base – Montagna, Collina and Marina. Galtung does not attach too much importance to his choice because he is not interested in the communities as such. This community study is placed firmly in the *genre* of 'community study as a method' – Galtung is only interested in the villages insofar as they provide him with usable data. Galtung's concern is similar to that of Banfield's. He wishes to use his study 'as a basis for some explorations in the theory of development'.[90] In particular he utilizes three concepts in order to understand the social process underlying the retardation of development – Sorokin's 'cultural mentality', Lerner's 'psychic mobility', and Banfield's 'amoral familism'. All these can be regarded as value orientations but Galtung asserts that 'it is insufficient to know *how many* have this or that value-orientation; one will have to know *who* they are. One answer to the question of *who* is to bring in more personality variables, but here the answer will be given in structural terms. *Distribution in the social structure* is the first step of what we have called structural analysis.'[91]

Sorokin's notion of cultural mentality is interpreted as a dichotomy of ideational and sensate characteristics. Put briefly, and rather crudely, ideational individuals see stability as essential and change as accidental, while their supreme goal is transcendental or to become 'God-like'.

[88] *Ibid.*, pp. 67, 68, 69.
[89] J. A. Davis, *op. cit.*, p. 346.
[90] J. Galtung, *op. cit.*, p. 4.
[91] *Ibid.*, p. 72 (emphasis in the original).

158   COMMUNITY STUDIES

Sensates view change as essential, stability as accidental – their supreme goal is to become 'Ideal-Man-like'.[92] Attitudes to change are, of course, of considerable importance to the advent of development. Using the data from his Sicilian village, Galtung concludes that 'sensate men are found at very different places in the social structure. Somehow the periphery seems to have an over-representation of sensateness. . . . One would not in general expect these people to have very much influence in society and since they are surrounded by ideationals one might also expect that with increasing age they would be easily absorbed in society and moulded into the general ethos.'[93] However, sensates are also found at the centre of society, particularly if, in addition they are poor. 'In other words, the sensates are particularly frequent among the discontented in the periphery and the centre. And these people in the centre should, in principle, have some power; if they would dedicate all their energy to the transformation of their societies according to their own blue-prints, then one would expect this to be consequential.'[94] But it is not, and this leads Galtung to consider emigration.

'First of all', Galtung notes, 'the desire to move is embedded in a cluster of experiences rather than in a cluster of other attitudes.'[95] Emigration is correlated with both experience of upward social mobility and previous geographical mobility, even if it is only within the village. There is a tendency towards polarization between 'stayers' and 'movers' – 'Once a mover, always a mover' – though this polarization is far from perfect. Since the movers are less involved in the community, they may be regarded as something of a liability for the village. This may reinforce their attitudes towards moving. The lower sections of society possess a weaker desire to move, particulary if they are downwardly socially mobile and if they are relatively well-to-do. Conversely those in the higher strata are likely to move if they are upwardly socially mobile, but not enough to become relatively rich. 'In other words, the simplistic hypothesis that the movers are poor people in the periphery is directly wrong, but the opposite hypothesis, that they are rich people in the centre of society is also wrong. The location is more complicated. . . .'[96]

We can break off here from Galtung's exposition briefly to consider Lopreato's *Peasants No More*, which is concerned with the effects of emigration on changing social class and conditions in the village of Franza in Southern Italy between 1959 and 1964. Lopreato shows that social mobility in Franza proceeds by a kind of spiralism. Individuals must 'get out' in order to 'get on' and the prevailing pattern is for the male head of household to emigrate in order to secure a better paid job,

[92] *Ibid.*, p. 33.   [93] *Ibid.*, p. 187.
[94] *Ibid.*   [95] *Ibid.*, p. 225.
[96] *Ibid.*, p. 227.

while his wife and children remain at home. The husband will then send remittances which allow the family to enjoy a higher standard of living in the village and may later return himself in order to take the wife and children abroad[97] with him. Having saved enough money abroad, the husband and the whole family may then return to the native village, using their savings to buy land and live off the proceeds. The family will thus re-enter the local social structure at a higher level. Lopreato confirms Galtung's findings that emigration does not involve the lowest or highest strata of the community, and indeed the position of the lowest stratum, 'the wretched', appears relatively to be deteriorating. However, the results of emigration can be seen in a broadening of the 'middle classes',[98] as the diagram shows (see overleaf).

Thus Lopreato concludes that, 'Inasmuch as the increase in social opportunities and the proliferation of social strata are to a large extent the results of emigration, it may be seen that one fundamental consequence of emigration has been a systematic or structural change in local society. In recent decades Franza has experienced not merely a circulation or exchange of personnel across the existing strata, which would in itself denote an essentially static social structure, but a reorganization of the structure through the actual development of additional social strata. Together, the new strata constitute what might be thought of as "the middle class". In matters of social mobility, in other words, emigration has been for Franza – and we might indeed generalize to the agricultural South as a whole – an effective functional alternative to the phenomenon of industrialization experienced elsewhere in more urban societies.'[99]

Such a system, however, drains the village of the individuals capable of changing the local social conditions. As Galtung puts it, 'These are the people who could potentially give the villages new directives and new directions, but their orientation seems not to lead them in that direction, but rather out of the village. . . . From the point of view of the villages this is most unfortunate; it means that the villages can only benefit from the social energies expended by individuals when they are making the more traditional moves up the social ladder, on the lower rungs so to speak. When they have come higher up and have acquired social potential and experience, even education and skill, then – if they are motivated to move further on – their energy is devoted to other social areas, out-

[97] 'Abroad' may be Northern Italy as well as the United States, Canada, Australia, Germany and Switzerland.

[98] Not that too much significance should be attached to this term, for Lopreato's analysis of status distinctions seems to owe a good deal to Warner's in Yankee City and is subject to similar criticisms (see below, chapter 6). However, the broad trends are fairly clear from Lopreato's data.

[99] J. Lopreato, op. cit., p. 188.

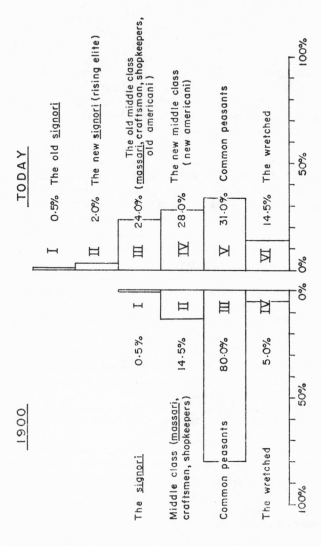

The Social Structure of Franza, around 1900 and today (from Lopreato, p. 196)

side the village and their constructive energy will be to the benefit of those other places.'[100] Such mechanisms are something to bear in mind when considering Banfield's explanations in terms of amoral familism, which is Galtung's next task.

Galtung modifies Banfield's conceptualization of amoral familism on four points. First, he prefers the term 'neo-familism', since the 'neo familist' is not the 'classical familist tied to an extended family',[101] and indeed is highly mobile in his thoughts and probably in his actions – he is ambitious. Secondly, this ambition does not necessarily make him a protagonist for local development since he is not concerned with changing society, but only his own position within society. In addition, his family orientation serves as a 'filter' which makes him less amenable to participation in other social activities. Thirdly, familism is related to *behaviour* rather than *attitudes* – more particularly, experience with geographical mobility seems to *predispose* for familism: an individual less rooted in the community is more likely to fall back on the family. (Banfield, on the other hand views the situation in reverse – familism causes lack of community action). Fourthly, familism is to be found primarily in the poor peasantry – and here Banfield's hypothesis is confirmed.

Galtung is now able to tie together the factors with which he has dealt in order to 'show that this particular distribution of value-orientations provides these societies with an almost remarkably efficient protection against change, an almost diabolical combination of factors that explains almost too well the absence of endogenous change in the region'.[102] Considerably simplified, the argument is that the middle strata of the local society – the sensates – are predisposed to change but are also in possession of a high degree of psychic mobility. They are thus inclined to be only loosely rooted in the community and are, to use a term of Rees', 'on the move and on the make'. Of the other two 'classes', however, the upper class are part of a national social network, while the poor peasantry are typified by a degree of introverted familism. Thus, even allowing for the large social distance between these groups, they lack any institutionalized interaction that would bring them together.[103] The only group for which the community would provide an appropriate locus of interest – being between the family of the peasantry and the national networks of the gentry – are the middle strata, and they are constantly being pulled away by economic advantages of emigration. Hence, as Galtung concludes, 'there is a conspiracy of value-orientation and social structure – against development and progress.'[104]

[100] J. Galtung, *op. cit.*, p. 227.   [101] *Ibid.*, p. 247.
[102] *Ibid.*, p. 254.   [103] See p. 151 above.
[104] J. Galtung, *op. cit.*, p. 263.

Ashworthy and Westrigg

Both Galtung and Lopreato show that the communities of Southern
Italy are far from being the essentially static entities that Banfield's
study implies. They show that economic backwardness need not imply
a social immobility and provide an important corrective to notions of a
static and unchanging countryside. Such re-interpretations have also
occurred in British rural communities, to which we now return. Following on his study of Gosforth, Williams investigated the village of
Ashworthy, the pseudonym of an agricultural community in Devon, in
1959. He characterizes Ashworthy by a condition of 'dynamic equilibrium', that is, that while the social structure *as a whole* appears relatively unchanged and unchanging in the absence of external stimuli,
within it constant and irregular changes are in fact taking place. 'Country
life, as exemplified by Ashworthy, is subject to piecemeal changes, is
constantly in a state of internal adjustment between one part and another.
This is a much less neat and tidy concept than the orthodox *Gemeinschaft* view of rural social structure.'[105] Williams' central problem is to
investigate how this equilibrium is maintained and, in addition, how
continuity is ensured, for Ashworthy is an area of family farming and,
as we have seen, continuity is of crucial practical and ideological
significance in family farming.

In contrast to Gosforth, Ashworthy has a very poorly developed class
structure. While 'some people have higher prestige than others . . .
there are no social groups that are or can be identified as belonging to a
particular social class.'[106] This should not be taken to mean that the
inhabitants of Ashworthy are unaware of class distinctions but that the
'idea that someone you have known all your life, been to school with,
and who has, perhaps, married a girl who is your first cousin, should be
in a superior social position merely because he has a better job, or more
money, or lives in a bigger house, is foolish and irrelevant to the
people of Ashworthy'.[107] This, however, does not apply to 'strangers'
and 'outsiders' to whom Ashworthy inhabitants apply class terms and
distinctions. The tight-knit social and kinship network means that
people are seen as wholes, that Ashworthy does have some aspects of
Gemeinschaft, yet the social structure is continually changing. Williams
also found that Ashworthy could not sensibly be treated as a social and
economic isolate since it was difficult to separate the parish from those
surrounding it.

There are three variables to be considered in the landholding system:

[105] W. M. Williams (1963), *op. cit.*, p. xviii.
[106] *Ibid.*, p. 7.
[107] *Ibid.*

the field pattern, the occupation of the land and the ownership of the land. In Ashworthy, 'the most striking characteristic of the land holding system is the way that it has been subject to piecemeal and irregular changes over a long period'.[108] Williams discovered that there were 589 changes in occupation between 1900 and 1959, of which 205 were within the parish and 218 were between Ashworthy and the surrounding parishes. The remainder were the result of what, in Gosforth, would have been termed 'offcomers' but in Devon are known as 'Up-Country Johnnies'. There was, then, a considerable migration of farm families. In addition, the system was not entirely hereditary for three reasons: families died out; agricultural workers bought land at the bottom of the 'agricultural ladder'; and non-farmers bought land (on the rung of the ladder they could afford). These changes in landholding and in the farm population reveal an essentially fluid situation which has clearly persisted for many years. The problem to be solved is how continuity of family farming is achieved in conditions of considerable change.

In fact, one solution to this problem in turn provides much of the explanation of the change itself. Under stable conditions, such as those described by Arensberg and Kimball in County Clare, it was suggested that the deep attachment to the land, in particular a piece of land, gives the economic and social system its central logic. In contrast to County Clare, Llanfihangel and Gosforth, however, there is no deep attachment to land in Ashworthy: farmers both move from and sell pieces of their farm and buy others. Williams argues that 'in this essentially changing situation continuity is achieved, ideally, by each farmer attempting to set up *all his sons* as farmers in their own right'.[109] As he points out: 'This method of ensuring continuity is quite inconsistent with a system based on the principle of keeping farms in the hands of the same family, since there can never be more than an occasional holding available for non-inheriting sons in any one generation.'[110] This conflict between the aims of immediate family continuity and the desire to establish non-inheriting sons on farms of their own lies at the root of the field situation in Ashworthy. The resolution of this conflict is made possible by the absence of deep attachment to the family land. Without this attachment there is no need to turn to the kindred to ensure inheritance and as 'the elementary family is a very imperfect instrument for ensuring biological continuity, there are some farms available for farmers wishing to find farms for non-inheriting

[108] W. M. Williams. The Social Study of Family Farming, *Geographical Journal*, Vol. 129, 1, March 1963, p. 63. (This article is based on Ashworthy data).
[109] *Ibid.*, p. 73.
[110] *Ibid.*

sons.'[111] There will, therefore, always be a movement of individuals, from farm to farm, this structural 'instability' being a feature of the system rather than a 'makeshift device'.[112]

In his study of Gosforth, Williams gives a fine analysis of social class divisions in the community, but it is static rather than dynamic. In Ashworthy, however, while a state of 'dynamic equilibrium' is detailed, there is virtually nothing about social class. For a dynamic study of social class in a rural community we must turn to James Littlejohn's study of 'Westrigg', an upland parish in the Cheviots consisting of 326 inhabitants. Littlejohn's study contains something rare in British studies – a strong historical bias. In particular he analyses the decline of the parish as a socio-economic unit. Littlejohn takes the turn of the century as his starting point, 'because many informants . . . could clearly recall social life as it was at that time'.[113] The inhabitants of the parish have, during the course of this century, been increasingly drawn into wider and less local social networks. However, not only have the internal relationships of the parish altered, but also the social relationships within the parish.

Seventy years ago, the children of Westrigg obtained little direct experience of the world outside the parish into which they had been born. It provided their total experience, and they left the village school to work in the parish. The parish was then not only a social unit, it was a political unit with rights over and duties towards the members. Littlejohn claims that Westrigg 'was a community within which by far the greater part of the individual's social and economic relationships were found. Or rather, his relations outside the parish were fewer than they are now.'[114] The relationships within the parish were cemented by the exchange of services, and by mutual aid and mutual entertainment. Nearly all the food eaten in the parish was produced in the parish itself and, apart from two or three retainers of the Duke, the minister and the schoolmaster, everyone in Westrigg was attached to a farm. The farm formed a small group within which the individual lived the greater part of his or her life. As Littlejohn puts it, exaggerating a little perhaps:

[111] *Ibid,.* p. 74.

[112] The term is Arensberg and Kimball's. Williams re-analysed his Gosforth data and looked closely at the studies of Llanfihangel and Country Clare and concludes that 'Continuity of land-holding over a long period and the placing of a high value on the family land which goes with it are characteristic of a *minority* of farmers' (*Ibid.*, p. 58). As was suggested in Chapter 3 Williams' emphasis on continuity may have been the result of his preconceptions about the community.

[113] J. Littlejohn, *Westrigg: The Sociology of a Cheviot Parish*, London, Routledge and Kegan Paul, 1963, p. 39. The fieldwork was carried out between 1949 and 1951. It was not published, remarkably, until 1963.

[114] *Ibid.*, pp. 44–5.

'Every adult knew the existence of everybody else.'[115] The relative independence of the parish from the outside world had its counterpart in an internal self-sufficiency and intensity of social relations. As all but three farms were owned by the Duke, it could be said by one old informant that, 'The Duke was the law up here.' The class system in Westrigg represented a hierarchy of economic power.

It is important to note, however, that even at the turn of the century, the influence of government – for example, in the Poor Law – was felt in the parish. Similarly the economic forces of national and international markets were also felt and some individuals did have social contacts outside the parish. Even so, 'The everyday social environment was provided by the farm and the family and the relatively contained network of parochial relations.'[116]

Since 1900, however, there have been some radical social changes. Firstly, parish control of education and the operation of the Poor Law have disappeared. Relationships between employer and employee have also altered, with the growth of collective bargaining taking the place of negotiations at an individual level and at hiring fairs. Finally inhabitants now have much more widely dispersed social networks stretching beyond the parish, and their relationships within the parish have altered accordingly. So the re-organization of the state administrative apparatus through various Local Government Acts and Education Acts has led to an increased 'citizenship', to use Marshall's term. Unionization has broken the bond that joined farm servant (itself now an archaic term) to his farm. Labourers no longer bargain alone but as representatives of an occupational category. The development of transport has meant that not only can the inhabitants of Westrigg escape from the parish both for work and leisure, but town tradesmen can also come to the village. There has also been a great expansion in the consumption of mass-produced goods.

These events chart the decline of the parish as a socio-economic unit. So rights which an individual once possessed by virtue of his membership of that unit, he now possesses by virtue of his membership of either the county or the state. As the parishioners' social contacts have widened so they are no longer dependent on the other members of the parish socially and economically. The processes of social change have disrupted if not destroyed, community so much so that Littlejohn can write that, 'the term "parish" now refers merely to a population living within a geographically defined boundary which has little sociological importance'.[117] One major consequence of these changes is that there are now

[115] *Ibid.*, p. 49.
[116] *Ibid.*, p. 59.
[117] *Ibid.*, p. 63.

few parishioners who know the existence of all others. As Littlejohn puts it, 'To be a parishioner is no longer to be an object of interest to all other parishioners.'[118] What has happened is that the relationships of the local social organization and network have been replaced by those of the modern industrial and economic system. So in contrast to other rural localities that have been studied in Britain, Westrigg has a class system, that is to say, work units are based on employer-employee relationships as in industrial communities and not on the basis of kinship ties.

The incorporation of both farmers and farmworkers into nationwide unions, the extension of the rights of citizenship, increased money wages and leisure hours, the buying of foodstuffs from outside the parish has also led to changes in the family. There has been a separation of the roles of father and employee because the family is no longer living on the farm. The personal relationship between master and servant has, Littlejohn argues, given way to a more impersonal one, so much so that they now confront each other as abstract administrative categories. There has also been a reduction in the number of social classes represented in the community, with a redistribution of power between them. The power of the landed aristocracy has declined and whereas the old system was accepted by everyone as the natural order of things, it has become increasingly questioned by the working class. Littlejohn uses the form of the community study to show the interrelated nature of macro-social processes working on the interrelations of social institutions in a locality. These processes have transformed the social relationships between the parishioners themselves and between them and the outside world. The general conclusion is that 'social class' has increasingly become relatively more important than 'community'. Littlejohn goes as far as to call the population 'industrial', though Westrigg is, of course, geographically very rural. Indeed, Westrigg, though an isolated rural village of just over 300 people, would seem to have more of the social characteristics of 'Ashton', a coal-mining community in Yorkshire (to be discussed below) than Llanfihangel or Ashworthy.

Coal Is Our Life

By including at this point Dennis, Henriques and Slaughter's study of Ashton, entitled *Coal Is Our Life*, we can illustrate the lack of necessary connection between geographical milieu and social relationships referred to by Gans and Pahl and included in Chapter 2. Frankenberg has even referred to Ashton, rather confusingly, as 'the town that is a village'. By this he means that 'Ashton remains a village, but combines multi-

[118] *Ibid.*, p. 67.

plicity of ties and sense of community with urban values and environment',[119] but identifying a multiplicity of ties and sense of community with non-urban values and environment is misleading, as we have seen from our examination of Westrigg. Ashton, in fact, far from being a village in the geographical sense, is more or less continuous with the built-up areas of neighbouring towns and, as we shall see, the social experience of the inhabitants is more limited by class than by geographical boundaries.

The data were collected in the early 1950s and it is avowedly a 'community study' influenced by social anthropology. Henriques is very sensitive to the implications of this approach and these methods, for he wrote in the introduction to the second edition: 'By its focus upon the "community" framework as such, this technique will tend to abstract from the societal framework of every level of social life.'[120] The example that he gives of the kind of problems that this leads to in *Coal Is Our Life* is that whereas relations between husband and wife, or the nature of leisure activities are 'viewed primarily from the standpoint of grasping their *interrelation* with the forms of activity and social relationships *imposed* by the coal-mining work upon which the community is based, this emphasis will tend to obscure the fact that each of these particular sets of relationships is extended beyond the community, in both space and time. *By itself*, the community study technique provides no way of measuring the significance of its findings against that which may be crudely described as these "external" factors.'[121]

Coal Is Our Life is, then, another example of using the community study as a method. It only indirectly asks, what kind of community is 'Ashton'? What is central is how do the peculiar features of coal-mining, for example, emphasize certain potentialities of the nuclear family form and inhibit others. It has to be recognized, though, that 'the influences upon behaviour within this form derive from a vastly bigger framework than that of a coal-mining community'.[122] The authors point out that the large-scale Yorkshire miners strike of May 1955, which occurred after the completion of their fieldwork, could only be explained 'at a series of higher levels of social interaction than that of the community'.[123]

The central features of the community life described by Dennis and his colleagues are the recurrent conflict and the attitudes of the miners, their cultural poverty and isolation, and the oppression of their wives.

[119] R. Frankenberg, *op. cit.*, p. 139.
[120] N. Dennis, F. Henriques and C. Slaughter, *Coal Is Our Life*, London, Eyre and Spottiswoode, 1956; second edition, which is referred to here, 1969, p. 7.
[121] *Ibid.* (our emphasis).
[122] *Ibid.*, p. 8.   [123] *Ibid.*

These are seen as the outgrowth of actual economic relations and work conditions. From the peculiar class situation and from the work situation, to use Lockwood's terms, of miners, much else follows. As the title of their monograph suggests, they are concerned with the consequences in the community of a way of life based on the mining of coal. Non-miners, and there are certainly some in 'Ashton', are only indirectly the concern of this community study. Coal, however, dominates the life of 'Ashton' – the dominant feature of the landscape is the spoil heaps and there is no point in the town from which they are not visible. Homes and mine-workings crouch under their shadow. To the observer, the spoil heap is the physical symbol of work and life in 'Ashton'. The first colliery opened in 1868 and without coal 'Ashton' would have remained a small agricultural village.

Most men in Ashton are miners, from this fact there are certain 'cohesive results'. This is not just mechanical solidarity arising out of the *character* of the industry, but also solidarity that has come through a long *history* of conflict. As Dennis *et al* remark, 'Common memories of past struggles will have undoubtedly helped to bind a community such as "Ashton".'[124] But whilst men have been thrown together by coal, it has exerted an opposite or centrifugal influence upon women. There is no work for them, other than housework. Dennis *et al* write about 'the centripetal' and the 'centrifugal' aspects of community: 'Clearly what is the "community" for one person may be much less than the community for another. Dispersive and cohesive influences impinge with varying degrees of power on different sections of the community. While for some women, working in Castletown and spending their time in Calderford the "community" may be very attenuated, for an old miner, Ashton may be very nearly the all-inclusive home of his being.'[125] Yet from data in this community study, it is possible to show that one out of every three miners in Ashton travels to a colliery outside the town to work and about one in five miners in Ashton pits comes in from outside. Though they are travelling to work, in the same industry with the same character and history, miners in Ashton are by no means locality bound.

However, over 60 per cent of the male working population of Ashton does work at local collieries. So Dennis *et al* stress that firstly, Ashton families have 'a common fate determined by virtue of their similar relationship through a wage-earning husband, to the coal industry'.[126] Secondly, miners are wage-earners and so have a similar class situation to millions of others in Great Britain, if not elsewhere, though this may

[124] *Ibid.*, p. 4.
[125] *Ibid.*, p. 17.
[126] *Ibid.*, p. 26.

be modified by local conditions. This leads to their third point: Ashton has peculiarities in terms of the local availability of alternative employment, the local market for coal and the actual physical conditions of coal-mining in the area. They consequently consider the miner and his family firstly as a member of the working class, secondly, as a member of the *mining* section of the working class and thirdly as an '*Ashton* miner whose life has a unique bias' resulting from the 'local' factors experienced in the sphere of work.[127] Their approach, then, is considerably more sophisticated than that of many community sociologists who have often only considered the individual 'unique bias' and then, in a somewhat cavalier fashion, extrapolated not just to other communities, but to the whole of society.

Their approach to the miner as a wage-earner is marxian. They write that: 'The miner enters the process of production by selling his labour power to an owner of capital.' and 'Just as the employer's ownership of plant, of means of production [and it should be noted they do not see that nationalization has changed this], would be of no value without the availability of labour, so given this ownership, the worker needs the facilities of employment offered by the employer.'[128] Here they are discussing a class experience, not a community experience and they write that 'when a man receives his wages every seven days, and these are on the whole not a great deal more than enough for comfortable survival, he is *bound* to work'.[129] The particular nature of coal mining makes this class experience more pointed. In a class-divided society, then, 'Ashton itself, far from being a microcosm of the national framework, is representative of only one part of it. To all intents and purposes, the inhabitants of Ashton are all of the working class. In relations to the stratification of our society they are all in the same category. In this, Ashton is typical of mining villages.'[130]

Mining is dark, dirty and dangerous. To stay alive and to earn good money on piecework, will involve close co-operation among workers, and the team of colliers underground 'is the hub of the social structure of coalmining'.[131] Years of hard work and social conflict between workers and bosses have, as Dennis *et al* describe, given rise to a social structure and an ideology in mining which are fraught with dissentions, contradictions and suspicions. The fact of common residence means that a man's workmates are known to him 'in a manifold series of activities and contracts, and often have shared the same upbringing'.[132] As Ashton is a single-industry town, the necessary solidarity at work is

[127] *Ibid.*, pp. 26–7.   [128] *Ibid.*, p. 27.
[129] *Ibid.*, p. 29 (emphasis in the original).
[130] *Ibid.*, p. 37.   [131] *Ibid.*, p. 45.
[132] *Ibid.*, p. 79.

carried over into extra-work attitudes and explains in large measure
the voluntary solidarity of the trade union associational life and the club.
The Miners' Welfare Institute, the 'welfare' and other working men's
clubs are the centre of leisure time activities in Ashton. The pursuit of
leisure is vigorous and predominantly frivolous and is without 'giving
thought for the morrow'. It is argued that this, too, is the result of the
miners work situation: its danger to life and limb, insecurity of income
and, for that matter, of work at all. As a miner remarks 'Well, we might
not be here another day.'[133] It is a boisterous culture based on drink,
talk, concerts and Rugby league football. There is in Ashton, as in many
much smaller villages, a common set of persisting social relations which
work to reinforce and reaffirm the social bonds developed at work.
Social relationships *engendered* at work are a characteristic, they argue,
of coal-mining that have been given added strength as a result of the
high degree of integration in mining villages. There are strong norms
and codes of behaviour. Close-knit social networks are effective agents
of social control.

It is against the work situation of mining that the family is discussed,
rather than for its own intrinsic interest. Family life derives its character
in Ashton from the large-scale framework of the community's social
relations, i.e. its basic industry and 'the relations which it enjoins on
Ashton's population, together with the institutional life that has grown
upon that basis'.[134] The most notable feature of family in the community
is the division of the sex roles, 'husband and wife live separate and in a
sense secret lives. Not only this, but the nature of the allotted spheres
places women in a position, which although they accept it, is more
demanding and smacks of inferiority.'[135] We are told that most Ashton
families have a continuous record of existence in the town for at least
fifty or sixty years. The ties of kinship and marriage are, therefore,
spread across the community. Friends and relatives live in close
proximity and it is claimed that 'Ashton has not yet reached a size where
changes [such as the building of a new council estate] can rupture the
system of face-to-face relations.'[136] Women's place is in the home,
men's at the pit. A boy brought up in Ashton is destined for the pit
even though 70 per cent of those interviewed said they would not en-
courage their sons to be miners.[137] A man's activities centre *outside* his
home. 'Home', as the workingmen's club comedian said, 'is where you
fill the pools in on a Wednesday night.' The women's activities centre
inside the home and in that of their relatives. Young girls see their
future in terms of being married and running a household. Joint

[133] *Ibid.*, p. 132.
[135] *Ibid.*, p, 228.
[137] *Ibid.*, p. 176.

[134] *Ibid.*, p. 171.
[136] *Ibid.*, p. 172.

entertaining by husband and wife is rare. It is argued that any development of affection and companionship is accidental. In a perceptive
section on 'the wage-packet' Dennis and his colleagues show that the
wife often does not know what her husband earns – she is just given her
'wage'. This is symptomatic of their relationship. The significant aspect
of the husband's participation in social life is its *isolation* from his
family which is reinforced by the exclusively male character of work,
union and club, pub and bookies office. Ashton would appear to be
confirming evidence for Elizabeth Bott's thesis that there is a relationship between close -knit social networks and segregated conjugal roles.[138]

Coal Is Our Life did not have as its aim the description of the whole
of the community. It does, however, show the interrelations of work,
leisure and the family within the locality. The authors write that it
would 'be entirely wrong to draw conclusions about the whole society
from the study of one English community'.[139] They particularly stress
that it is difficult to deal adequately with social change through the
medium of the community study (although an attempt was made, in
Banbury). Their monograph shows that as communities increase in
size, the significant social experiences of the inhabitants will be limited
by social class. This is especially true where the intrusion of social class
into the community is the result of *national* rather than local changes.

The People of the Sierra

The relationship between the local and the national is becoming a
pervasive theme of community studies – the effect of national decisions
on the locality has been seen in Westrigg and Ashton. A further study
which concerns itself with the relationship between state and community is J. A. Pitt-Rivers' *The People of the Sierra*, which concerns
Alcala de la Sierra, a small Spanish town of 2,045 people in the mountains of southern Spain.

Pitt-Rivers begins with a straightforward description of the countryside and town. The streets and not the houses or halls are the social
centre of this community. One of the prime conditions of the social
structure of central and southern Spain is to live in a physically compact community. *El Pueblo* means both the place and the people who
belong to that place. It also means 'people' in the sense of proletariat
'for the rich do not belong to the *pueblo*'. Thus, Pitt-Rivers can write
that the 'conception of the *pueblo* as a human community is expressed
in a geographical idiom'.[140] There are neighbourhoods within the

---

[138] E. Bott, *op. cit.*   [139] *Ibid.*, p. 246.
[140] J. A. Pitt-Rivers, *The People of the Sierra*, Chicago, Phoenix Books, 1963,
p. 7.

pueblo which have legal status. Membership of a neighbourhood, each with its patron saint, entitles a man to vote in the municipal elections, to hold municipal office and to participate in the privileges of the community such as common pastures. The sentimental attachment to the *pueblo* is 'counterbalanced, as might be expected, by a corresponding hostility towards neighbouring *pueblos*'.[141] There are myths about fighting between *pueblos*, though Pitt-Rivers doubts whether these enmities are anything more than a piece of folk-lore which people enjoy repeating. The slight differences in culture, in slang and pronounciation between *pueblos* are significant 'for they are the ways whereby membership of the community is defined'.[142] Pitt-Rivers argues that the basic premise of the Andalusian peasant's political thought is the moral unity of the *pueblo*.

Pitt-Rivers then turns to the relationships of the *pueblo* with the outside world. The *pueblo* is run by officials, who are mostly outsiders and who 'are only temporarily part of the community. Neither the mayor, nor the priest, nor the judge, nor the secretary of the Town Hall, nor the Secretary of Justice, nor the Chief of Posts, nor three of the five schoolmasters, nor the doctor, the vet or the chemist, nor the State tax-collector are sons of the *pueblo*, nor the head of the municipal guards nor any of the civil guards.'[143] As in many communities, these people feel less solidarity with the *pueblo* 'for whether sons of the *pueblo* or not, their ambitions and interests, both social and material, revolve within far wider horizons'.[144] In contrast, the lives of the working people are contained within narrower horizons. Some of the *pueblo* have nicknames 'that define a person in his relationship to the community, define him by his origin, his family, his place of upbringing, his office or his outstanding characteristics in the eyes of the people'.[145] This leads to the system of *el vito* or informal sanctions. Professional people, however, are known as 'the chemist' or 'the vet' and so on.

The links with the outside world are in terms of mechanical solidarity with the mountains, where there are kin ties and with whom Alcala shares the same culture, but in terms of organic solidarity with the plains, with whom there are economic links. Within the community, social control is tight. Public opinion is very powerful; the inhabitants refer to *el quedron* or the 'what-they-will-say'. Pitt-Rivers argues that: 'The tensions of the internal structure are projected outside the group where they serve, as an exterior threat, to strengthen the group's solidarity.'[146] The social institution of scapegoating, like that of gossip, both of which are found in Alcala, implies a degree of proximity and

[141] *Ibid.*, pp. 8–9.   [142] *Ibid.*, p. 13.
[143] *Ibid.*, p. 16.   [144] *Ibid.*
[145] *Ibid.*, p. 167.   [146] *Ibid.*, p. 29.

co-operation – you cannot be blamed if you have not somehow been involved. This proximity leads to a completeness of human relations: people are seen as wholes. Within Alcala the 'sanction of public criticism is exercised not as in open society by a number of separate groups which largely ignore one another, but by a single group, the *pueblo*'.[147] There are, however, no techniques for co-operation between *pueblos*; there is no Kula, no exogamy and no county cricket league.

Pitt-Rivers' discussion of stratification in Alcala seems at first sight rather strange. Classes are discussed in terms of their contacts with the outside world. By this approach there are only two classes: the 'ruling group' and the rest. The 'ruling group' may express solidarity with the *pueblo* against other *pueblos*, with other 'ruling groups' against 'inferiors', or with either or both against central or regional government. Unlike communities in Britain, for example, there is no variation in accent between social classes and where the *pueblo* divides up at all it tends to divide along the lines of sex and age differentiation only.[148] The only way to change one's status in Alcala – not to be confused with seeking money – will be to leave the *pueblo* and to seek a place in wider Spanish society.

Within the *pueblo*, and those that identify fully with it, the majority of male occupations are connected directly with the land. There are clearly gross inequalities: two-thirds of the total area is owned in 25 properties of over 100 hectares, while 800 properties between them share the remaining 400 hectares. In Alcala, in contrast to many peasant communities, there is a 'lack of a mystical attitude towards the land'. There is a 'value system of a people who dwell in towns from which they go out to cultivate the earth, but who do not love it'.[149] Occupations are not hereditary. While everyone in the *pueblo* is conceptually equal, the distribution of wealth is far from equal in Alcala. Money itself is morally neutral but 'most ways of spending money other than in satisfying the needs of simple living involve going away from the *pueblo* and are regarded as wicked'.[150] The ways in which money is made (i.e. class) and the ways in which it is spent (i.e. status) are, in Alcala, subject to moral judgement.

Somewhat surprisingly for such a static population, kinship ties in this community are weak. In Alcala, few people can give an account of their kin beyond their first cousins. There is a lack of mutual rights and obligations outside the elementary family, so that while kinship 'is an excellent basis for friendship, it is not in itself an important element in the structure of their society'.[151] Friendship in this community of

[147] *Ibid.*, p. 31.   [148] *Ibid.*, p. 78.
[149] *Ibid.*, p. 46.   [150] *Ibid.*, p. 62.
[151] *Ibid.*, p. 6.

equals is based on voluntary reciprocity and not on the prescribed reciprocity of ranks. Performance is, therefore, everything, for the friend who fails ceases to be a friend. The friendship system is, as Pitt-Rivers points out, of the greatest practical utility. 'It is a commonplace that you can get nothing done in Andalusia save through friendship. It follows then that the more friends a man can claim the greater his sphere of influence; the more influential his friends are the more influence he has.'[152] He demonstrates this proposition through a long and involved analysis of a dispute over irrigation water in the community. What this shows is that 'The institution of friendship, based on the moral notion of inequality, and the free exchange of favours, builds up, in situations of material inequality, a structure of patronage which links up the authority of the state through the economic power of certain individuals to the network of neighbourly relations.'[153]

There are thus two principles of political structure in the *pueblo*, equality and authority. The basic conflicts in Alcala are between the values of equality and authority. The former is associated with the relationships of neighbours among people who live together and the sanctions of gossip and personal contact. This is particularly associated with the female sex. Authority is associated with the male sex and the quality of manliness justifies the subjection of neighbourly values, for it is recognized as necessary to defend order and enforce the rule of right.[154] However, political authority belongs to the state. It is wielded for the most part by outsiders who do not belong to the *pueblo* and so do not always enjoy legitimacy. Matters of government are the business of the state not the *pueblo*, and are regarded 'as something dangerous and immoral which sensible people have nothing to do with'.[155]

Pitt-Rivers faces the problem at the end of his monograph about the delimitation of his community and says that 'one should delimit the area of one's data according to the techniques which one intends to use'.[156] Having done this the question arises of what the system of social relations is within the community. In addition, how is this system affected by being part of the wider society? Pitt-Rivers' answer to the first is 'founded upon an evaluation of physical proximity which not only orders the growing group within it, through conceptions like the neighbour or the *pueblo* but also runs through every aspect of its culture . . . [resting] upon the assumption that there is no difference in the quality of man, that by nature all are equal'.[157] The answer to the second question is that the community is part of the wider society and is sub-

[152] *Ibid.*, p. 40.   [153] *Ibid.*, p. 154.
[154] *Ibid.*, p. 158.   [155] *Ibid.*, p. 159.
[156] *Ibid.*, p. 208.   [157] *Ibid.*, p. 209.

ject to the state and to persons 'allied to those powers whose non-
membership of the community enables them to escape the sanctions
whereby the values are maintained'.[158]

Glossop and Banbury

The relationships between state and locality can be taken further by
reference to two studies of small towns in England – Glossop and
Banbury.

Glossop, like Westrigg, but in contrast to Ashton, was for many
years – up to the turn of the century at least – a local interaction status
system, and not a community based on one social class. Birch's study of
Glossop, *Small Town Politics*, only sets out to be a partial view of the
community, in this case its political life. There is, for example, virtually
nothing about the family in Birch's book. However, while Birch and
his colleagues may initially have set out to study one institution in a
community, they were also forced to discuss its interrelations with other
institutions. This was one of the first examples of an increasingly
familiar theme within the genre of community studies, that of con-
stituency politics at the grass-roots.

The research was a team effort, nine investigators besides the author
being listed. Files from the local newspapers and other documentary
materials were explored and they interviewed 'nearly all the persons
holding influential positions in public life'[159] – about eighty in all. We
are not told how they were selected.[160] Meetings were attended and
extra census data were obtained from the Registrar-General. Six
hundred interviews, a 2 per cent random sample drawn from the
electoral register, were conducted. In addition, thirty members of each
of the three political parties were drawn randomly and interviewed.
Their techniques, then, are the typically eclectic ones of community
studies, but they had the great advantage that instead of the research
team having to be 'jacks of all trades' (and masters of none), a trained
historian did the historical research, an accountant concerned himself
with the municipal finance and a single investigator was allocated to
each political party. What they describe, would, if it had been written
about by Maurice Stein, be called the eclipse of Glossop as a

[158] *Ibid.* The connection between them involves the law which, though
universal, has to be applied in the local context. Pitt-Rivers expresses this
relationship in the form of a syllogism: see p. 210.

[159] A. H. Birch, *Small Town Politics*, Oxford, Oxford U.P., 1959, p. 6.

[160] It is interesting to note, in the light of the discussion in Chapter 7 on
community power, that it appeared to the investigators to be self-evident who
these people should be.

community.[161] It is characterized by increasing government centralization and by locally-owned firms becoming associated with national or
even international combines. The Welfare State and various Education
Acts have led to the disappearance of local voluntaristic and par-
ticularistic social services. All this, Birch says, has 'inevitably had a
disintegrative effect on local community life'.[162] Local differences,
however, do remain and what is called 'the enduring strength of local
ties' alters and effects local behaviour. It is thus sufficiently self-
contained and isolated 'to have a distinct community life of its own',[163]
eighty per cent of its employed residents working within its boundaries.

Glossop was really the product of the Industrial Revolution. Industrial relations were peaceful despite the work situation of the mills
which, though less than satanic, were still unpleasant, and wages were
low. Harold Perkin, who wrote this chapter, argues that the cause of
industrial peace 'is to be found in the superior industrial relations of the
Glossop masters, in their success in maintaining contact with their
workers, not only in the mills, but outside in the churches and chapels,
the reading-rooms and the clubs, at public lectures and on the sports
field'. Here was a community where 'The masters demanded a loyalty
that went far beyond obedience in the mill, and they seem to have
received it.'[164] In Glossop 'Antagonisms . . . were not between classes
but between rival religious groups, representing complete vertical
sections through the class structure.'[165] Here, as in nineteenth century
Banbury, it was Tory-Anglican against Liberal-Non-Conformist – a
rivalry that benefited the town, for as one leading manufacturer built
a cricket pavilion, another sponsored the football club and so on,
through the library, swimming baths and parks. At this time the way
to the top in Glossop was by making money in business and by 1900 the
fortunes of Glossop depended upon nine large firms, eight of which
manufactured cotton. All their owners were very prosperous and
locally resident. Thus, in the not-too-distant past, Glossop 'was a well-
integrated and largely independent community in which local people
controlled its government as well as its industrial and social life'.[166]

It was the inter-war depression that disrupted this cosy, hierarchical
social structure. During the 1930s unemployment rose to 67 per cent
and the population of Glossop actually declined. As Perkin writes
' . . . the loss to the towns' morale and to its social and political life was
severe. The places of the old owner-managers of redoubtable character,
independent opinions and large resources were not filled by the most

[161] For an hitherto totally overlooked description of this process, see E. R.
Roper-Power, 'The Social Structure of an English Country Town', *Sociological
Review*, 1937.
[162] *Ibid.*, p. 2.   [163] *Ibid.*, p. 4.
[164] *Ibid.*, p. 21.   [165] *Ibid.*, p. 22.   [166] *Ibid.*, p. 4.

benevolent of professional managers, even where they were resident in
the town. The community, which had once been a well-endowed
patriarchy, found itself within a decade a stricken democracy of equals.'[167]
Glossop was saved economically by the war. The rather simple social
hierachy of the *ancien régime* has been replaced by one more complex
as a result. *Small Town Politics* was one of the first British community
studies, along with that of Banbury, to appreciate the *local* significance
of the so-called 'managerial revolution'. In Birch's words, there has
arrived 'a new middle-class of professional and managerial people whose
influence is great and whose social and political attitudes are quite
different from those of the self-made business men and the voluntary
ladies distributing charity, whose places they have largely taken'.[168]
Often these mobile members of the middle class would be only
'temporary visitors' to the community, who did not expect to stay:
they are, to use Watson's[169] term, 'spiralists'.

Spiralists, who have often come up through the grammar schools,
rarely make their careers in their home towns. 'People who get ahead
tend to become geographically as well as socially mobile and to join the
increasingly large class of professional and managerial workers who do
not have strong roots in any local community.'[170] Birch discovered that
only 7 per cent of grammar school leavers who took further education
were subsequently employed in Glossop. There are, of course, professional and managerial workers in the community, but they have
rarely worked their way up in the town in which they were born. 'Most
of them secure advancement either by moving from one post to another,
which may well be in quite a different area, or by promotion within an
organization which has branches in several places.'[171] Sixty per cent of
the professional and managerial workers were immigrants to the town,
compared with only 35 per cent of the adult population as a whole.
They are neither 'rooted' in the community nor are they generally
interested in acquiring prestige among the townspeople. Thus, Gloss-
opians tend to emphasize the importance of the distinction between
'natives' and 'immigrants'. Locals were thought to be different. The
newcomers[172] are not an élite in the sense that the industrialists were:

[167] *Ibid.*, pp. 30–1.   [168] *Ibid.*, pp. 3–4.
[169] See W. Watson, 'Social Mobility and Social Class in Industrial Communities' in M. Gluckman (ed.), *Closed Systems and Open Minds: The Limits
of Naïvety in Social Anthropology*, Edinburgh, Oliver and Boyd, 1964.
[170] *Ibid.*, p. 35.   [171] *Ibid.*, p. 37.
[172] It should be noted that in contrast to Stacey, Birch really only discusses the middle-class newcomers. What Birch fails to realize is that he has
too closely identified changing attitudes and orientation with one group living
in the community when these changes may be far more widespread and significant. This point will be pursued below in relation to Stacey's argument on
Banbury.

they do not spend their money conspicuously. In any case, they are not wealthy by earlier standards and whilst 'the economic gap between them and the industrial workers of the town is smaller than it was, the cultural gap is somewhat greater',[173] a result of their higher educational standards and more cosmopolitan outlook. There is no concensus about who are the most influential people in Glossop – and 25 per cent of those interviewed could not name anybody they thought was influential in the community. Many, however, hark back thirty years to the days before the Depression, when the force of the town's earlier social structure was still felt in the town. For example, Birch and his colleagues argue that the heavy Conservative vote amongst older people 'reflects the social structure of the town as it was a generation ago'.[174]

In analysing the political life of Glossop, Birch is concerned to contrast the present situation with that which existed two generations earlier. The changes that have occurred are summed up by saying that 'we have moved from a society that is locally organized with some functional organization imposed, to one which is functionally organized with local ties cutting across this with less and less effect'.[175] The national has increasingly taken over from the local with economic and political centralization. What Birch calls 'the new men of power' – industrial managers, civil servants, trade union officials and professional politicians – have come into and taken over the local community. They derive their income from salaries not profits. The significant point for the sociology of the community is that 'there is no necessary connection between success in their profession and status in the community in which they happen to be living'.[176]

As a full community study, *Small Town Politics* is obviously deficient in several respects. The pre-existing social structure, we are told, continued to exert its influence, for example on local voting behaviour, and yet there are few data on the continuation of the old institutional interrelations. Changes in the values and behaviour of the working class are dealt with in far less detail. There is not a full account of the interrelations of voluntary associations with religious and political institutions. Yet in this community study, Birch locates and analyses the *local* consequences of significant *national* changes within the restricted focus of the political life of the community. That this is a partial account can be seen by a comparison with Stacey's study of Banbury which was carried out slightly earlier than the Glossop study.

Banbury, unlike Glossop, was not a product of the Industrial Revolution. It was a market town and a coaching centre, a community of inns and taverns and stores. In the late nineteenth century it also

[173] *Ibid.*, p. 39.   [174] *Ibid.*, p. 26.
[175] *Ibid.*, p. 184.   [176] *Ibid.*,

manufactured turnip cutters for the rest of the world. It was never dominated, like Glossop appears to have been, by competing industrialists. For the first three decades of this century, Banbury was stagnating, if not in actual economic decline, and its population was actually declining in the 1920s. This was clearly a period of stabilization of social relations, and things stayed as they were. People would have been 'known' – the population of the town was just over 13,000 in 1931, almost the same as it had been in 1901. There had been a rapid growth in the town between 1861 and 1871 which corresponded with the establishment of the agricultural implement foundry mentioned above, but this was followed by sixty years, or three generations of stability. It would seem that this led to a local social structure very similar to that described by Birch and his colleagues for Glossop, where status was total and pervasive,[177] and where a person was more important than what he did, though it can be questioned if this would have been wholly the case. Kinship, as in Ashton and Glossop, was also important. Margaret Stacey calls this social structure the 'traditional' social structure, insofar as it is 'traditionally legitimized' by an appeal to the past – 'things have always been like this'. There was in the town, she argues, 'an established group, a group bound together by common history and tradition, with a recognized social structure and having certain common values [of] . . . conformity, stability, conservation of established institutions'.[178] This traditional structure was held together by what Stacey refers to as the 'many cross-threads of personal relationships'. But, like Glossop, there were 'vertical' politico-religious divisions between Anglican-Conservatives and Free-Church-Liberals, rather than 'horizontal' divisions of social class. Thus the middle-class members of traditional Banbury 'were followed and supported by the traditional working class',[179] who were tied to the former by their personal relationships, at work and in the community, and at church or chapel. They shared the same values and the traditional working class 'were not inclined to trade unions or Labour politics, *accepting* their position and the right of the middle class to lead'.[180] They were, in Mogey's term. 'status assenters' not 'status dissenters'.[181] The traditional working class 'provided the rank-and-file support in business and social life which made it possible for traditional Banbury to carry on . . . they did not rebel or agitate for change'.[182] But clearly, from the

[177] See Chapter 6 for an elaboration of this point.
[178] M. Stacey, *Tradition and Change: a Study of Banbury*, Oxford, Oxford U.P., 1960, pp. 167–8.
[179] *Ibid.*, p. 169.
[180] *Ibid.* (our emphasis).
[181] See J. M. Mogey, *Family and Neighbourhood*, Oxford, Oxford U.P., 1956.
[182] M. Stacey, *op. cit.*, p. 169.

evidence of the founding of the Labour Party, there were some members of the working class, and the middle class for that matter, who did not accept the traditional Banbury way of doing things.

Whilst many traditionalists are Banburians, however, not *all* traditionalists are natives of the town and not *all* native Banburians are traditionalists. The traditional social structure can always absorb a limited number of immigrants who are prepared to behave according to the traditional standards and to accept the traditional values. And, of course, many newly arrived members of the middle class have done just that and have been absorbed. Similarly, it is clear that some locally born Banburians do not accept their place and are outside this traditional social structure. This point must be stressed, as both Birch and commentators on Stacey seem to have over-emphasized the 'locally born/migrant to the town' division. This is a gross over-simplification of Stacey's thesis. However, there would appear to be a limit to the number of new arrivals a traditional local social system could absorb in a short time, even if they all wished to be absorbed.

Stacey's community study of Banbury started with the desire to chart the effects on the town of the introduction of large-scale industry – an aluminium factory. There were at least two aspects of this industrial arrival that are sociologically significant: both the work situation and ownership situation in the aluminium factory were relatively alien and novel to Banbury. It was a large plant, whereas the bulk of Banbury's industry was relatively small. This fact, together with its international ownership and the presence of professional managers, meant that the traditional particularistic, 'gaffer to man', social relationships were unlikely to be present. It also operated a shift system and the specific tasks to be carried out in the factory were hitherto unknown in the town. The second aspect was that the bulk of the workers at the aluminium factory were immigrants to the town so that, whereas Birch and his colleagues concentrate on the social consequences for the community of middle-class emigration from and immigration into the town Stacey, whilst not overlooking the middle class, lays greater stress on the arrival of large numbers of working-class 'immigrants'.

It is not irrelevant to point out that this was during the 1930s and many new aluminium workers came from areas of high unemployment, notably from the coal fields. Indeed, among those interviewed in Stacey's community study are ex-miners from both South Wales and Yorkshire. The previous work and community experience, discussed earlier in the section on Ashton, sharpened by a period of unemployment, were not conducive to fitting easily into Banbury's traditional social structure. The social consequences for the community were not just those described by Birch for Glossop but were more far-reaching, as in Banbury there were bitter and unsuccessful strikes over union recognition at the aluminium factory. The local Labour Party leaders, though not aluminium factory workers, were also immigrants to the town who had arrived in the late 1920s. By the beginning of the War the new factory was employing over a thousand men, so that no longer could it be *felt* that everybody was 'known' and could be placed in the traditional local social structure. Also these new arrivals did not accept the lead of the local middle class – they were non-traditionalists in Margaret Stacey's terms.

In *Tradition and Change* 'an attempt was made to relate the parts to the whole'.[183] Margaret Stacey's approach is therefore holistic and she is concerned with the configurations of the local interrelations of social institutions. She was inspired both by the works of the Lynds and by the classical anthropological monographs on the Trobriands and the Nuer. The main method of work used for the study was participation in the life of the town and each fieldworker (there were two besides herself) took a different sphere. However, Banbury was a town of 19,000 when it was studied and so it was felt, reasonably, that 'participation and discussion with people met in the daily round are by themselves inadequate for a town of [this] size. . . . Without the techniques developed by the statistician and the sociologist in their more specialized studies of complex societies, it would not be possible to apply the social anthropologists' methods to a place of this size.'[184] So, as well as scrutinizing the published records of the town, over 1,000 households were interviewed (a 20 per cent random sample) to determine population composition, family and household composition, religious and political adherence. Though Stacey's approach is holistic she does not treat Banbury as an isolate nor does she claim to deal exhaustively with every aspect of the life of the town.

Banbury was not chosen as being either typical or peculiar in its social characteristics. Stacey says that the choice of the community was 'in a sense fortuitous', as she had lived in the town for a number of years. This is a very important point. It implies that as an 'ordinary' inhabitant of the community, she can but only have had some views – albeit sociologically informed, but not based on systematic investigation – about what she calls the 'interesting social problem'. In her words, Banbury was 'small enough (just under 19,000) for all its leaders in whatever activity to be readily known. It has a long history and traditions of its own. It shows the stresses and strains as a result of its sudden growth (in 1931 the population was under 14,000) and relations of the long-established residents with the large number of "foreigners" who

183 *Ibid.*, p. 5.
184 *Ibid.*, p. 11.

182 COMMUNITY STUDIES

came to man the large-scale modern factory in the 1930s presented an interesting social problem.'[185] But she, too, was a 'foreigner' and it would seem likely from her own analysis of the local social system, that the majority of her social relations were with other 'foreigners'. It should be remembered, however, that she lays far less stress than is sometimes thought, on the Banburian-immigrant situation than on the difference in values and orientations. It seems likely that she herself was a 'non-traditionalist', an outsider, not sharing local values. What is more, she had been in the town for a number of years and so not only would she have formed an impression as to what the community was "like" but some parts of the community would also have 'placed' her. This would, of course, have led to certain difficulties in the fieldwork. These were overcome, in part at least, by working in a team.

Tradition and Change is an unparalleled analysis of the local inter-relation of social institutions. The tight, close-knit social structure of the relatively small pre-1930 town, in which 'Family, together with place of origin and associations, such as religion and politics, was the test by which people "recognized" or "placed" each other',[186] was still apparent in 1950. There were still 'small, private enterprise firms in which the owners take a direct part', in contrast to the non-traditional factory or shop organized on a large scale with remote ownership and control.[187] Traditional industry puts considerable emphasis on par-ticularistic relationships, and traditional shopkeepers feel they can rely on the personal support of their customers. Traditional industries are ill-organized by trade unions. There is a *tendency* for those Margaret Stacey calls traditionalists to be *locals* in Merton's sense, but those of higher social standing always had social relations extending well beyond the town. There is a similar tendency for the non-traditionalists to be *cosmopolitans* in that 'their frame of reference extends beyond [Banbury]',[188] this being especially true of the career-minded middle-class immigrants. In industry they are 'progressive' and see the tradi-tionalists as 'hide-bound', the traditionalists on the other hand, will refer to their 'new-fangled' methods. Despite the non-traditional social structure being based on universalistic, as opposed to particularistic, values the aluminium factory still had a marked predilection for ex-public school managers. It was not, therefore, as Stacey herself stresses, 'entirely unaffected by traditional values'.[189] Traditional industry, however, was part of a total local social structure in contrast to non-traditional industry which, whilst it was related in particular ways to particular sections of the town, was also related nationally and inter-

[185] *Ibid.*, p. vii.   [186] *Ibid.*, p. 12.
[187] *Ibid.*, p. 21.   [188] *Ibid.*, p. 32.
[189] *Ibid.*, p. 33.

nationally. As in Westrigg, increasingly 'the managers, the workers, the industry . . . are distinct and abstractly conceived groups'.[190]

The consequence of the expansion of the non-traditional sector is that Banbury, and by implication other communities, 'may less and less be thought of as a whole society, but rather divided with sections, *parts of larger wholes in a much wider society*'.[191] In contrast to the traditional social structure, economic, social, political and religious values are not closely linked. Stacey demonstrates this linkage in her justly famous diagrams of the interlinking of associational membership with political and religious institutions. She shows the traditional division between Conservative/Anglican and Liberal/Non-Conformist and the social isolation of the Labour Party and the Trade Unions. As in Glossop, the influence of class on voting behaviour is mediated by the traditional social structure, those members of the working class who are employed and spend their lives in the traditional sector having a marked tendency to vote Conservative. The consequence of the traditional, non-traditional division on the class structure of the community is that Stacey found it impossible to construct a 'simple *n*-fold class system' into which everybody could be placed. There was no consensus about the criteria on which social status should be given or received *between* as opposed to *within* the opposing sectors of Banbury's social structure.[192]

Stacey sums up her view of Banbury by saying that 'the town is bisected two ways: it is cut down the middle by a line which divides traditional from non-traditional; it is cut across the middle by the line which divides the middle from the working class'.[193] The key indicator of non-traditionalism that she takes is Labour voting, in either class and the indicator of traditionalism in the working class is *not* voting Labour. She reports that the most profound cleavage 'is found at the point where the three factors of traditionalism and non-traditionalism, social class and politics come together. This is the point where the maximum social distance and also social tension between groups is found'[194] – in other words, between the non-traditional, Labour-voting members of the working class and the traditional, Conservative-voting members of the middle class.

Stacey would reject, and so do we, Frankenberg's view that Banbury approximates to a microcosm of Britain, [195]yet there are some general lessons to be learned from her community study. These relate particularly to her notion of a traditional social structure. This is a social

[190] *Ibid.*, p. 37.
[191] *Ibid.*, p. 3 (our emphasis).
[192] This will be discussed in much greater detail in Chapter 6.
[193] M. Stacey, *op. cit.*, p. 173.
[194] *Ibid.*, p. 175.
[195] R. Frankenberg, *op. cit.*, p. 155.

system 'characterized by the close overlapping of leadership in formal associations; by the accordance of status on a totality of factors, public service and family position being at least as important as occupation; by the high value which is placed on the maintenance of established institutions and associated with this, the relatively low value placed on enterprise and "getting on" in the material sense'.[196] There are clear parallels with the social structure described by Brennan, Cooney and Pollins in south-west Wales, Mitchell in Devon, Mogey in St Ebbes in Oxford and Willmott and Young in Bethnal Green;[197] also, it should be pointed out, with Warner's *assumptions* about Yankee City and some aspects of Springdale described by Vidich and Bensman.

Margaret Stacey, for example describes the social structure of south-west Wales as 'Banbury through the looking-glass'. 'The close overlapping of leadership occurs, not among middle class anti-socialists, but is an overlapping of leadership in the trade unions and non-conformist chapels.'[198] What is traditional in Swansea is non-traditional in Banbury. What Brennan *et al* call a 'local system'[199] has values which at a fundamental level are similar to Banbury and which equally are being challenged. In Swansea, though, this challenge is not the newly arrived working class but 'a section of the middle class [which] is outside the "local system" '.[200] Stacey's point is that even in a society like ours – highly integrated, or centralized in Birch's terms, and highly industrialized (and therefore, relatively highly mobile, both socially and geographically) – 'given enough time, stability and continuity, the outlines of such a traditional society are likely to develop in any area. . . . [A] group of people living together in the same place over a period of two or three generations without major upheavals will develop a customary way of life connected with and upheld by a network of face-to-face relations in which kin plays a part.'[201] Elias and Scotson[202] have generalized about the same process, though they rely more heavily on physical mobility than on common values. They analyse in detail how social relations develop under the conditions of relatively high mobility into communities. However, they show how the image of 'established'

[196] M. Stacey, *op. cit.*, p. 178.

[197] T. Brennan, E. W. Cooney and H. Pollins, *Social Change in South-West Wales*, London, Watts, 1954; G. D. Mitchell, 'The Parish Council and the Rural Community', *Public Administration*; Winter, 1951; P. Willmott and M. Young, *Family and Kinship in East London*, London, Routledge and Kegan Paul, 1957; J. M. Mogey, *op. cit.*

[198] *Ibid.*, p. 178.

[199] *Ibid.*, p. 99.

[200] *Ibid.*, p. 181.

[201] M. Stacey, *op. cit.*, p, 182.

[202] N. Elias and J. L. Scotson, *The Established and the Outsiders*, London, Cass, 1965.

groups, both middle and working class tends to be 'focused on the best (minority) whereas the image of outsiders is focused on the worst (minority)'.[203] This would seem to apply to all local social systems: for example, he established that in South Wales they were working class, whereas in Banbury they were middle class. Stacey's conclusions and Elias and Scotson's general argument show how what the latter call 'micro-sociological studies'[204] can suggest pregnant hypotheses for the study of wider societal processes. Certainly it is not feasible to study communities as isolates and the external connections of local social systems is one of the central problems. This is dealt with in more detail in the next chapter.

[203] *Ibid.*, p. 7.
[204] *Ibid.*, p. x.

6

Local Social Stratification

Introduction

THE authors of two recent community studies which were discussed in some detail in the previous chapters, were quite explicit that it was not possible to place all those living in those localities into a single social stratification system. It was found that Banbury, a community of 19,000 when it was first studied by Margaret Stacey in 1950, did not have 'a simple *n*-fold class system'. That is to say, the total population cannot be placed in a series of horizontal groupings, members of each group being assumed to have parity with each other and able to recognize each other as social equals *if they should meet*. Nor is it possible to place people upon one social status scale, ranked on a basis of commonly agreed social characteristics.[1] It should be noted that there is an assumption that local stratification systems are *interactional*. This is in marked contrast to national stratification systems which are *attributional*. This raises an important empirical problem about the size of a community; put simply, how big can an interactional system be?

There would seem to be a limit to the number of individuals who can be in direct relationship with each other, though the stability of the community obviously is an important factor affecting whether or not individuals in that community *feel* that they know each other. It could be quite reasonably argued that Banbury, with a population of 19,000, would just be too big for there to be a totally interactional stratification system especially, as has been discussed earlier, as there had been a large influx of immigrants to the town. Yet it was also found in 'Springdale', a community of 2,500 of whom 1,700 lived in the township, that even for this 'relatively simple rural community there is no single standard for social stratification'.[2] Vidich and Bensman point out that a single

[1] M. Stacey, *op. cit.*, p. 144 (emphasis added).
[2] Vidich and Bensman, *op. cit.*, p. 94.

stratification system presupposes knowledge which makes assessments possible – again they are stressing an interactional system. Both Stacey and Vidich and Bensman distinguish between 'local' knowledge, what someone living in the community knows, and the 'sociologists' knowledge, what they as the fieldworkers and analysts know. No Springdaler can 'place' all other Springdalers by a single standard, not only because even in so small a community the inhabitants literally do not know enough about their fellows to do so, but also because the locally predominant ideology lays so little stress on economic differentiation.

However, Vidich and Bensman do categorize *all* Springdalers, by an intriguing application of the basically Keynesian distinction between attitudes to investment, saving and consumption. Similarly, though Margaret Stacey does not precisely quantify the numbers and proportions of families by her various social class categories and social status groups, she nevertheless produces a large chart onto which all those living in Banbury could be placed.

Clearly then, a distinction can be made between the local model of the stratification system 'in the heads' of those living in the community which, while important data, should not be confused with the sociologists' model. It might be helpful, though potentially misleading, to call the first a *local subjective* model and the latter a *scientific objective* model. It will be seen below that much confusion has followed from not keeping these distinct. For example, some 'local subjective' views of the community stratification system may approach or even be identical with the sociologist's 'scientific objective' model. There might, in this case, be a temptation for the fieldworker to adopt all the views of informants who appear to share his model of the system. But other 'local subjective' models will be very divergent from the sociologists' model in which case the fieldworker usually has little difficulty in spotting them for what they are. A maxim that was stressed in the chapter on community study methods was that both an informants' and a fieldworker's position in the local social structure would determine what he would see. There are checks that the fieldworker can operate that his informant cannot, and so there is really no excuse for the sociologists to uncritically adopt the views of a particular or even a collection of informants.

One final distinction must be made by way of introduction. When sociologists discuss stratification, they usually attempt to distinguish, analytically at least, between 'hard' and quantifiable data, like income or amount of property owned, and 'softer' qualitative data like attitudes and style of life. This again is sometimes called the difference between 'objective' and 'subjective' stratification, but more properly the distinction is between class and status. Local subjective models of local stratification may well contain both elements of class and status. It would be more helpful, however, if the sociologists kept these dimensions separate, for if the confusion between 'local subjective' and 'scientific objective' stratification systems is confounded with a confusion between class and status as well, then not only does conceptual chaos reign, but it makes the task of comparing community stratification systems well-nigh impossible.

Class, as an analytic category, can and should be kept distinct from status. A class is an abstraction and a categorization which may in rather special circumstances become a group. Status, in contrast, is far less likely to be a categorization. In a community it will in many circumstances refer to a group. When community sociologists have been discussing stratification, regardless of their terminology, they have often been talking about 'status groups' and not class. And when Stacey, and Vidich and Bensman, for example, claim that there is no single stratification system in the communities they studied, they mean first and foremost that there is no single system in the community by which the relative standing of status groups can be judged. However, because class is an abstraction and not necessarily coincident with the perceptions of those living in the community, it is in one sense easier to argue for a single local class system. Béteille, for example, has shown clearly in the Indian village he studied that the class system related to the means of production, in this case the exploitation of land, was different to the caste system, related to ritual beliefs and reflected in patterns of commensality or interaction.[3] Vidich and Bensman, using their Keynesian class model, also produce a single categorization of the local class system in Springdale and similarly demonstrate that the local status system, though *related* to this model, differs from it. Neither were fully recognized in the locality. James Littlejohn discussed the changes in Westrigg consequent upon the intrusion of a (national) class system displacing a (local) status system based on interaction. Those living in Westrigg now confronted each other as members of categories, though in this community study there is less information about local subjective perceptions of the stratification system. When Margaret Stacey wrote of Banbury that 'it is not possible to construct a class system into which everyone may be fitted',[4] she was in fact writing about the local status system, for her chart shows that at

[3] Andre Béteille, *Caste, Class and Power : Changing Patterns of Stratification in a Tanjore Village*, University of California Press, 1965. See below pp. 208–217, for an extended discussion of this brilliant community study (London, Cambridge U.P., 1966).

[4] Stacey, *op. cit.*, p. 164.

some abstraction it would be possible to apply a single (and marxian) model. Her point is that this is neither very helpful in understanding the local ordering of social relations nor does this simple model enter, to any great extent, into the local subjective model. In a single class model, as Béteille shows, an individual may, in fact, have several positions and these may change from year to year. It was unlikely that these changes radically altered a particular individual's interaction pattern, nor his perception of the local stratification system.

Lloyd Warner and his Critics

In contrast to Stacey, and Vidich and Bensman, there is the position of Lloyd Warner who, in his *Yankee City* volumes, has articulated his influential and highly criticized view of social stratification. Though highly provocative, his approach can serve as a vehicle for a full discussion of the central problems involved. Full consideration must also be given to the so-called 'Warner class scheme' in the light of the above discussion, as Warner clearly is able to produce a single 'class' system for the communities he studied. A brief introduction to, and some straightforward criticisms of, Warner's approach were given in Chapter 3. The following is not a simple reiteration, however, as he and two colleagues have written another book solely on this topic. One's suspicians are aroused by its title: *Social Class in America: The Evaluation of Status*.[5] This should put the reader on his guard against the conceptual confusion that this title implies, which is the more surprising as there are numerous references to both Karl Marx and Max Weber. The book is really written on three levels: it is a political tract, a manual of procedure for the measurement of social status, and a theoretical treatise.

Firstly, and this will be dealt with most briefly, it is an attack on 'the American Dream'. Whilst the book is an attempt to cool 'the bright and warm presence of the American Dream that all men are born free and equal', as will be shown below it has a markedly 'conservative' bias. Everyone in the American Dream has the right and often the duty to try to succeed and to do his best to reach the top. Warner points out that the dream's two fundamental themes and propositions, 'that all . . . are equal and that each . . . has the right to the chance of reaching the top, are mutually contradictory, for if all men are equal there can be no top level to aim for, no bottom one to get away from, there can be no superior or inferior positions, but only one common level into which all Americans are born and in which all of them will spend their lives'.[6]

---

[5] W. Lloyd Warner, Marchia Meeker and Kenneth Eells, *Social Class in America: the Evaluation of Status*, New York, Harper Torchbook, 1960 (first published 1949).   [6] *Ibid.*, p. 3.

'Americans, though, realize from their own (local community) experience that this is not so, but despite the presence of social hierarchies which place people at higher and lower levels in American communities'[7] the 'rags to riches' saga appears to prove that enough of the Dream is true. Yet Americans 'have little scientific knowledge about the powerful presence of social status and how it works for good and evil'. And so the [incredible] aim of the book is 'to provide a corrective instrument which will permit men and women better to evaluate their social situations and thereby better adapt themselves to social reality and fit their dreams and aspirations to what is possible'.[8] Thus it can be said that, whilst he emphasizes mobility striving, he also stresses the necessity of individuals adjusting to their situation in life where mobility is not possible. He is advocating the desirability of fitting the individual into the class system rather than considering the possibility of changing the system. However, one aim of his book is to make the stratification system more visible, and this is the second aspect to be discussed.

What this book does, it is claimed, is to provide a way of measuring status and particularly one's own status in a community. As an introduction to a discussion of social class in America there is a discussion of stratification in Yankee City (17,000), Jonesville (6,000), Old City (Deep South) (10,000): all are, of course, relatively small and relatively stable communities and Jonesville was a company town to boot. The kind of bias that this leads to is suggested by, for example, Warner's insistence that whilst economic factors *are* significant and important they are not sufficient 'to predict where a particular family or individual will be or to explain completely the phenomena of social class'. In Warner's view money had to be translated into *socially approved behaviour and possessions* and 'they in turn into intimate participation with and acceptance by members of a superior class'.[9]

Warner writes that 'talking to and observing the people of [from his own and novelists' accounts of] communities demonstrates that they too know how real these status levels are, and they prove it by agreeing among themselves about the status levels and who belongs to them in their particular city'.[10] The local stratification system is, then, viewed by Warner as an *inclusive mono-dimensional* system *recognized* by all the community. It would seem that he has moved very rapidly from a 'scientific objective' model of stratification to a local subjective model. His emphasis on social approval and intimate participation show clearly that he is talking about an *interactional* stratification system, and his rejection of what he calls 'economic factors', that he is not dealing with

---

[7] *Ibid.*, p. 4.   [8] *Ibid.*, p. 5.
[9] *Ibid.*, p. 21.   [10] *Ibid.*, p. 6.

an *attributional* system. If, as he claims to believe, Jonesville *is* America, it is not unreasonable for him to impute its local stratification system onto America. Yet, as will be shown below, some doubt can be thrown on the assumption that he satisfactorily analysed even that community's local stratification system. What Warner has done is to extrapolate a mistaken view of a local stratification system onto the whole of American society. All his examples are taken from some *local* context, for example, the exclusion of a man from a particular club, and from interactional *status* systems. Whilst what he describes undoubtedly occurs in many communities, this is at best only very indirect evidence of the workings of class in American society taken as a whole. Warner recognizes inter-community variations in stratification – for example, old stable towns will differ from a metropolis like Chicago – yet he claims that 'systematic studies from coast to coast in cities large and small and of many economic types indicate that, despite the variations and diversity, class levels do exist and that they conform to a particular pattern of organization'.[11] What it means to belong to what he calls a 'particular level' in the social class system 'of America' is 'that a family or individual has gained acceptance as an equal by those who belong in the class. The behaviour in this class and the participation of those in it *must be related by the rest of the community* as being at a particular place in the social scale'.[12] Some of the empirical difficulties with this approach can be readily appreciated if, instead of visualizing Yankee City or Jonesville, the area described by Zorbaugh in *The Gold Coast and the Slum* is considered. Many of those living in Chicago Near North Side were unaware of each others' existence. How would the *mafiosi* of 'Little Sicily' rank those living on Lake Shore Drive and vice versa? Certainly not by interaction. Similarly, it will be remembered that in Levittown, analysed by Gans, there were three class cultures 'each of which will consider itself to be of most worth, if perhaps not of highest status in the community'.[13] It might be more realistic to stress the differences between communities rather than their similarities, and certainly to be very wary of extrapolation from one sort of community to the whole of society.

Warner compares the task of the student of the social status structure[14] with that of the ecologist, whose first task in a community is to produce maps, and he says correctly that the 'map can represent nothing more

[11] *Ibid.*, p. 24.
[12] *Ibid.*, p. 23 (our emphasis).
[13] Gans, *op. cit.*, p. 132.
[14] We are deliberately following their usage of terms for various forms of stratification and have made no attempt to impose what we would consider to be some consistency.

about the territory than the knowledge he possesses. . . . Structure and status analysts can also construct scientific representations (or maps) which represent *their* knowledge of the structure and status inter-relations which compose the community's status system.'[15] The two methods that Warner uses to draw his 'maps' of the local stratification system are called Evaluated Participation (EP) and the Index of Status Characteristics (ISC). He claims that together they provide accurate procedures for 'measuring' social class and the class positions of individuals, for validating results obtained and 'for translating social class and socio-economic status categories into terms which are *interchangeable*'.[16]

EP is 'posed on the propositions that those who interact in the social system of a community evaluate the participation of those around them, that the place where an individual participates is evaluated and that the members of the community are explicitly or implicitly aware of the ranking and translate their evaluation of such social participation with social class ratings that can be communicated to the investigator'.[17] The EP is based on six techniques for rating an individual's social class position:

1. *Rating by matched agreements:* informants are asked to rank named social classes and their individuals are assigned to particular classes. When there is a high amount of agreement the analyst will know that 'the class system . . . is strong and pervades the whole community'.[18]

2. *Rating by symbolic placements:* individuals are rated into a particular class because they are identified by informants with certain superior or inferior symbols.

3. *Rating by status reputation:* individuals are rated 'because (informants say) he has a reputation for engaging in activities and possessing certain traits which are considered to be superior or inferior'.[19]

4. *Rating by comparison:* individuals are rated 'because informants assert he is equal, superior or inferior to others whose social-class position has been previously determined'.[20]

5. *Rating by simple assignment to a class:* individuals are rated because one or more *qualified* informant assigns the individual to that particular class. (How an informant *qualifies* we are not told).

6. *Rating by institutional membership:* individuals are rated by their membership of certain institutions which are ranked as superior or inferior (but how? the student may reasonably ask).

[15] Warner, *et. al.*, *op. cit.*, p. 34.
[16] *Ibid.*, p. 35 (our emphasis).
[17] *Ibid.*, p. 35. It should be noted that they are in fact unproven assumptions.
[18] *Ibid.*, p. 37.   [19] *Ibid.*, p. 37.
[20] *Ibid.*, pp. 37–8.

What is quite clear is that Warner abdicates from having what was called earlier a 'scientific objective' position at all. The analysis of any problem in sociology cannot make people's opinions of that problem its point of departure. It is one thing to be wary of imposing categories onto reality but quite another to say that not only 'must we try to see the problem from the point of view of the informants', but also 'that they are the final authorities about the realities of American social class'.[21] Lipset and Bendix, for example, in a classic caustic remark say that all he had done is to 'systematize the gossip and rumour of the town'.[22] For surely no resident of Yankee City or Jonesville knows that much about the interaction patterns of the community. Other than the upper class, the other five classes are much too numerous to permit that degree of personal acquaintance which would alone make a system of interlocking status evaluations feasible.

ISC is primarily an index of the earlier disparaged socio-economic factors. It is meant to be 'objective' cheap and simple. ISC was used in both Yankee City and Jonesville 'where it correlated highly with class',[23] It is based on occupation, source of income, house type and dwelling area. But 'it is not the house, or the job, or the income, or the neighbourhood that is being measured, as much as the evaluations that are *in the backs of our heads* – evaluations placed there by our cultural tradition and our society.'[24] Each component of this index is broken down on a seven point scale and then summed – the scale is *nominal* for dwelling area and house type, *ordinal* for occupation, and *interval* for income and so breaks just about every rule in the index construction book. The scales are weighted (it would appear somewhat arbitrarily) as the example below shows. The score for an individual is the sum of his scores on each dimension times the weight of that dimension. The range of possible scores is from 12 (very high) to 84 (very low). Warner's example is as follows:

	Rating $\times$ *Weight* =
Status Characteristic	*Weighted Rating*
Occupation	$2 \times 4 = 8$
Source of income	$3 \times 3 = 9$
House type	$2 \times 3 = 6$
Dwelling area	$3 \times 2 = 6$
	Weighted total 29

---

[21] *Ibid.*, p. 38.

[22] S. M. Lipset and R. Bendix, 'Social Status and Social Structure: a re-examination of the data and interpretations', *British Journal of Sociology*, 1, 1951, p. 156.

[23] We take this to mean the E.P. index.   [24] *Ibid.*, p. 40 (our emphasis).

The conversion table for Jonesville is as follows:

Weighted Total Ratings	Social Class Equivalents
12–17	Upper class
18–22	Upper class probably, with some possibility of upper-middle class
23–24	Intermediate: either upper or upper-middle class
25–33	Upper-middle class
34–37	Intermediate: either upper-middle or lower-middle class
38–50	Lower-middle class
51–53	Intermediate: either lower-middle or upper-lower class
54–62	Upper-lower class
63–66	Intermediate: either upper-lower or lower-lower class
67–69	Lower-lower class probably, with some possibility of upper-lower class
70–84	Lower-lower class

Warner argues that though EP and ISC measures two different factors[25] EP is the more basic. ISC was shown in Warner's community studies, though, to have quite a high predictive power on social class participation.[26]

The bulk of the remainder of Warner's *Social Class in America* consists of detailed instructions for using Evaluated Participation and

[25] The former identifies the actual social-class group with which an individual is found to participate in the community, whereas the latter rates certain socio-economic characteristics 'which it is thought (i) play a part in determining what the social class participation will be and at what level it will occur and (ii) are in part determined by the level of social participation'. (*Ibid.*, p. 42.)

[26] There has been an attempt to apply the I.S.C. method to an English community, by W. M. Williams, in Gosforth. Despite Warner's claim that it can be used anywhere, it was in fact a failure when Williams used it. The four dimensions of the I.S.C. were found not to correlate highly with class in Gosforth. The importance of this finding is increased as it will be remembered that Williams' usage of the term 'class' is very similar to that of Warner's and meant something like an 'interacting status group'. Williams writes that 'when applied to the housing estate (in Gosforth) every family received exactly the same rating in "housing" and "area lived in" and all but a few had the same rating in the other categories as well'. It would appear, therefore, that the people of this housing estate are of the same 'socio-economic level' and that 'in socio-economic terms one class is exactly the equivalent to another, so that the concept is valueless to an understanding of the social class system of this very common type of community. In fact, he stresses, 'the housing estate showed every evidence of possessing a highly developed form of class distinction'. (*Op. cit.*, p. 213.)

the Index of Status Characteristics. He takes passages very similar to the 'profiles' discussed in Chapter 3 and analyses them in great detail against these two indices. To add to the previously voiced suspicions he gives practical instructions on using the indices through the medium of an analysis of *Babbitt* and social class in Zenith. It is interesting to note that when Warner correlates his two indices he finds it very high (0·97).

The third and final contribution of this book is the theoretical chapter on 'several types of rank'. It is made quite clear that Warner realizes and appreciates that there are other forms of ranking system besides that detailed above: caste, for example. The system he has described is but one *type* of stratification, he argues – with this there can be little disagreement. The basis for differentiation of stratification systems which he adopts is, firstly, the amount and quality of *mobility* between positions in the system and, secondly, the *pervasiveness* of the stratification system in 'the life of a society'.[27] The classification that he can then produce is as follows (somewhat simplified).

	Pervasive and General	Mixed	Limited
High mobility (open)	1	2	3
Neither open nor closed	4	5	6
Low mobility (closed)	7	8	9

American communities (and by implication American society) falls mainly into box number one, except in the deep South where there is no mobility across the 'colour caste' line and so in some senses they would fall in box 7. It must be stressed that Warner is using a very limited and specific definition of class, but what this typology provokes is the seeking of reasons for movement along the two axes. If this is considered it may be possible to provide a classification of local stratification systems. Warner's discussion of class is now being limited, as seems reasonable, to local interactional status systems. It is possible to produce from this typology propositions that can be treated as hypotheses:

(a) the smaller and the more stable a community (meaning economically and in terms of population turnover) the lower the mobility and the more general and pervasive will be the local interactional status system (what Warner calls class), and conversely

[27] Warner *et. al.*, *op. cit.*, p. 258.

(b) the larger and the more unstable (both meaning economically and in terms of population turnover) the more mobility and the less pervasive the local interactional status system.

However, though this approach allows for significant differences between communities, one problem that should be faced is that for many people in localities of any size the locality itself will not be a significant reference group. For example, in Springdale, it was possible to distinguish entrepreneurial and bureaucratic segments of the community, neither of which could precisely rank with the other. For the former, in Springdale as for some of those called 'traditionalists' in Banbury, the local community *was* a significant reference group, but for the latter and for some of the non-traditionalists in Banbury it was not. There may well be communities where there are several status hierarchies which, while they all use the community as a reference group, would not be comparable with each other. What is clear, however, is that there can be living in quite small communities quite large segments of the population who are not members of local interactional status groups. It would not be possible for the fieldworker to collect their 'local subjective' models because they do not have any. Warner himself provides, suprisingly perhaps, some evidence on the differences felt by a newcomer to a community – and it might be added, on the differences between cities and the kind of communities studied by Warner. We are told that Mr Donnelly came to Jonesville from a large city. 'It seems to me', he said, 'there's quite a difference in the type of relation you have in a big and a small town. In large cities people aren't so closely connected with one another. In small towns the people know all their neighbours. They are more closely connected. They can see everything you do. And they follow all your goings and comings.'[28]

Pfautz and Duncan's 'Critical Evaluation of Warner's Work in Community Stratification'[29] lays most of the blame for the shortcomings of his approach on his anthropological orientation. This has been discussed in some detail in Chapter 3. They comment in addition, 'More is involved here than the tendency shared with many American sociologists to confine studies to the local community level for the sake of ease of gathering data. The traditional anthropological perspective of Warner *et al* together with their studied indifference to previous sociological literature leads them to a failure to distinguish between "community" on the one hand and "society" on the other.'[30] Their criticisms are interesting as both the authors of this paper were brought

[28] *Jonesville*, p. 29.
[29] *American Sociological Review*, 15, 1950.
[30] *Ibid.*

up in the Chicago School in its later days. It was pointed out in Chapter 4 that Warner could have benefitted from a close reading of the Chicago monographs before he went into the field. The seeming sufficiency of Warner's anthropological ethnographic approach kept him isolated from a considerable body of literature on social stratification and hence he failed to discern the crucial problems that it had raised – particularly the multi-dimensional nature of stratification.

Pfautz and Duncan are particularly critical of some of Warner's technical deficiencies, for example, they point out that as the EP Method necessarily depends on interview data, 'It is incumbent on the investigator to be quite specific regarding the sampling.'[31] Warner gives no information about sample size, selection or characteristics. It can rather alarmingly be gleaned from *Democracy in Jonesville* that though the 'upper class' was 3 per cent of the population of the community it comprised 13 per cent of the sample used to work out EP. Pfautz and Duncan write strongly that 'altogether it would appear that unscientific sampling practice vitiates to a considerable extent the claims for the ISC as an instrument for determining class level by the criteria of EP'.[32] If Warner's science is suspect, so equally is his theory, as Warner's classes are not necessarily the same phenomena with which Mosca, Marx or Weber were concerned. And Warner's critics also point out that confusion enters the picture when the protagonists of the prestige class define their concept on the basis of such criteria as intimate association, culture, way of life, etc. and then, because they fail to find group closure and intimate participation on the national level, conclude that power classes do not exist – or as is the case of Warner, assume that the study of (local) prestige classes encompasses the whole field. Merton has argued that if Warner and his associates 'intend only to assert that *contemporary* income, wealth and occupation are insufficient to assign all members of the community to their "correct" position within the prestige hierarchy their evidence is adequate. But this is a perilously narrow conception of an "economic" interpretation. Unfortunately [there are no] case studies of families who, *over a period of generations*, have not had their claims to upper-upper status validated by "economic" criteria which must serve as means for maintaining the behavioural attributes of that status.'[33] Despite Warner's emphasis on *mobility* as being a crucial differentiating criteria for ranking systems

31 *Ibid.*

32 *Ibid.*

33 Quoted by Ruth Rosner Kornhauser in her 'The Warner Approach to Social Stratification' in Lipset and Bendix, *Class, Status and Power*, first edition, p. 246. It is interesting to note that this article was omitted from the second edition of *Class, Status and Power* and one by S. Thernstrom substituted.

and being a vital element in the American Dream, there are hardly any figures in the five *Yankee City* volumes on how much mobility takes place and at what points in the class system. The only data are contained in the fictionalized profiles. Anyway, it will be impossible to assess social mobility on the basis of what people believe that mobility to have been.[34]

What is more, Warner has also biased the supposed objective ISC criteria – for example, by taking house type as a criteria of rank. This matter of class bias is much more serious than technical deficiencies in sampling. This point has been argued in two papers by Lipset and Bendix in the first volume of the *British Journal Of Sociology*. They argue that there is no analysis of the status structure as it actually exists, but only the way in which the status structure looks through the eyes of upper middle and upper class residents. For example, the emphasis is on 'acting right' and not just having money. There is clearly evidence – for example, in *Deep South* – that the upper groups made finer distinctions than the lower groups. In *Yankee City* we are told that 'the greater the social distance from the other classes, the less clearly are fine distinctions made'. Similarly it is clear from the designations used by one group about the others that the criteria for judgement vary from class to class: the lower groups making designations primarily in terms of money, the middle classes in terms of money and morality and the upper classes giving more emphasis to style of life and ancestry. So it seems that what Warner has produced is a *composite* version of the prestige hierarchy which is built from the varied perspectives of the local residents and, despite all Warner's protestations, was more *his* construction than the community's. Kornhauser asks 'why does Warner describe a large number of classes when only the upper strata recognize that many? Why are six divisions more "real" than the three or four that are recognized by the local strata? Why has Warner adopted the view of class held by the upper and upper middle class when members of the lower middle, upper lower and lower lower classes (the vast majority of the population) are said to base *their* rankings

---

[34] The best thing for a small town resident to do in order to improve his position to be socially mobile is to migrate. This is both well known and unmentioned as far as we can ascertain in any of Warner's voluminous writings. Social geographical mobility are just a convergence of terms, one often implies the other (see Colin Bell, *Middle Class Families*, London, Routledge & Kegan Paul, 1968). Warner implies (wrongly as shown by Thernstrom and discussed in Chapter 3) that relatively few people moved up in Yankee City. There were many who moved in and out of Newburyport on their way up. There will always, therefore, be a serious limitation to what community studies, particularly if they are naïvely ahistorical, can tell us about social and geographical mobility.

solely on money.'[35] The answer seems to be that Warner himself adopted the view of class held by the upper and upper middle class so that class is not what *all* people say it is, but what *some* people say it is. Lipset and Bendix point out that nine of his ten informants in Jonesville were upper middle class and so his community study reveals 'the perspective of the social climbers just below the upper crust of small town society. To people at this level class appears as a matter of interpersonal relations, manners, family and so on. It is not polite to suggest that class is a reflection of one's economic position. . . .'[36] His one working-class informant said he 'saw class as purely a matter of income and power'. They claim, therefore, that Warner's classes far from being 'real entities', as he frequently stresses, are the results of his conceptual scheme and his methods. The concepts used reflect the social reality primarily as seen from the perspective of the higher strata.

Does the 'upper-upper' of one community equal the 'upper-upper' of another? Warner's answer would seem to be in the positive. But it is clearly difficult to demonstrate. There is, then, the problem of extrapolation from and between communities. However uniform the smaller communities that have been studied are, and however universally the social classes extend, the community is still part of a wider culture. The upper and perhaps most significant strata are *not* represented at the very local level, but are to be found in large urban centres, in the American case, Boston, New York and Washington. Yankee City, Old City and Jonesville do *not* represent a microcosm or a sample of the United States: they contained no industrial leaders, no bankers, no big politicians, etc., who are surely central to a consideration of the *national* class structure. The upper classes in small communities are but pseudo-elites taking their powers and prerogatives within the narrower context of the local community. How this is done is considered in the next chapter.

It will be remembered that one assumption of the Warner approach to stratification was that the community was *the* reference group in this matter and that part of the preceding argument has been to show that this assumption is questionable. One approach, that of Bernard Barber in his paper, 'Family Status, Local Community Status and Social Stratification: Three Types of Ranking',[37] has been to conceptualize the community as only one of several ranking systems which are *independent* and not general or pervasive. Barber adopts what has become known as a functionalist position on social class: 'Social class position is the relative place in a hierarchy of such positions that an

[35] Kornhauser, *op. cit.*, p. 249.
[36] Lipset and Bendix, *op. cit.*, p. 162.
[37] Bernard Barber, *Pacific Sociological Review*, 4, No. 1, 1961.

individual and his immediately associated family of wife and dependent
children has as a result of the differential evaluation that people in
society make of the relatively full time, functionally significant role that
he occupies'[38] (i.e. his occupation). Barber treats social class so defined
as but *one* independent variable, i.e. not in principle more or less weighty
than family or local-community status. Family status depends upon the
societal evaluation of family-specific role functions though Barber's own
criteria of what constitute 'good' or 'bad' families are no less value-
laden than some of Warner's.[39] Barber wants to distinguish 'family
status' from what Warner calls 'social class position' and stresses its
independence. The 'old families' in Yankee City and Old City had high
'family status' which is analytically separate from both their social class
(as defined by Barber) and their local community status. Indeed what
distinguishes the upper upper from the lower upper classes in the
Warner scheme is the former's higher family status. This is also the case
in Springdale where the upper class's ancestors performed outstanding
services to community but they themselves have declined in the local
social hierarchy.[40] Barber's third independent variable, 'local community status' will be coterminous with family status, he argues, 'where
a society is so small that the local community and the total society are
coterminous'.[41] In modern industrial society, though, the local community and the larger society diverge. In this case, which Warner
apparently fails to understand, 'individuals and families will be evaluated
by two different standards, one for the contributions made to the local
community, a second for contributions made to the larger society'.[42]
The 'X' family in Middletown, discussed in Chapter 4, can be taken as
an example of a family with high community status. In the Lynds'
words, 'they symbolize the city's achievements'. In most communities
there is a cleavage between old and newcomers, between, in Elias and
Scotson's terms, 'the established and the outsiders'.[43] This is not always
directly related to length of residence in the community, but is related
to what Barber calls 'local community status' which in turn, he argues, is
related to identification with and service to the community. A point he
fails to grapple with is the one made earlier, particularly in relation to the
commuter villages analysed by Pahl,[44] that the established and the
outsiders may not agree on their evaluation of positions on any of

[38] Barber, *op. cit.*, pp. 3–4. That this formulation is highly contentious cannot
be gone into here.
[39] See, for example, *ibid.*, p. 5.
[40] Vidich and Bensman, *op. cit.*, pp. 66–7.
[41] Barber, *op. cit.*, p. 7.
[42] *Ibid.*, p. 8.
[43] See their book of the same title.
[44] See below pp. 206-208.

Barber's three ranking systems let alone the local community status ranking. *A priori* it seems unreasonable for newcomers to accept automatically the local community status ranking system that by definition evaluates them as 'low'.

Barber's conceptualization of the *independence* of ranking systems is, however, analytically useful. These three ranking systems are certainly 'lumped' together by many community analysts when, for many of those living in the community, the community itself will not be a significant reference point. Professionals are high on social class ranking but may be totally unconcerned about the actual community in which they live. There has been an interesting and stimulating attempt to elaborate upon what Barber would have called in his paper local community status by Plowman, Minchinton and Stacey in their paper 'Local Social Status in England and Wales'.[45] This is an insightful and ambitious attempt at systematic inter-community comparison which illustrates both the potential gains of the comparative approach and the ever-present difficulties. They survey twenty-one British community studies (containing data collected from 1946–59) and conclude that there is 'evidence for the existence both of systems of local social status and of forms of local social status not constituting systems'.[46] They follow the Weberian division between class, status and power. They are mostly concerned with the second, occasionally with the first, and the last (they claim) not at all. They wrote that 'when we use terms such as "status groups" or "status level", we should be understood to be referring to *social* status within localities'.[47] They discuss their findings under four headings: traditional status systems in England, non-traditional status in England, social status in Wales (which will not be discussed here) and social status in English working-class localities.

Social status will be organized locally into a system, they argue, where people meet regularly in a locality 'in which people would have places and believe accordingly'.[48] Gosforth and Banbury both have evidence of such a system, its characteristics being that the system had a generally recognized hierarchy of places, consisting of discrete levels rather than continua. Though there may be 'frontier groups', the members of which are difficult to place precisely, social mixing rarely spreads over more than a very limited range of the hierarchy. Not all these levels may be recognized by all inhabitants of the community, they suggest (in contrast to Warner's argument but, as has been seen, consistent with his data). Particularly there may be differences between

[45] *Sociological Review*, 10, No. 2, 1962.
[46] Plowman *et. al, op. cit.*, p. 161.
[47] *Ibid.*, p. 162 (emphasis in the original).
[48] *Ibid.*, p. 164.

the farm and non-farm population. Differences between status levels are differences between 'ways of life' and involve 'difference in manner, attitudes, beliefs, expectations, patterns of child rearing, relations between sexes, patterns of visiting, range of travel and kind of work and degree of responsibility'.[49] Status within this system is *interactional*, but newcomers are placed, initially at least, by their *attributes*. They wish to call this type of system 'traditional' from Max Weber's concept of traditional as opposed to rational-legal or bureaucratic and charismatic legitimacy, based on the belief in things as they have always existed. It does not indicate the age of the system. This is also a *total* status system or, in the term used above pervasive, in that there is a tendency 'for individuals to have similar status in different spheres of activity'.[50]

However, in contrast to Warner, they argue that 'everyone in a locality need not belong to a local system'[51] and that there may well be parts of non-traditional status systems present in the locality. Banbury provides evidence of people who are outside the total, traditional local social status system. Non-traditional status is not a single system: 'it is an unorganized set of levels'.[52] It is attributional and not interactional 'and involves uncertainty about status boundaries and resentment at status rejection'.[53] There is not a total or pervasive system: status in one sphere does not necessarily carry over into another. It is quite possible, though, for traditional and non-traditional status to co-exist in the same community. A characteristic they also claim of working-class localities is that evidence of local total social status is hard to find. They discover 'respectability' to be a widespread style of life and suggest that it is 'a claim to status'.[54] It involves the rejection of the 'roughs'. Between these two extremes are 'ordinary' working-class people. Old, stable working-class areas show signs of the total status lacking on new housing estates. Plowman *et al*'s crude broad divisions of the majority of the population, in contrast to the relatively fine divisions usually elaborated within the middle class, suggest that the working class are those the sociologists write about most and talk to least.

Mobility can be individual (including the family of the actor) or group, between generations or within a generation. Mobility is easiest between generations on an individual basis in an attributional system. It is at its most difficult on a group basis within a generation in an interactional system. Almost certainly this kind of social change is rarely generated from within a locality, but must derive from wider, perhaps national or even global social changes. Plowman and his colleagues point out that 'it must be difficult to change one's socia

[49] *Ibid.*, p. 165.   [50] *Ibid.*, p. 167.
[51] *Ibid.*, p. 171.   [52] Stacey, *op. cit.*, p. 72.
[53] *Ibid.*, p. 187.   [54] Plowman, *et. al.*, p. 178.

status within a (local and total) system, since everyone already knows one's place'.[55] This is relevant to the earlier discussion of Warner, for Yankee City, as he describes it, has all the characteristics of a local and total status system and so it would seem that the most likely means to social mobility would be emigration to another community where one's original status is unknown or counts for less. This, as has been pointed out, he does not consider. Whilst there may be 'places' in the local traditional status system for immigrants (clergy, doctors and so on), as like as not they will become one of the fragments of a non-traditional status system present in the locality. The useful term 'cross mobility' is coined for 'mobility between a local system and non-traditional status and it may involve important changes in attitudes (say between localism and cosmopolitanism) without necessarily altering the level of status'.[56] It is also possible, but more difficult, to be 'cross mobile' into a local status system

Shils has listed the conditions under which, if the status position of each individual in a locality were to be ascertained, they could be ranged in a single distribution. These are the conditions for total local social status and though they seemed to have occurred, say in pre-1930 Banbury and in pre-1950 Gosforth, some doubt must be cast on whether they are met by Yankee City. This list may serve as a measure against which to put community. There must be, Shils argues:

'(a) an evaluative consensus throughout the society regarding the criteria in accordance with which *deference* is allocated;

(b) cognitive consensus throughout the society regarding the characteristics of each position in each distribution and regarding the shape of the distribution of entitlements;

(c) consensus throughout the society regarding the weights to be assigned to the various categories of deference entitling properties'.

Where these three conditions exist, there would also exist a consensus between the judgement a person makes of his own position and the judgements which others make about his position:

(d) equal attention to and equal differentiation by each member of the society of strata which are adjacent to his own and those that are remote from it – which presupposes rather hopefully, equal knowledge by all members of a society about all other members;

(e) equal salience of deference judgements throughout the society;

(f) equivalence of all deferred judgements'.[57]

[55] *Ibid.*, p. 188.
[56] *Ibid.*, p. 193.
[57] E. Shils, 'Deference', in J. A. Jackson (ed.), *Social Stratification*, Cambridge, Cambridge U.P., 1968.

If the term community or locality is substituted for society in the above quotation it can be readily appreciated that these conditions will rarely be met, and were not met, in Yankee City.

Housing Classes and the Local Social System

There has recently been, however, a totally different approach to local stratification that starts from class, rather than status. This is the approach to what have been called 'housing classes'. It has been used to show how local stratification can be analysed as a *system* in communities which are not totally *interactional* systems, particularly by Rex and Moore in Birmingham and Pahl and his students in Kent.[58] This approach is the opposite of the abdication of Warner in favour of the conceptions of informants and represents an ambitious sociological attempt to bring together the work of the Chicago ecologists (see Chapter 3) and Max Weber. The theory of housing classes emerged out of Burgess's concentric zone theory. It will be remembered that he posited (and the Chicago School spent a decade describing) four zones or rings outside the CBD – a zone of transition, a zone of working-class housing, a middle-class residential zone and what we would now call a commuter zone. Rex rejects as too vague Burgess's explanation based on the general notion of 'competition', but like the Chicago school considers the historical evolution of the physical urban structure up to the present day as the essential starting point for analysis. He, in the case of Birmingham, considers the growth of industry and the segregation of residential areas in the nineteenth century between 'the captains of industry' and the rows of red brick working-class cottages. 'Mutual aid rather than property gave security to the inhabitants in this [working-class] area and when that mutual aid was expressed in political terms in the socialism of the city hall it was greatly to enhance the power of the established working classes in their struggle for housing and living space.'[59] Around the turn of the century a 'hard way of life', that of the growing numbers of white-collar workers, emerged between these two. Their houses were abandoned in the inter-war suburban migration. Rex writes that 'in the twentieth century, however, the great urban game of leapfrog begins. The types of housing (mentioned above) pass to other residential and commercial areas and support new differentiated styles of life while their original inhabitants open up new de-

[58] See first and foremost, J. Rex and R. Moore, *Race, Community and Conflict*, Oxford, Oxford U.P., 1967. Also Rex's paper, 'The Sociology of a Zone of Transition' published in Pahl's *Readings in Urban Sociology*, Oxford, Pergamon, 1968. See also the essays by Pahl in his *Whose City?* London. Longman's, 1970.

[59] Rex (in Pahl), *op. cit.*, p. 213.

sirable housing options further from the centre.'[60] The 'captains of industry' go to classy detached houses in inner suburbia, white-collar workers move to 'inter-war semis' and the working-classes move to council houses 'modelled on those (houses) of the white-collar people but are distinguished by the fact that once a week a man from the council calls for the rent'.[61] There are, then, three ways of life and of housing that are considered to be both normal and desirable in the city. Though 'less desirable and normal is the way of life of those who inhabit the inner zone'[62] which includes those 'left behind' in single household slum property together with the deviants and recent immigrants to the city, who are forced by the constraints of the housing market into the multi-household dwellings of the 'zone of transition' that surrounds the inner zone.

In Rex's view the 'basic process underlying urban social interaction is competition for scarce and desired types of housing. In this process people are distinguished from one another by their strength in the housing market or, more generally, in the system of housing allocations'.[63] Rex modifies Weber's notion of differential placement in a market situation to include differential placement with regard to a system of bureaucratic allocation, and from this he arrives at the notion of housing classes. The housing classes, which may in fact be in conflict with each other at the local level that Rex distinguishes, are:

1. The outright owners of large houses in desirable areas.
2. Mortgage payers who 'own' whole houses in desirable areas.
3. Council tenants in council-built houses.
4. Council tenants 'temporarily' housed in slum houses awaiting demolition.
5. Tenants of private house owners, usually in the inner ring.
6. House owners who must take lodgers to meet loan repayments.
7. Lodgers in rooms.

The crucial class struggle in housing will, in the first place, be for either a mortgage or a council tenancy. Size and security of income are vital to the first, 'housing need' and length of residence are vital to the second. Failing to gain admission to either of these two housing classes will almost invariably involve residence in the 'zone of transition'. The Birmingham situation analysed by Rex and Moore was empirically complicated by an urban-rural culture change. The housing classes listed above are also arranged in a hierarchy of prestige and status and will have a definite ecological position in the city. Rex and Moore have shown that it is possible to analyse a social system as large and complex

---

[60] *Ibid.*, p. 213.
[61] *Ibid.*, p. 214.
[62] *Ibid.*
[63] *Ibid.*

as that of Birmingham in a conceptually clear and empirically accurate manner. They demonstrate that in class terms it is possible to treat the community as a single system, but they never suggest that it is a single all-inclusive status system such as that described by Warner.

A further example is Pahl's ideal type 'commuter-village' near London, based on data collected by him in both Hertfordshire and Kent.[64] He distinguishes six groups, all to be found living in the village, yet in some cases they would be socially invisible to each:

1. *Large property owners* who are tied to the village by tradition and property and yet have considerable financial and other interests elsewhere. They may well be members of a national if not international upper class. Whilst their wives open village fetes and they may receive deference (especially from group 6 below) their reference group for class and certainly their interactional patterns are not bounded by the village.

2. *The salariat:* these are business and professional people who have defined 'for themselves a village-in-the-mind',[65] and whilst it is therefore important to them that they live in *a* village, *what* particular village is largely irrelevant. Group 6 below may be important props to their definition of the stage but their subjective class model will be related to 'people like themselves', i.e. others with a bureaucratically organized career. Like those discussed in Chapter 3 living on Crestwood Heights, the career not the community is their reference group.

3. *The retired urban workers with some capital* who are likely to use their past not their present community as a reference group.

4. *Urban workers with limited capital income* 'who do not particularly want to live in this settlement type but, owing to the high price of urban land are forced to seek cheaper housing "in a village" '.[66] Pahl calls these 'reluctant communiters' and they may be very similar to Gans Levittowners. They certainly will not use their present local community of residence as a reference group.

5. *Rural working-class commuters* who have a house but not work in the village and are forced to seek employment elsewhere. They are more likely to be similar to the rural commuters described by Frankenberg and Littlejohn who, whilst they would have local interaction, their knowledge of the 'other' class (in economic terms) would be very limited.

[64] R. E. Pahl, 'The Rural-Urban continuum', *Sociologis Ruralis*, 6, 1966, reprinted in Pahl, *Readings*. See also his *Urbs in Rure* London, Weidenfeld and Nicolson, 1965, and 'Class and Community in English Commuter Villages', *Sociologis Ruralis*, 5, 1965.

[65] Pahl (1966), *op. cit.*, p. 271 (in his *Readings*).

[66] *Ibid.*, p. 272.

6. *Traditional ruralites*: a 'minority element of local tradesmen, agricultural workers and so on whose residence and employment are both local. There may be close kinship and other links with group 5 and in practice it is difficult to distinguish between them sociologically.'[67]

If the social networks of these groups were collected it could be shown that their interaction is rarely bounded by the locality. All but the last two groups are likely to have what have been called 'loose-knit' social networks, meaning that it is likely that relatively few of their friends know each other and that their friends do not know their kin and both do not know the husband's colleagues. In this social situation it is highly likely that they will not have a 'local subjective model' of the local stratification system and that their 'class position', in Warner's meaning of the term, will not be 'pervasive' or 'general'. Or at least, it need not be if they themselves do not want it to be. In contrast, groups 5 and 6 will have close-knit networks – meaning that their friends know their kin and each other and they may even work with each other. In such a social situation, within this group, it may well be possible to utilize Warner's approach, but their evaluation of groups 1 to 4 is likely to be both vague and untrustworthy. Clearly there is some value for the community sociologist knowing how the groups *feel* about each other but, as they neither interact nor have the knowledge upon which to make judgements, nor for that matter care very much about the other groups, it is difficult to see how they can be, in Warner's words, the 'final authorities about the realities of social class'. But it should be realized that the subjective approach is only one way of looking at stratification and there are potentially dangerous value judgements in deciding which subjective opinion to take if they are divergent. It is, however, possible for the sociologist to make a 'scientific objective' analysis of the local stratification system of a commuter village. This Pahl does by considering the differential relation of groups to the housing market (and this at least is regional and not locality bound) and he shows that the amount of spatial constraint operates differentially for each of these six groups, so that the amount of choice becomes more limited further down the scale.

The work of Rex and Moore and that of Pahl suggests that one fruitful approach to local stratification is in terms of a socio-ecological system. This is a system of constraints, both social and economic, that operate differentially on different classes and have spatial consequences. This approach, though one way to analyse local stratification as a single system, suggests that it is unlikely that there will be a concensus of

[67] *Ibid.*

'local subjective' models of stratification. The absence of mutually recognized and understood hierarchically arranged interaction patterns in the community does not imply that there is nothing for the student of stratification to study in the community. This can be underlined by reference to one of the most rigid stratification systems – the Indian caste system. The caste system, may, on the face of it, imply such constraints on individuals that their behaviour can only be examined in the context of their caste rather than their locality. Indians have always had membership of groups that extend outside their community, especially those related to the caste system. This has led Dumont to ask 'Is the village indeed the social fact which it has for so long been assumed to be?'[68]

Caste and Community

Villages are exogenous, castes, by definition, are endogenous. Villages will, therefore, be linked by kinship but intra- rather than inter-caste. Redfield is ambivalent about the answer to the question posed above, for he clearly attributes some 'community' characteristics to castes: 'the principle elements of the countrywide networks of India consist of familial and caste associations that persist through generations. The associations connect one set of villages with another or some of the families in one village with families corresponding in culture and social status in other villages. It is *as if* the characteristic social structure of the primitive self-contained community had been dissected out and its components spread about a wide area.'[69] For this reason, the village, it has sometimes been argued, is not a significant unit of study. However, a simple point can be made against this: castes and sub-castes (*jatis*) do have, in fact, what are occupational names. *Jatis* are innumerable, small, local endogenous groups. Their titles may originally have represented their place in the local division of labour, but their tasks have changed to meet the *community*'s needs. *Jatis* live in the same village and *do* interact, the most important indicator being that they have changed jobs related to the local village needs regardless of caste, and so 'lampmakers' are now 'shopkeepers', 'farmers' became 'metalworkers' and so on. Nevertheless, Dumont has argued that caste is the proper unit of study. Srinivas and his colleagues have argued that this point of view is 'perhaps ignoring the bonds which arise from the occupational interdependence of hereditary groups, from the continued sharing of

[68] L. Dumont in a review article on Indian Village Studies in *Contributions to Indian Sociology*, 1, 1957, p. 23.
[69] R. Redfield, *Peasant Society and Culture*, Chicago (and London), University of Chicago Press, 1956, p. 34 (our emphasis).

common experience – flood, famine, epidemic, feast, fast and festival – and from an investing of territorial areas with religious values. Caste unity and village unity are both real: members of the same caste are distinguished territorially, while members of the same village are distinguished on the basis of caste.'[70] What needs to be discovered is how these groups with extra-community ties are related to each other in the villages. The principle vehicle for this exposition will be the village Sripuram in Tranjore, South India, reported on by André Béteille in his monograph, *Caste, Class and Power*. Béteille recognizes that for three reasons it is very difficult to separate what is internal to the village and what is part of what he calls 'the milieux'. *Social relations* overflow the boundary of the village both easily and extensively – especially links of kinship and affinity. *Economic relations* cut across the boundary, for example, landowners live outside the village, the agricultural surplus has to be sold outside, land comes on to the market. The village is progressively becoming part of the wider Indian economy. And finally, *political relations* extend outside the village as it is both linked to the local government structure and the villagers are members of political parties that are at least state-wide.

As suggested by the title of his book, Béteille is centrally concerned with stratification. Caste is, of course, the basis of the traditional social structure in Sripuram. The population of the village was, and still is, divided into unequal ritual statuses. How far this also dominates the economic and political life of the village was the empirical question that Béteille set out to answer. As the caste system is one of enduring *groups* whose mutual relations are governed by certain broad principles, they can be located with relative ease. They are named and have well-defined boundaries. However, as we shall see, the principles that govern their mutual relations are very complex. The caste system is reflected in the ecology, and although certain areas of village life are relatively 'caste-free' the settlement pattern of Sripuram continues to reflect the basic cleavages of the traditional caste system. Classes, on the other hand, are *categories* of persons occupying a specific position in the system of production, for example, landowners, agricultural labourers and tenant farmers. Caste and class overlap but there are also cross-cutting relationships at a number of points. Power is analysed by Béteille in both formal and informal groups, and he claims that it required an analysis of the social networks of interpersonal relations which cut across those of caste, class and party. Traditionally in Sripuram, and in many other Indian villages, the cleavages of caste, class and power tended to run in the same grooves.

[70] M. N. Srinivas, Y. B. Damle, S. Shahani and A. Béteille, 'Caste: a trend report and bibliography', *Current Sociology*, 8, No. 3, 1959, p. 141.

There are three reasons why there are now more cross-cutting ties. The first is that the formal education system increasingly works on universalistic principles and so allows non-Brahmins and Adi-Dravidas ('untouchables') to be socially mobile and to get, for example, white-collar jobs. Indeed, the partial rejection of this new educational system by the Brahmins in favour of their own more traditional tuition of their children has worked to their disadvantage in that, whilst they may be accomplished in the Sanskrit scriptures, they fail to get the qualifications needed to compete in the modern labour market. The second reason is that, unlike in the past, land has come onto the open market and non-Brahmins have been able to buy it and so the exploitation of land has been freed from the structure of caste. The third reason is that, especially since Independence in 1947, new situations of government have been created in India and so there are new bases of power. One man one vote gives the *numerically* dominant caste a great deal of power, whereas in the old system the *ritually* and socially dominant caste held power in the village community. What has happened in Sripuram is that, in the terms of the American political scientist, Robert Dahl, there has been a change from a system of cumulative inequalities to one of more dispersed inequalities.[71] Whereas in the past wealth, power and prestige were intimately combined in the same set of individuals, they are now dispersed and new social strata have risen to power.

In Béteille's terms, this is a change from a *closed* social system to an *open* one.[72] Caste society is the classic example of a closed system, with caste, class and power combining in the same way. Caste once played an important part in every important sphere of village life and so the social, economic and political life of Sripuram was dominated by the Brahmins. Béteille cogently argues that there will be associated with the transformation from a closed to a relatively open system a differentiation of institutional structures which had earlier been subsumed under a more comprehensive framework. For in the traditional system, class and power were subsumed under caste, but now in Sripuram, and by implication in many other Indian villages, class and power are relatively autonomous and there is a greater range of possibilities for different combinations of caste, class and power. Indeed, Béteille questions whether it is legitimate to talk about class in societies where economic relations have been governed by traditional obligations and inherited status. The differentiation of the class system in Sripuram

---

[71] See for example, R. Dahl, *Who Governs?* New Haven, (and London), Yale U.P. (paperback edition), 1963. This is discussed in some detail in the next chapter.

[72] See Béteille, 'Closed and Open Social Stratification', *European Journal of Sociology*, 7, 1966.

has been brought about by the introduction of the cash nexus and the development of market mechanisms, especially land. There has been a change in the location of power, firstly away from the Brahmins to the more numerous non-Brahmin castes and secondly, away from castes altogether to village councils (*panchayats*) and to political parties, and so power now cuts across caste.

This is an overview of the principle social changes that have occurred in Sripuram, illustrating the confrontation of the local – the traditional social structure of the village, dominated by caste and therefore by the Brahmins – with the national, dominated by class. This confrontation has modified the nature of the community. Sripuram now has a different sort of local social system to that which it had at the turn of the century. These social changes will now be considered in more detail.

In Sripuram, as in Sparkbrook and elsewhere, people who are close to each other in the social system tend to live side by side, and people whose social positions are widely different live apart. Physical distance can fequently be seen as a function of structural difference. In Sripuram the village plan reflects some of the basic unities and cleavages in the social structure. Where the Brahmins live, the *agraharam, is* the village for the Brahmins. The settlement pattern everywhere is relatively resistant to rapid social change and so it provides a good point of entry for studying the traditional social structure.

The Brahmins live close to the river, because this has religious merit, in a tight nucleated settlement. The rest of the inhabitants are more dispersed. Sripuram means different things to different people. If the Brahmins were asked what the population of Sripuram was, they replied 'about 100 families', and when they were told by Béteille that there must be at least 300 families in the village, the Brahmins said that this was so only if the non-Brahmins and Adi-Davidas were included. The non-Brahmins at first included themselves and the Brahmins as inhabitants of the village, not the Adi-Dravidas. In fact, the population of the village was made up as shown in the table:

	Households	Numbers
Brahmins	92	341
Non-Brahmins	168	688
Adi-Dravida	89	371
	349	1400

The Brahmin and Adi-Dravida streets were the most distinctive whilst the non-Brahmin streets were more dispersed and heterogeneous.

The Brahmin area, the *agraharam* is very dense, for they live in close physical proximity to one another. There is an intimate social life. Brahmins wish to be close to each other as they appreciate the feeling of security it gives. This proximity facilitates their participation in the numerous socio-religious activities that dominate the Brahmin way of life. It allows their children to be brought up in 'the right atmosphere'. Béteille is prepared to call the *agraharam* a more or less exclusive community. No non-Brahmin has ever lived in the *agraharam* in Sripuram. In other villages when one has moved in, *all* the Brahmins have moved out. However, the *agraharam* is open to Brahmins from any other part of the country. It should be remembered that the Brahmins themselves are not homogeneous, there are numerous sub-castes and lineages that can be distinguished. However, they all have an overweaning consciousness of their own cleanliness which they contrast with the dirty habits of others. Non-Brahmins are not aware of these divisions, to outsiders they are a caste, not a group of castes. The same applies to the 'untouchables' which, as a group, has fine internal divisions of which outsiders are unaware. In the *agraharam* of Sripuram there were twelve endogenous sub-divisions.

The Adi-Dravida are considered by learned Brahmins to be outside Hindu society. As if to emphasize their social exclusion, they reside on the fringes of the village, in the *cheri*. The *cheri* is rarely visited by Brahmins and some Brahmins are not clear whether the *cheri* is part of Sripuram or not. This lack of awareness on the part of the Brahmins reflects an important social reality: that social perception is limited by the nature and intensity of social interaction. So the 'village', to reiterate, means different things to different people. The *cheris*, like the *agraharam*, though on the opposite end of the scale as they are squalid, are physically homogeneous.

Where the non-Brahmins live is more dispersed. They have more 'structural' space in Sripuram and so have more physical space. Non-Brahmins have no corporate life so there is a comparative lack of spatial compactness. There is, however, a tendency for the individual castes and sub-castes to live in compact blocks.

Is Sripuram, then, a unity? Béteille thinks that there is unity only in a very limited sense of the term. It is a unit in a physical sense but far less in a social sense. The primary cleavages are between Brahmin, non-Brahmins and Adi-Dravida and each of these units, he claims, is a unit in a far more fundamental sense than the village as a whole. However, as he goes on to demonstrate, this does not mean that there is nothing for the sociologist or the anthropologist to study in Sripuram, just that it would be mistaken to start calling the village as a whole a 'community'. Despite these cleavages it is not possible to understand what is happening in the confrontation of the local with the national without taking the village as a whole. One simple example: the *panchayat* hall, where the village council met was located, before Independence, in the *agraharam*. The *panchayat* was dominated by the Brahmins and most non-Brahmins and all Adi-Dravidas were excluded. Since Independence and one man one vote, all *panchayat* presidents have been non-Brahmins and the location of the hall has shifted, and so now the Brahmins find themselves automatically excluded. The physical divisions of Sripuram still represent the traditional caste divisions regardless of changes in the class structure of the village.

Positions in the caste structure are fixed by birth and are to this extent immutable. In the past, birth in a particular caste fixed not only ritual status but also economic and social position. Though when Béteille studied Sripuram, it was possible to achieve a variety of economic and political positions in spite of birth into a particular caste, caste still set the limits to the choices open to a particular individual. Castes are in Béteille's definition, 'a small and named group of persons characterized by endogamy, hereditary membership and a specific style of life which sometimes includes the permit, by tradition, of a particular occupation and it is usually associated with a more or less distinct ritual status in a hierarchical system'. Brahmins believe that they are a different race, ideally they should have light skins and refined features. As Hindus remark 'dark Brahmins and light Pariayas are not proper'. A dark-skinned Brahmin girl is a burden to her family as they will find it difficult to find her a husband. The physical differences between non-Brahmins and Adi-Dravidas are marked but are of less significance because they are not the basis of a political ideology and are not posed in racial terms. Caste is much more relevant in the *local* setting: in large cities like Madras and Calcutta it is not possible to distinguish castes easily, though castes can be visually recognized and distinguished in the villages, especially by other villagers who *know* each other, i.e. can place each other in the local social structure.

Brahmins can be contrasted with both the non-Brahmins and the Adi-Dravidas firstly by their culture: the former are heirs to a literate Sanskrit tradition, the latter are not. Tamil, in Sripuram, is the language for all except the Brahmins. Secondly, their rituals serve to express in dramatic form, not only the unit within a group, but the cleavages between different sections of it. A key here is the pattern of commensality, for castes never eat together, though they do, of course, in restaurants and cafés in large towns and cities. In Sripuram, the entire social world is divided up so as to constitute a segmentary structure in which each segment is differentiated from others, each segment forming a unit within which commensality is more or less freely allowed.

The ideal and traditional division of labour in Sripuram was that the

Brahmins were the landowners, the non-Brahmins were the cultivating tenants and the Avi-Dravidas were the agricultural labourers. Now, not all Brahmins are landowners and not all landowners are Brahmins. However, no Brahmin does manual work. Occupation is an important component in the style of life of the inhabitants of Sripuram and generally the 'lower' the status of a person the more likely it is that he will do manual work. In the village there are beginning to be competing systems of prestige: the system of occupational prestige familiar in most industrialized societies competes with that of status honour in a caste hierarchy, which is legitimated through tradition and established over generations. Within the broad tripartite divisions of Sripuram it is difficult to decide between sub-castes in terms of rank. This ambiguity makes possible social mobility intra-caste, but inter-caste mobility is impossible within a locality. Geographical mobility has made 'passing' getting away with a claim to a higher caste, easier, but this can only happen where an individual is *not known*, i.e. outside the locality in which he was born and brought up.

Inter-caste relationships are played out on the local stage. Castes are autonomous as far as kinship and marriage are concerned, but they are functionally dependent in other spheres, especially in economic relationships. They do, after all, represent (or appear to have done originally) the local division of labour. It should be expected that whilst castes are characterized by mechanical solidarity, the village itself is characterized by organic solidarity. A partial answer to the village/caste question is that they are *both* unities but of a different sort. A complex set of ties binds the Brahmins, non-Brahmins and 'untouchables' of the village in a web of economic interdependence (how, otherwise, do Brahmins live in an agrarian economy when they are ideologically forbidden to touch the plough?), and political interrelations for the village provides a framework within which different castes interact in various political processes.

The relations of production in Sripuram consist essentially of the relationships between categories of persons contributing in different ways to the process of agriculture. Landowners, their tenants and the agricultural labourers, together with their interrelations, constitute the agrarian class structure of the village. The processes of production require the interaction of different categories of people. The relations of production create cleavages as well as bonds between classes and persons and these partly coincide with other cleavages of the social structure – for example, that of caste – and partly cut across them. The fundamental cleavage in an agrarian economy will be between the owners and non-owners of land. In Sripuram there is a separation between the ownership and cultivation of land. In 1961 India passed a law forbidding the ownership of more than thirty acres of land and although there is widespread evasion, this forced some land onto the market in Sripuram.

There are two types of *rentier* landlord in Sripuram – resident and absentee; neither invest their profits in the productive process and together they own 75 per cent of the land. The rest of the land, and the proportion is increasing, is farmed by its owners – smallholders resident in the village who do invest their profits in their land. The majority of the village works on but does not own land. Yet it should be noted that 'farmer', 'tenant' and 'agricultural labourer' are conceptual categories, for the same individual is frequently all three. This multiple class affiliation, as Béteille points out, pulls people in different directions preventing class interests from becoming sharply focussed and classes from being clearly ranged against one another. These categories are very dynamic. An individual described by Béteille was a tenant one year, an owner/cultivator the next, and an agricultural labourer the next. This kind of mobility impedes the development of class consciousness and so conflicts are often posed in terms other than class, i.e. caste. The productive processes, as outlined by Béteille, have brought *into* existence social relations between different classes of people. This gives a kind of 'vertical' (his term) unity to the village, making landowners, tenants and agricultural labourers dependent upon one another. People having a diversity of backgrounds and interests are brought into relationship with each other by virtue of their complementary roles in the system of production, *and* between the people of the village and the outside world. These ties are further extended through the disposal of the agricultural surplus produced from the village.

Power in Sripuram has been distributed like this:

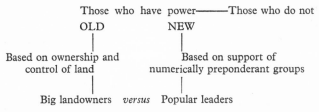

The old bases of birth and ritual status are giving way to the new bases of numerical support, party membership and contact with officials. As has been explained above, the ecological divisions af Sripuram reflect caste divisions. These in turn reflect the ward divisions which therefore reflect political representation. In the hierarchical traditional social structure, social distances were clearly and rigidly defined. There was hardly any scope in this structure for people at the polar extremes to sit together, let alone to discuss together. This was not a basis for

equality, though the past 'consensus' was based on a tacit recognition of
the superiority of some groups and the inferiority of others. Consensus
was imposed on the former by the latter. When, as by the time Béteille
studied Sripuram, the hierarchical values of the caste society were
increasingly questioned, this 'consensus' was tending to evaporate. So
the *panchayat* was increasingly characterized less by 'consensus' and
unanimity than by domination and unequal participation. Political
strength in Sripuram now depends on caste, class, numerical support
and connections with influential people outside the village, to ensure
an important position within it. Béteille concludes that the 'most
important feature of the new political order is the emergence of networks
of interpersonal relations which ramify in every direction. The creation
of new political opportunities and new bases of power has provided
congenial conditions for the development of elaborate networks of
patronage. Such networks serve to link the village with territorial units
of increasingly wider scope, and they also provide interlinkages between
caste, class *panchayat* and political party.' In other words, the new
political order has created a different sort of local system, that is far
more complex and tightly knit than the previous systems based, as it
was, on a rather simple form of organic solidarity.

Whereas castes in India can be seen as having most of the characteristics usually ascribed to communities, classes do so only under
specific historical and social conditions. Béteille does not want to imply
that what he categorizes as classes in Sripuram are in conflict. Their
high degree of common personnel makes this unlikely together with the
existence of other alignments, particularly those associated with caste –
the overlap of class and caste means that a particular conflict is often
as much a conflict between Brahmins and non-Brahmins as between
landlords and tenants. Béteille is prepared to call the Brahmins of the
village a community, but claims that 'it would be inexact to speak of
all Brahmins or even all Shri Vaishnavas (a Brahmin sub-caste) as
constituting a community'. Castes are seen, then, as only constituting
communities at the local or narrow regional level.

In Sripuram the relationships between the classes are changing but
as Béteille has shown, these changes have not kept pace with changes in
the distribution of power. The ownership of land has shifted in only a
small way, from the old *rentier* class to the emerging class of farmers.
Power has shifted decisively from the traditional elite of the village into
the hands of the new popular leaders. The new bases of power are to
some extent independent of class and caste, as numerical support is
most important now, though class and caste ties may be a way of
mobilizing this support, for numerical support must be organized.
Caste has more immediate relevance in mobilizing political support than

the division into landowners, tenants and agricultural labourers – they are like 'communities'. In contrast, classes in Sripuram are not characterized by areas of common residence and a particular style of life, and are therefore less likely to develop common political values and orientations than castes. Since Independence there has been persistent discrimination against Brahmins, which has been an additional factor in their feelings of consciousness and unity. It has, however, been an anti-Brahmin movement rather than class conflict between landowners and the landless that has dominated political life in Sripuram. The forces of democracy have turned the tables on the Brahmins. The Adi-Dravidas, the 'untouchables', also have considerable political unity.

In conclusion, the traditional social structure of Sripuram was simpler. The caste system subsumed the organization of production and the distribution of power. Now class positions are relatively autonomous and power has, in Béteille's words, 'detached itself from the caste-matrix'. This does not mean that there is no relationship between power and caste, just that it is more complex. He has shown in his community study which other factors, in addition to caste, are of importance to the distribution of power. The result of the confrontation of the local with the national in Sripuram has been a change from a relatively static social order to a more dynamic one in which the economic and political systems gradually detach themselves from caste and acquire a relatively autonomous character.

Béteille succeeds in demonstrating that there is something worth studying in even the most stratified communities where there is a complete absence of consensus on local-subjective models of that community by all the inhabitants. However, the investigator will not be able to rely on his informant, if he ever could, to tell him all there is to know and he will have to bring his own concepts to the data. That this, too, is problematical is the theme of the next chapter.

7

Community Studies,
Community Power
and Community Conflict

Introduction

THE community has been the subject of an acrimonious debate that has involved a significant proportion of professional political and social scientists. This debate, about 'community power', so called, has been full of both sound and fury. However, it signifies something.[1] The general lessons to be learned are about the close relationship of ideology, theory and methodology. This is a central theme in community studies for, as has been shown, they are frequently both normative prescription and empirical description. This debate, conducted on an almost medieval theological scale, has shown signs recently of becoming confused and rather silly.[2] Underlying it, though, are real problems that must be faced by the sociologist of the community: about how he should go about his work, what is evidence, what is the significance of findings and so on. The community has been a battlefield and it is necessary first to decide what is being fought about, then who is doing the fighting. Their tactics and the more general strategies will be analysed, and a tentative and unfortunately rather inconclusive result will be declared. The precise location of this battle is in part already familiar through some of the communities that have been discussed in Chapter 4, for example Middletown and Yankee City. Still other communities have been analysed in order to attempt an answer

[1] We are resisting the suggestion that it is a tale told by idiots.
[2] See for example the recent exchanges in *The American Sociologist* between Terry N. Clark *et al.*, and Nelson Polsby on 'Wissenssoziologie', *American Sociologist*, 1968 and 1969.

to the particular questions posed by students of community power. Most of these communities have, in fact, been in the United States, and most of their analysts have been Americans. The debate has been followed with interest from this side of the Atlantic and is beginning to influence the work done in communities both by political scientists and by sociologists in this country. As yet, though, it is difficult to exchange data with the Americans as few communities have been studied with their precise problems in mind. It is interesting to speculate upon why this should have been so, for at first sight it is somewhat surprising.

As has been seen in the previous chapter, many community studies have made significant contributions to sociological knowledge on stratification. It is also virtually unquestioned that stratification is a multi-dimensional phenomenon. Every first-year undergraduate knows of the distinction usually attributed to Max Weber between class, status and power. The conventional wisdom can be summed up briefly like this: class is usually viewed in a more or less marxian manner as relating to the economic sphere, or the means of production. This is, of course, frequently trivialized into just meaning how much money people have, or what their job is. Status, is viewed as the 'social' dimension, as being about what people do with their money, and as being about consumption rather than production, in that familiar phrase 'style of life'. Power, however, is not so simple (nor for that matter are class and status). There is much more disagreement about what it means and how it should be measured. It is not even agreed that this 'third dimension' was intended to be called 'power' by Max Weber: it has been argued that the correct translation should be 'party' and that 'power' should be understood to be involved in all three dimensions of stratification.[3] Whilst British community studies have certainly been concerned with stratification, and at least have provided perceptive descriptions in terms of class and status, power seems somehow to have been largely ignored. Certainly politics in communities has been discussed, but political parties have tended to be treated as though they were like voluntary associations. The socio-economic characteristics of their membership are described along with the formal organization of the party, yet what the parties actually do has received far less attention. Power has not been defined as a significant problem area. The reason

[3] See for example the concluding note to John Goldthorpe and David Lockwood's 'Affluence and the British Class Structure', *Sociological Review*, 1963; W. G. Runciman's *Social Justice and Relative Deprivation*, London, 1965, and his 'Class, Status and Power' in J. A. Jackson (ed.), *Social Stratification*, Cambridge, 1968. Also Geoffrey Ingam's critical note on the last in *Sociology*, 1970.

for this would seem to be as follows: the community can be clearly
divided into social classes and status groups. The limits of the latter are,
by and large, set by the former. The middle class occupy a preponderance of the formal positions in the voluntary associations, religious
bodies and the political parties except the Labour Party (and sometimes even there). Politics reflects the class divisions of the community.
It is one of the central clichés of British social science that class tells us
more about voting behaviour than any other variable. Politics (and by
implicit extension, power) are what the political parties do. Political
parties are the extension of social classes, tempered by local traditions
and when you know about stratification you know most of what there
is to know about politics. When you know about formal politics (meaning
what the political parties do) you know all there is to know about power
in the community.

There are other reasons for the lack of emphasis on power in British
community studies; most communities that have been studied have
been very small and cannot realistically have been seen to contain
within them much power over their own futures in comparison with
'higher' authorities: their Rural District Council, County Council and
even Whitehall and Westminster. It may be that British communities,
especially in comparison with American, are so much 'communities of
limited liability' that local power has not been thought worth studying.
Until recently, virtually no *large* British town has been studied as a
whole at all. Of fifty-four studies in United States analysed by Walton
in 1966, with reference to the work that had been done in them on the
problem of community power, twenty-eight had populations of over
50,000, and seventeen over 100,000.[4] For comparable material on
Britain we must await the current work being done in Birmingham,
Sheffield, Aberdeen, Colchester and elsewhere.

The fact that large towns in which one would expect significant
'amounts' of power to be located (and therefore analysed) have not been
studied until recently in Britain is, however, probably less relevant
than the preconceptions, predilections, and procedures used in studying
British communities. In Britiain, politics is a formal game played, it
would seem, almost entirely by the rules. It is remarkably uncorrupt.
This is not in any way to suggest that politics in the United States *are*
more corrupt, just that they seem so. From popular accounts one can
be forgiven for believing that what goes on publicly is less relevant than
what goes on privately. What about the Mafia? What about 'bossism'?
These are the questions which a British political scientist or sociologist
would ask if he were presented with an account of politics in New

[4] J. Walton, 'Substance and Artifact: The Current Status of Research on
Community Power Structure', *American Journal of Sociology*, 1966.

Jersey or Chicago or Detroit, in terms of the socio-economic characteristics of party members and key activists. Beyond this is the fact
that the formal structure of local government in Britain and America
is so different. As Newton has pointed out, 'it is an interesting co-
incidence that whereas England and Wales have about 1,400 separate
local authorities, New York City alone also has about 1,400.'[5] He
quotes Wood who has written of the American situation: 'Within the
single social and economic complex we have come to call a metropolitan
area, hundreds and hundreds of local governments jostle one another
about. Counties overlie school districts, which overlie municipalities,
which overlie sanitary and water districts, which sometimes overlie
townships and villages. Except for the special purpose "districts" each
suburban government maintains its own police force, its fire stations,
its health department, its library, its welfare service. Each retains
authority to enact ordinances, hold elections, zone land, raise taxes,
grant building licences, borrow money and fix speed limits. . . . By
ordinary standards of effective responsible public services, the mosaic
of suburban principalities creates governmental havoc.'[6] British city
government, at least in its formal aspects, is relatively unified and
consolidated.

Brian Green, in one of the few British studies of community power –
in 'Georgian City' – wants to distinguish between what he calls *prescribed* as opposed to *structural* power.[7] The former is an automatic
attribute of those holding official positions of authority within the *formal*
power structure of a community: elected councillors and mayors, and
senior permanent officials of local government. Structural power refers
to the ability to set conditions, make decisions and take actions in the
context of the community. The empirical question therefore is, to what
extent are those who wield structural power also those who wield
prescribed power? It should not be assumed, but seems to be in British
community studies that discuss politics, that the prescribed influentials
of a community are also those wielding structural power. There might
well be 'hidden powers' behind the elected and appointed officials. This
is the basic problem about community power. The answer to the
question asked by one school of American community power analysts –
'who runs this town?' – has often been held to be self-evident – those
who are elected and fill the top positions. This method of studying

[5] K. Newton, 'City Politics in Britain and the United States', *Political
Studies*, 1969, p. 209.
[6] *Ibid.*, quoting R. C. Wood, *Suburbia: Its People and Their Politics*, Boston
1958, pp. 9–10.
[7] B. S. R. Green, *Community Decision-Making in Georgian City*, unpublished
Ph.D. thesis, Bath University of Technology, 1968.

community power, called by the commentators on the community power debate, the *positional* method, seems to beg important questions and can only really be the starting point for an investigation.

One of the most important lessons to be learned from community studies in general and the community power controversy in particular, is that the methods used and the basic questions asked are closely related to what is discovered substantively. It has been suggested that in the study of community power the methods may even determine the findings. It is therefore necessary to examine closely the methods used and the questions asked. The two principle approaches and what divides them can be summarized like this:

	A	B
Discipline	Sociology	Political Science
Method	Reputational	Decision/Issue Analysis
Power Discovered	Pyramidal	Factional/Coalitional/ Amorphous
Ideology	Elitist/ stratificationist	Pluralist

A, chronologically, was prior to B and B was in many ways a reaction to A, and so A will be discussed first. Prior to 1953 and Floyd Hunter,[8] it is claimed by Bonjean and Olsen that the answer to 'who governs a community' would have been the same by both social scientists and the lay public: those occupying important offices, and elected politicians.[9] They were assumed to be those making the key decisions which directly or indirectly affected the lives of most other community residents. Hunter's achievement was that he was one of the first who seriously challenged the assumed relationship between office holding and decision making at the community level, between prescribed and structural power.

The Elitist Approach

From his book, *Community Power Structure: A Study of Decision Makers*, can be dated the current community debate. As the debate is about ideology, method and findings it will be necessary to consider all

[8] Floyd Hunter, *Community Power Structure*, University of North Carolina Press, 1953, References in this book will be to the Doubleday Anchor 1963 edition.

[9] Charles M. Bonjean and David M. Olsen, 'Community Leadership: Directions of Research', *Admin. Science Quarterly, IX*, 1964. Reprinted in R. L. Warren, *Perspectives on the American Community*, Rand McNally, 1966.

COMMUNITY STUDIES, POWER AND CONFLICT   223

three. The locale for Hunter's study is 'Regional City' and is, in fact, Atlanta, the State capital of Georgia, a city of over half a million people. It is very relevant to point out that Hunter had lived and worked in Atlanta for at least five years before his study: he had been Executive Director of the Community Planning Council for Atlanta. His analysis will, therefore, be tempered by a deep local knowledge of what it was *really* like trying to get things done in Atlanta. This, as will be seen, is an important point as it is frequently suggested that Hunter only asked hypothetical questions about issues and the policy of his leaders (in fact, as a careful reading of his book will show, this, too, is not so). It is of course, also open to readers of Hunter's book to suggest that his local knowledge would have given him a distorted view of the community: having occupied a particular, special position (within the power structure we might also notice) he would have developed a special view of the social system. However, clearly Hunter had been in a position to see a great deal of the action in Atlanta; a good deal perhaps, but clearly not all.

Consider, first, Hunter's preconceptions as stated in his book: he felt that policies on vital matters affecting community life ' . . . are acted upon, but with no precise knowledge on the part of the majority of citizens as to how these policies originated or by whom they are really sponsored. Much is done, but much is left undone. Some of the things done appear to be manipulated to the advantage of relatively few.'[10] He found this situation to be in contrast to 'the concepts of democracy we have been taught to revere'. In wanting to strengthen democracy Hunter was arguing for the strengthening and broadening of 'the line of communication between the leaders and the people' [Hunter uses the word 'power' to 'describe the acts of men going about the business of moving other men to act in relation to themselves or in relation to organic or inorganic things'.[11] He clearly wants to make power both more accountable (i.e. legitimate) and visible. Perhaps the central point of his orientation is revealed when he wrote that his aim was to find out 'who are our *real* leaders' and to discover 'how they operate in relation to each other'.[12] There is a strong suggestion here that 'our real leaders' are not who they seem to be, perhaps not who we elect and that perhaps these real leaders act together as a *group*].

How did Hunter set about his task? What methods and techniques did he use and were they appropriate to the tasks that he set himself? It is at this point that many of the most persistent criticisms of Hunter have been made. For clearly, if his techniques are inappropriate to the

[10] Hunter, *op. cit.*, p. 1.
[11] *Ibid.*, p. 2.
[12] *Ibid.*, p. 1. (our emphasis).

problem he set himself then his findings are just wrong. It has also been argued that the task he set himself was the wrong one anyway, but this point will be dealt with below. In all the voluminous literature now running into literally hundreds of articles and books on community power, one vital point about Hunter's techniques seems to have been overlooked. At the end of his book there is an appendix on 'Methods of Study'. Most of his appendix is about a 'dry run' (his term) of his methods in 'Poplar Village' – a community of about 7,000 in population. There would seem to be serious doubt whether techniques suitable for, and developed in a community of this size are immediately applicable for studying a city with a population of over half a million.

There were two problems to be solved as far as Hunter could see: first, which community leaders should be interviewed (that there are leaders is held to be self-evident) and second, what questions should they be asked 'that would yield data pertinent to power alignments and dynamics within a given community'.[13] He started from positions of formal authority although it was felt that some leaders might not work through formally organized groups ' . . . getting leaders from organizations would be a good start toward turning up leaders who might operate behind the scenes'.[14] Lists had to be secured (this is a central procedure) of prominent people in the civic organizations, business establishments and office holders in politics, and much more contentiously, of 'persons socially prominent and of wealth status' (sic).[15] It should be noted, then, that there is an immediate confusion between power and status. If this is confused in the mind of the investigator, how much more likely that it is confused in the minds of his respondents. Lists of the town's civil, governmental, business and status leaders were secured after being somewhat arbitrarily shortened as they were felt to be too long (200 business leaders in a community of 7,000!) and were given to six judges. These judges were all persons 'who had lived in the community for some years and who had a knowledge of community affairs'. This might be satisfactory in a small community where everybody was 'known' but less so in a large city. The judges were asked to select from each list, in rank order of importance, ten persons of influence. (No reason is given for why ten and not five or twenty) 'who in your opinion are the most influential persons in the field designated – influential from the point of view of ability to lead others'.[16] They were given the opportunity to include others not on the list if they wanted. There was a high degree of agreement among the judges as to who the top leaders were in the four fields. 'The decisions of the judges had given a basic list of forty persons to interview in the community.'[17]

[13] Ibid., p. 256.   [14] Ibid., p. 256.
[15] Ibid., p. 256.   [16] Ibid., p. 258.   [17] Ibid., p. 259.

Incredibly Hunter also identified forty leaders in Atlanta, a city over seventy times larger.

These forty leaders were then interviewed, sociographic data were collected from them, and they were asked who were the five top leaders. Questions were also asked which were designed to get the degree of interaction of each person with others on the list. It should be noted in the light of some frequently voiced criticism that Hunter did ask about their relationship to two recently-made decisions in the community. He also asked the very value loaded question of the leaders, 'In your opinion how do the men on the list operate in relation to community projects: in the forefront of affairs, behind the scenes or in other ways?'

'The methods of getting basic lists of power personnel, and of using judges to cut the list to *manageable interviewing proportions*, were used in Regional City much as in Poplar Village.'[18] In Atlanta he used fourteen judges to give their opinions on who were top leaders, and again there was a high correlation in the choices. The judges, we are told (and this is all that we are told) represented three religions, were male and female, young and mature, business executives and professional people, and Negro and White. In a masterly understatement, Hunter writes: 'It was felt that the number of judges should be larger in Regional City than in Poplar Village because of the size of the community and because elements of bias were highly possible in so large and complex a community.'[19]

The advantages of Hunter's techniques are that they are cheap and quick. However, they have been strongly criticized. Wolfinger, for example, says that they are little more than an elaborate version of the techniques of asking local inside-dopesters for a quick run-down on the local big shots.[20] It is not clear whether the leaders identified by Hunter have influence in certain specific areas or general influence. Given that other studies, for example, those of Digby Baltzell in Philadelphia[21] have shown that the social elite is not the political elite, it is particularly unfortunate that Hunter's techniques do not really allow him to be able to distinguish between the two. How can the knowledge of the 'judges' be guaranteed? As d'Antonio, Erlich and Erickson comment acidly, ' . . . some people distort reality . . . some who should know what is going on don't . . . others accept gossip as gospel and pass it on as the

---

[18] *Ibid.*, p. 261 (our emphasis).

[19] *Ibid.*, p. 262.

[20] Raymond Wolfinger, 'Reputation and Reality in the Study of Community Power', *American Sociological Review*, 1960.

[21] Digby Baltzell, *Philadelphia Gentlemen*, Glencoe, Free Press, 1958 (London, Collier-Macmillan, 1966).

latter'.[22] How can the gossipers be sorted out from the gospellers?
Hunter's techniques have been generally labelled 'reputational' – this
is apt for they do seem to be more informative about who has a reputation for power. Is this the same, though, as who really wields power?
Hunter clearly believed that he was getting at real power. It does seem
to be encumbent on the users of these techniques, however, to demon-
strate the relationship between perceived and actual power structures.
Hunter takes for granted precisely what must be proved, and as
Kaufman and Jones argue, 'by his practice, he predetermined his
findings and conclusions . . . that there is a small group ruling the city
is not demonstrated but presupposed and this presupposition relieved
Hunter of the obligation to develop any objective measure of power'.[23]
Perceived power structure could be a starting point but not a conclusion.
Polsby has stressed that the central methodological issue is one of
appropriateness. Are respondents being asked questions to which they
can give answers capable of unambiguous interpretation and can they
give competent testimony? Are their responses, if correctly interpreted,
capable of answering underlying questions about community decision-
making processes? If the answers to these questions are positive, then
the reputational method is clearly an appropriate tool of community
power research. 'If not, as the weight of evidence and argument seem
to suggest, then the method can be discarded.'[24]

Nevertheless, it is necessary to outline Hunter's principal findings for
it has been against these as much as his techniques that many of his
critics have been reacting. Hunter paraphrases a past American
President when he writes, 'The business of Regional City is business.'
It is perhaps, then, not surprising that he found a predominance of
businessmen among the top leaders of Atlanta. In fact, the forty leaders
were made up of eleven directors of large commercial enterprises, seven
bankers, six professionals (five lawyers and a dentist), four governmental personnel, two labour leaders and five persons 'who have civic
or social organizational leadership capacities and yet do not have business
offices or similar places in which they conduct their day-to-day affairs'.[25]
These forty people 'represent a definite *group* . . . and a very important
one in Regional City'.[26] He conceptualizes a 'power pyramid' but

[22] W. V. D'Antonio, H. J. Ehrlich and E. C. Erickson, 'Further Notes on the
Study of Community Power', *American Sociological Review*, 1962, p. 849.
[23] H. Kaufman and V. Jones, 'The Mystery of Power', *Public Administration
Review*, 1954, p. 205.
[24] Nelson Polsby, 'The Study of Community Power' in the *International
Encyclopaedia of the Social Sciences*, Vol. 3, Macmillan & Free Press, 1968, p. 159.
[25] Hunter, *op. cit.*, p. 13.
[26] *Ibid.*, p. 61 (our emphasis).

'seriously doubts that power forms a *single* pyramid. . . . There are *pyramids* of power in this community which seem more important . . . than *a* pyramid.'[27] This important *caveat* seems sometimes to be forgotten by his critics. He worked out a sociogramme among his leaders to demonstrate that they were a group. He also stressed that these leaders were highly visible[28] (not, it should be noted, covert) and this is even true of the businessmen who take a prominent part in Atlanta's civic affairs. However, 'within the policy-forming groups the economic interests are dominant.'[29] Atlanta was not, though, a single community and Hunter had to carry out a parallel exercise in the Negro 'subcommunity' (his term).

Hunter goes on to emphasize what he calls 'the more private aspects of power'[30] and shows that these men do indeed make decisions in exclusive clubs and over the dinner table. He discusses *actual* projects, but instead of collecting his own data about them asks the leaders about their role and their view of that of others. Interestingly, the redevelopment of Atlanta was the most important project as it was in New Haven, the locale of the principal 'pluralist' study discussed below. However, data from Hunter and Dahl's study are in no way comparable, collected as they were from different academic positions and with different techniques. The general stance, techniques and conclusions of Hunter will be discussed again below, in the light of other studies that share his view of the community power structure.

Delbert Miller has used techniques very similar to those used by Hunter to compare the power structure in Bristol (England) with Seattle.[31] This would seem to provide an interesting test of the techniques, as it has been suggested that the techniques used to study community power determine the findings regardless of differences between *real* power structures. The formal difference between English and American local government has been commented on above. This, together with the difference in the histories of the communities, would *a priori* make it surprising if they had the same kind of power structure. Peter Drucker has commented 'Pacific City (Seattle) . . . has never in its life known any leadership [it is] an overgrown timber camp', whereas Bristol is 'the oldest, next to Venice, maritime oligarchy in the world . . .

[27] *Ibid.*, p. 62. (emphasis in the original).
[28] *Ibid.*, p. 81.
[29] *Ibid.*, p. 82.
[30] *Ibid.*, p. 170.
[31] D.C. Miller, 'Decision-Making Cliques in Community Power Structures: a comparative study of an American and an English City', *American Journal of Sociology* 1958-9; 'Industry and Community Power Structure: a comparative study of an English and an American City', *American Sociological Review*, 1958.

228   COMMUNITY STUDIES

and has an unbroken history of being a merchant city from before Roman times'.[32]

The size of the leadership groups in the two cities was very similar, fifty-nine in Seattle and forty-seven in Bristol. However, he describes the former as a 'stratified pyramid', the latter as 'coalitional'. It was discovered that Seattle had many of the characteristics of Atlanta: policy-makers were drawn from business-men, but religious and educational leaders played a larger role. It was discovered that Bristol had relatively specialized decision-making elites (in the plural). The interests of the business sector were becoming more diverse as outside interests entered the city's economy (characterized by absentee-ownership) and as a new, politically largely neutral, managerial class developed. At the same time new influence groups were entering the political arena in the form of union, educational, managerial, political and governmental leaders. There was in Bristol, he discovered, 'no single solidary elite and no hierarchical dominance based on one institutional sector. The pattern of personal influence is best described as a kaleidoscope of recognizable faces shifting in and out of coalitions as conditions change.'[33] Miller distinguishes *top* influentials: persons from whom particular members are drawn into various systems of power relations according to the issue at stake, and *key* influentials who are the sociometric leaders among the top influentials. However, one reason for the difference in his findings to those of Hunter may well be that he secured *nine* (as opposed to four) lists in nine institutional sectors in the communities studied: business and finance, education, religion, society and wealth, political and governmental organizations, labour, independent professions, cultural institutions and the social services. It is less surprising that, say, religious and educational leaders appear in the community power structure, as he set out to specifically include them and Hunter did not.

The question that Miller posed to 'top influentials' was: 'If you were responsible for a major project which was before the community that required decision by a group of leaders – leaders that nearly everybody would accept – which ten on this list would you choose?' Those most nominated are called 'key influentials'. The point that must be made is that the key influentials seemed to be picked for their unanimous acceptability and not because they initiated and sanctioned policies. There is no evidence in Miller's paper at all, for either Bristol nor Seattle, of the *actual* initiation and sanction of any community policy. There were just twelve key influentials in Seattle which, as Polsby

[32] Quoted in W. V. D'Antonio and H. J. Ehrlich (eds.), *Power and Democracy in America*, Notre Dame, Notre Dame U.P., 1961, p. 107.

[33] Miller, *American Journal of Sociology, op. cit.*, p. 309.

points out, 'seems ridiculous in the hub of American's North West. If these twelve key influentials were truly influential on an appreciable number of issues in Pacific City, then it seems unlikely that they would have had any time or energy left over to run their own businesses. If their influence was in fact restricted to only one or two issues, then Miller should have told us what these issues were.'[34]

Though Miller's techniques are open to criticism, clearly it cannot be said that they completely determined his findings for he found different power structures – coalitional in Bristol, pyramidal in Seattle. There were further differences in Seattle, for the nine-member council was not the crucial centre of power in the community and rarely made decisions until various interested groups had fought out the issue amongst themselves. Decision-making in Bristol took a very different form. As Miller says, 'It seems clear that the council is the major arena of community decision . . . community organizations play important roles in debating the issues, but there are definitely secondary or supplementary activities.'[35] However, both are 'stratification' or 'elite' models of community power.

The Pluralist Approach

As has been seen in the previous chapter many community studies, not explicitly concerned with community power, have described the local patterns of stratification. The 'stratification approach' to community power – the viewing of power in the community as an extension of social stratification – has been subject to a sustained critique by Nelson Polsby in his book *Community Power and Political Theory*. He argues that sociologists have tended to see a stratified society in which the socio-economic elite dominates politics. This is as true in Middletown, Yankee City and Jonesville, in which 'community power' was not the prime concern of the investigator, as in Atlanta and Seattle, where it was. Polsby sets out to argue the pluralist case, from elitist data, which in itself is no mean task. The evidence on which the pluralist case is based will be considered below when Dahl, Wolfinger and Polsby's work on New Haven will be detailed. In 1957 Polsby, then a graduate student, set out to explore the literature on community power as part of the exploratory work to be done before starting to investigate the power structure of New Haven. He discovered that instead of accumulating a neat set of propositions constituting a reliable body of knowledge, he met with several problems. This was not because of the diversity of

[34] Nelson Polsby, *Community Power and Political Theory,* New Haven, Yale U.P., 1963, p. 65.
[35] Miller, *American Sociological Review, op. cit.,* p. 15.

the literature, though it was certainly empirically varied. He found that, at a certain level of generality there was what he calls an 'extraordinary unanimity that scholars displayed in upholding certain propositions about community power'.[36] His fundamental conclusion was that not only were these propositions wrong but also they could not be supported on the evidence produced by these studies themselves. The measure of Polsby's achievement was that he showed that the implicit assumptions made about the nature of community power in these community studies are at the very least doubtful and perhaps just plain wrong, not with additional data but from the stratificationists' or elitists' own data.

He follows Dahl's usage of the term power: as the capacity of one actor to do something affecting another actor, which changes the probable pattern of specified future events. Empirically this can most easily be envisaged in a decision-making situation. 'Where decisions are choices between alternative courses of action leading to outcomes A and B, an actor can be said to possess a certain amount of 'power' if, by acting on others, he changes the comparative probability that the outcomes will take place. The amount of power the actor has in this situation is expressed by the magnitude of the changes he introduces.'[37] It follows from this approach that the analyst of a particular decision – and it is implied that power cannot be analysed without analysing particular decisions – needs three kinds of data: first, who *participates* in decision-making, second who *gains* and who *loses* from alternative possible outcomes and third who *prevails* in decision-making. This last, Polsby argues, is the best way to determine which individuals and groups have 'more' power – it is like an experimental test of capacities to affect outcomes. So Polsby breaks down the question 'who runs this town?' into 'who participates, who gains and loses and who prevails in decision-making'.[38] He makes the innocent sounding remark that findings that pretend to scientific acceptability must be verifiable, i.e. 'they must refer to events in the real world, accessible to more than one competent observer . . . [and] must be put in such a form that in principle it is directly or indirectly subject to disproof by an appeal to evidence'.[39] He would also like the findings on community power to be verifiable by observation. Polsby takes his definition of power (see above) and the stratificationists' axiom that 'American communities may be divided into two groups (classes) which differ with respect to socio-economic status'. This axiom can be made operational or researchable by saying

[36] Polsby (1963), *op. cit.*, p. 3.
[37] *Ibid.*, pp. 3–4.
[38] *Ibid.*, p. 5.
[39] *Ibid.*, p. 5.

that 'the upper socio-economic class has more power than the lower class'. He goes on to say that reference must be made to specific decisions in which particular outcomes were affected by members of the classes into which the population is divided and that the conditions under which it can be demonstrated that the higher class has or does not have more power than the lower class must be *stated* (preferably in advance).

Polsby is arguing that there are common empirical presuppositions among many researchers into community power. He goes as far as to call these presuppositions 'embryonic political theories'. And what sociologists presume to be the case will to a very large extent influence both the design and the outcome of their research. Lloyd Warner wrote in *Jonesville* that 'the political organization fits the rest of the social structure . . . curving or bulging with the class lines of the body politic' of the community.[40] That sums up what Polsby calls the 'stratification theory' of community power, 'since it suggests that the pattern of social stratification in a community is the principal, if not the only, determinant of the pattern of power'.[41] According to Polsby stratification studies make five assertions about power in communities. These are:

1. *The upper class rules in local community life:* whilst definitions of the upper class vary, all stratify communities on some basis other than power, e.g. income, occupation, social participation, consumption (see the previous chapter). The common assumption is that 'the group with the highest social-economic standing has the most power' and that 'a high social-economic position is the base of most community power'. The stratificationists have a neapolitan ice-cream view of society and just below the upper class are the civil leaders and the politicians.

2. *Political and civic leaders are subordinate to the upper class:* they are subordinate in that they have less power and they take their orders from the upper class.

3. *A single 'power elite' rules in the community:* it is a small group, selected by means other than majority vote. It is also an omnicompetent elite, in that its powers are distributed over a large number of significant community decisions. It is a socially homogeneous group being made up of members of the upper class.

4. *The upper class elite rules in its own interests:* this is by no means satisfactory to the other classes which implies the final characteristic of community power asserted in stratification studies.

[40] W. Lloyd Warner, *Democracy in Jonesville*, New York, Harper Row, 1949, p. xviii.
[41] Polsby, *op. cit.*, p. 8.

5. *Social conflict takes place between the upper and lower classes:* so it
would seem that conflicts are along class lines rather than on any other
basis.

Polsby's five assumptions are drawn out of the largely sociological
literature on communities. Each can be cast in the form of a testable
hypothesis. He found that evidence contrary to these hypotheses is
frequently ignored and that anyway the methods of study do not
adequately test these hypotheses. He goes on to consider in detail
eight community studies: Middletown, Yankee City, Elmtown-Jones-
ville, Philadelphia, Regional City, Bigtown, Cibola and Pacific City,
several of which have already been discussed in this book (see above
and Chapter 4). Space permits only the consideration of two of his cri-
tiques, Middletown and Regional City which have been chosen for their
importance in the field of community studies generally.

The Lynds, according to Polsby, accept all five of the generalizations
that he listed. He comments though that 'one of the Lynds' greatest
contributions is the care and responsibility with which they recorded
data that disproves each of the propositions of stratification theory, in
spite of the fact that they themselves adhere to these propositions'.[42]
They recorded the activities of the 'X' family and the 'inner business
control group', the power of which was based on the 'pervasiveness of
the long fingers of capitalist ownership'. It would seem that even in
the 1920s businessmen tended to monopolize community prestige at
the expense of city political officials. The Lynds wrote that 'local business control sat astride both parties', and they commented that 'the
lines of leadership and the related controls are highly concentrated'.
There was the famous statement about the 'X' family, 'If I'm out of
work, etc. . . . ' (quoted in Chapter 4). The Lynds were certainly puzzled
that conflicts between the classes did not take place more often in
Middletown, yet they do detect some indicators of class cleavage.

However, Polsby notes that there was also the 'Y' family who chose
to withdraw from public life. Also there were striking examples of the
importance of Middletown's political organizations in determining
policy outcomes (which contradict propositions one and two above) –
the rejection of the sewage disposal plan against the wishes of the business class, and the prevention of political reform again against the wishes
of the businessmen. They also give evidence of 'special purpose', as
opposed to omnicompetent elites. The ruling elite varies in composition
from issue to issue. This point also contradicts the fourth proposition
in that at various times 'values were distributed in different ways to
groups within classes, to lower rather than higher classes and to groups

[42] *Ibid.*, p. 15.

cutting across class boundaries'.[43] Clearly also conflict was not always *between* classes, as when the Lynds report that workers and management rejected unionization. But as Polsby shows, the Lynds' data never confront their working propositions which are not stated directly anyway. Their evidence and arguments are also odd in that it would seem that the inner business group only prevails on 'important' issues which are likely to be (by definition) those issues on which the inner business control group prevails.

The substantive findings of Floyd Hunter in Regional City – Atlanta – and the methods used to achieve them have been discussed earlier in this chapter. Perhaps the key phrase from *Community Power Structure* is that 'the test for admission to this circle of decision-makers is almost wholly a man's position in the business community in Regional City'.[44] They were the 'initiators', 'the men in the under-structure of power become the doers'.[45] 'The inner workings of many organizations . . . are actually operated in the interests of the political and economic status quo.'[46] It has already been argued that Hunter's basic questions presupposed his answers: that there was a *group* who ruled, that perceived power was actual power. This is leaving on one side the essentially arbitrary nature of his techniques. As Polsby puts it: 'He provides no standard by which the panel's [of judges] work can be judged and no reliable guidelines which the panel can follow in its work.'[47] A great deal of Hunter's interview data tends to discredit the notion that there was a homogeneous, discrete, top leadership group in Regional City. For example, the Negroes had low economic and social status and yet by virtue of their solidarity were very powerful. The nine issues that Hunter discusses demonstrate that different groups were active on different issues and there was certainly more than occasional conflict *within* the elite group.

Polsby concludes that he cannot 'on the evidence, conclude that the upper class ruled, that political and civic leaders were subordinate to them, that there was a power elite, that the interests of a single class were served by community policies, or that social conflicts sharply divided the classes'.[48] Hunter, though, claims that all five propositions were true in Regional City. There are not, as Polsby agrees, enough data to attempt formulating an alternative description of power in Atlanta.

Robert Dahl, together with Raymond Wolfinger and Nelson Polsby,

[43] Polsby, *op. cit.*, pp. 20–1.
[44] Hunter, *op. cit.*, p. 79.
[45] *Ibid.*, p. 100.
[46] *Ibid.*, p. 258.
[47] Polsby, *op. cit.*, p. 52.
[48] *Ibid.*, p. 55.

has studied New Haven with different presuppositions and different techniques and has come up with different findings to those of the stratificationists.[49] Their first question was not 'who runs this town?' but 'does anybody run this town?' Their method can be called 'the issue-outcome method' and their presuppositions and their findings, pluralist, though Polsby somewhat confusingly calls both 'pluralist'. A set of 'key' decisions (it will be seen below that this may well be the achilles heel of the pluralists) covering a number of issue-areas were studied and re-constructed. Those who successfully initiated or opposed key proposals were taken to be most influential in the community. According to Dahl, this method enables the investigator to penetrate behind official positions, reputations, or participation and to use admittedly somewhat crude operational tests, which enable him to weigh and compare the power of different individuals or groups. The method, because it reconstructs decisions, should also suggest how influentials became influential, indicate the sources or bases of their influence, what coalitions or factions they form, and what tactics and strategies they employ to initiate or oppose proposals. In other words, Dahl and his colleagues hope that their methods will not only be informative about who the influentials are, but also – and this is an important point – how they work to exercise their influence. 'Pluralist' methods then claim to reveal not just the structure but also the process of power.

The whole emphasis of their work is different to that of the stratificationists. They wanted to explain certain *events* which took place in the community, events relating particularly to urban redevelopment, public education and political nominations. Their methods were varied: participants in and observers of each 'issue-area' were interviewed and asked to describe the events in which they were involved, their roles and the roles of others. Wolfinger virtually moved into the mayor's office for a year. They interviewed, though, in all, only forty-six persons, 'who had participated actively in one or more of the key decisions'.[50] but mailed questionnaires to over 1,000 sub-leaders. This last had such a high non-response as to be almost unusable.

Dahl and his colleagues, as befits political scientists, have reintroduced the community politician. The stratificationists regarded him merely as an agent of interest groups and especially of the elite. They stress that the gifted political entrepreneur would always be able to make himself felt. As far as 'social structural' explanations are concerned they doubt, in contrast to those discussed by Polsby, that inequalities in resources are cumulative. They doubt, too, that leaders always cohere and form

[49] Robert Dahl, *Who Governs?*, New Haven, Yale U.P., 1961.
[50] *Ibid.*, p.334.

a group; instead leaders are seen as tending to divide, conflict and bargain. They sum up the changes that have occurred in New Haven from
the eighteenth century to the time when they studied it, in the phrase,
'from oligarchy to pluralism'. 'In the political system of the patrician
oligarchy, political resources were marked by a cumulative inequality:
when one individual was much better off than another in one resource –
social standing, legitimacy, control over religious and educational
institutions, knowledge, office. In the political system of today, inequalities in political resources remain, but they tend to be *non-
cumulative*. The political system of New Haven, then, is one of *dispersed
inequalities*.'[51] But who rules in a pluralist democracy? To answer this
question they turn to analyse issues in New Haven. Of the three mentioned above, only one will be dealt with in detail here: urban redevelopment. This was 'by most criteria the biggest thing in New Haven',[52]
but significantly very little happened until it became attached to the
political fortunes of an ambitious politician. As Dahl writes: 'In origins,
conception and execution, it is not too much to say that urban redevelopment has been the direct product of a small handful of leaders.'[53]
There was no great surge of popular demand. Dahl feels that there was
a possibility that those he calls 'Economic Notables' could, if they had
been more unified, influential, skilful and dedicated, have provided the
dominant leadership and co-ordination. However, their support was
only a necessary not a sufficient condition for aggressive action by city
officials.

Mayor Lee of New Haven needed a positive issue with which to
confront the voters after two narrow losses in campaigns in which he
felt he had concentrated too much on the shortcomings of his opponents.
Urban redevelopment in New Haven was not just a social experiment,
but also a political experiment in which Lee sought to discover whether
sufficient political support could be rallied behind such a programme.
When elected Lee, after some difficulty, appointed a head to his Citizens
Action Commission (CAC). This Commission was filled with what
Lee referred to as the 'biggest muscles' – heads of big business firms,
representatives from Yale, banks, labour, Yankee Protestants, Italian
and Irish Catholics, Jews and prominent politicians (from both parties).
The important point is that the influence of this conglomeration of
economic, status, ethnic and civic leaders on the making of urban
redevelopment policies was negligible. Its function was to create and
legitimize an atmosphere of being above politics for the whole programme. The technicalities of urban redevelopment were the responsi-

51 *Ibid.*, p. 85.
52 Polsby, *op. cit.*, p. 70.
53 Dahl, *op. cit.*, p. 115.

bility of the Redevelopment Agency and were co-ordinated by an office, created by Lee: the Development Administrator. The major substantive decisions on urban redevelopment were made by the man who held this office, the executive director of the Redevelopment Agency and Mayor Lee. Most of these decisions were made in secret. These men were not, of course, completely unrestrained, there were Federal and economic restrictions on their actions. There were also political constraints – particularly that Mayor Lee's political popularity, as measured by his electoral majorities, could not be jeopardized. Anyway, there was virtually no opposition to urban redevelopment in New Haven. What was achieved, though, was by virtue of the ingenuity, hard work, skill and expertise of the Mayor and his principal assistants.

The full significance of these findings can only be really appreciated when considered with other issues. An analysis of these issues makes quite clear that participation in the making of most community decisions is concentrated in the hands of a few but that *different* small groups normally make decisions on *different* community problems. There were élites but not an *élite*. Government officials are the most likely of all participants to overlap issue areas. This is in marked contrast to the stratificationists who Polsby in particular was criticizing for assuming and indeed, claiming to show the power repeats itself in different issue-areas. It was possible in New Haven to define, in stratificationists' terms, both an economic and a social elite. And what is more *some* of them *were* found to be active in the issues analysed by Dahl – for example, 15 per cent of the members of the CAC were also members of the economic or status elite – but then very few members of the CAC had any direct individual importance in shaping the redevelopment decisions Taking all three issues it was difficult to show that an elite of high status or great wealth ran New Haven – rather as in the case of members of other New Haven groups, some participated, but most did not. The second presupposition of the stratificationists, that the politicians were subordinate to the upper class, was unsubstantiated in New Haven – instead the CAC could be seen as a 'front' for the Mayor and not vice versa. In each of the three issue-areas studied, entirely different decision-making processes could be identified and so the third assumption also falls. Polsby says strongly that 'in order to say that New Haven was ruled by a single power elite, we must find a small group, not selected by some democratic means, which was united in its policy aims and consistently got its way in more than one significant policy area. We could not find such a group in New Haven.'[54]

But in whose interests were decisions taken? A central weakness of both the stratificationist and pluralist position is that it is almost im-

[54] Polsby, *op. cit.*, p.90.

possible to answer Polsby's question 'who gains?' The benefits and costs to any individual or group of policy outcomes are diffuse and intangible and perhaps impossible to evaluate sensibly without making all sorts of highly questionable assumptions. There was, however, no evidence in New Haven of a united upper class in opposition to others in the community and there were, in Dahl's view no major social conflicts between the upper class and those below. All five of the assumptions drawn out of sociological studies of community power have not only been weighed in the balance of their own evidence but also in that from New Haven, and have been found wanting. As Polsby said, they 'were irrelevant and untrue in New Haven and at least misleading and questionable in other communities',[55] and the general approach 'encourages research designs which generate self-fulfilling prophesies . . . leads to systematic misreporting of facts and the formulation of vague, ambiguous, unrealistic and improbable assertions about community power'.[56]

Why then, should stratification theories persist? There seem to be three possible explanations. There are strong reasons for rejecting the first – that stratificationists are victims of their personal preferences – and for accepting the other two. Stratification theory is a deceptive intellectual framework because it *assumes* of power what can be *demonstrated* of prestige or life chances: that the variable is quantifiable and unequally distributed; that individuals and /or groups are ordered transitively regarding it; that all nuclear family members enjoy equal amounts; and that it is intergenerationally transmittable. Second, that the five key suppositions are *logical* derivatives of the basic presuppositions, axioms and definitions of stratification theory (for example, as noted above: 'the upper class rules because the upper class is at the top of the economic and status hierarchy, and capacity to realize one will [or prevail in decision-making] is indexed by class and status position') but are *empirically* false.

There are large and damaging assertions and so the alternative approach recommended by the critics must be considered in detail. It is claimed that no assumptions are made in the pluralist approach, and that an attempt is made to study specific outcomes in order to determine who actually prevails in community decision-making. But what issues? How shall they be chosen? The pluralists claim that by studying significant issues, for example in New Haven, Dahl, Wolfinger and Polsby claim that by studying nominations by the two political parties (which determined who held office), the urban redevelopment programme (the largest in the US measured by past and present outlays *per capita*),

[55] *Ibid.*, p. 98.
[56] *Ibid.*, p. 112.

public education (the most costly item in the city's budget), they would have discovered a ruling elite if there was one. If it did not show itself on these issues then it was not much of a ruling class. This, as will be argued below, is questionable. Pluralists hold that power is not only tied to issues but that issues are both fleeting and persistent, so it is important to take account of the time dimension. This, in fact, they do and they have made a significant contribution in stressing the time-bound nature of coalitions. Implied in this point is that pluralists focus on actual behaviour, preferably studied at first hand.

What can be said against the pluralists? Criticism can be levelled on ideological grounds first. Take this statement by Polsby: 'In the decision-making of fragmented government – and American national, state and local government are nothing if not fragmented – the claims of small intense minorities are usually attended to.'[57] Go tell 'em that in Harlem or Watts. Naïve pluralism can be very silly. Dahl has made the same kind of remark, though more cautiously: 'Nearly every group has enough potential influence to mitigate harsh justice to its members, though not necessarily enough influence to attain a full measure of justice.'[58] The pluralists have, in fact, been far more open about the ideological preferences than most stratificationists.

Their techniques are pragmatically difficult. It is not altogether conceivable that there will be, say in British cities, the equivalent of Mayor Lee who will let the researcher sit in his office. The pluralist methods are costly and time-consuming but if that is the price that has to be paid for knowledge, so be it. That is even more reason for making sure that it is knowledge. In the article on community power by Polsby, in the *International Encyclopaedia of the Social Sciences* it is interesting to note that whilst he exposes the reputational techniques to fairly ruthless criticism there is no discussion of pluralist techniques in the section headed 'methods of research'. It is as if they are self-evidently correct yet several questions remain, one of the most important of which is: what issues are to be studied? Bonjean and Olsen have suggested that one advance would be to classify issues along five dimensions: unique or recurrent, salient or non-salient to leadership, salient or non-salient to community publics, affecting action possible or impossible, local or cosmopolitan.[59]

Polsby's criteria for identifying 'significant' issues appear straightforward: how many people are affected by outcomes, how many different kinds of community resources are distributed by outcomes, how much, in amount, of resources are distributed by outcomes, who

[57] *Ibid.*, p. 118.
[58] In D'Antonio and Ehrlich (eds), *op. cit.*, p. 89.
[59] Bonjean and Olson, *op. cit.*, p. 288.

drastically present community resource distributions are altered by outcomes.[60] These all seem quite reasonable conditions. Issues must be strategic in that they affect the whole community and not merely a small section of it. These issues would affect the material and ideal interests of a whole range of community organizations, bodies, groups and individuals, who could therefore be expected to participate directly or indirectly in the controversy surrounding an issue, However, in New Haven, the issues which were studied by Dahl were not strategic in this sense, and as Bachrach and Baratz have pointed out, the economic and social notables were uninterested in two of the three key issues.[61]

Bachrach and Baratz, in their justly celebrated paper, 'The Two Faces of Power' have suggested that whilst the elitists ignore both, Dahl and his colleagues only examine one. Whilst accepting the pluralists' critique of the elitists, especially that elaborated by Polsby and discussed above, they make two damaging criticisms of the pluralists' approach. The first was that mentioned above, that the pluralists' 'provide no *objective* criteria for distinguishing between "important" and "unimportant" issues arising in the political arena'.[62] Secondly, they suggest that Dahl is only concerned with one face of power – the largely public one. The pluralists, they claim, take no account of the fact that power may be, and often is, exercised by confining the scope of decision-making to relatively 'safe' issues. Dahl, they say, is only concerned with those who have the power to sucessfully initiate and oppose proposals, but ignores those who have the power to squash proposals before they have even become public issues. By concentrating on issues that have actually arisen, it is not possible to study the second face of power – what they call the 'politics of non-decision-making'.[63] Community power studies must, then, concern themselves not only with those who influence decisions, but also with those who decide what issues are to be raised, and those who effectively prevent some issues from becoming public issues, and those who decide what formal rules are to be laid down which determine how the issue should be fought. 'Some issues are organized into politics while others are organized out.' Quoting from the same author, Schattschneider, Bachrach and Baratz go on to discuss the 'mobilization of bias' and the primary method for sustaining a given mobilization of bias is non-decision-making.[64] The central point against the pluralist

[60] Polsby, *op. cit.*, pp. 95–6.

[61] Peter Bachrach and Morton S. Baratz, *Power and Poverty: Theory and Practice*, London, Oxford U.P., 1970, p. 12.

[62] *Ibid.*, p. 6.

[63] *Ibid.*, p. 9.

[64] *Ibid.*, pp. 43–4, quoting E. E. Schattschneider, *The Semi-Sovereign People*, New York (and London), Holt, Rinehart-Winston, 1960.

position is that it assumes, without demonstrating, that public decisions
are more important than private decisions. Empirically it will, of course,
be very difficult or impossible to find out what issues are suppressed
and by whom.

Harry Scoble, in a perceptive review of Polsby's book, has worked
out the consequences of these empirical and the theoretical deficiencies
of the pluralist position. 'Using the exact same methodology as Polsby
advocates, two cities of identical size, growth rate and so forth are
studied and the researcher finds that these are identically low [there have
not yet been any real suggestions how this should be quantified and so
comparisons will tend to be difficult to achieve, and subjective] overlap
from one scope to another, that only the mayor participates significantly in more than one scope in both cities, and that the pre-
vailers represent similarly different ethnic stocks. But one city's public
decisions (especially those determining tax collections and public
expenditures) are contingent on decisions made collectively in Detroit
which set the level of operations of the dominant local automobile plant,
while the other city is not so dependent. The fact that present methods
would lead to classifying both communities as equally pluralist tells us
more about our methods than it does about the system.'[65]

Scoble's last sentence would be a fitting epitaph for the whole
community power debate. It is unfortunately true that the conflicts in
this debate have drawn attention and interest away from the substantive
topic of community power. There is, for example, after nearly two
decades work and literally hundreds of articles and books, no clear way
of differentiating by means of empirically verified propositions which
state clearly and unambiguously the various conditions under which
different findings hold. Clearly communities on both sides of the
Atlantic do differ in their politics, yet no-one has satisfactorily related
community differences to local decision-making processes. Spinrad
makes the same point when he writes that 'the relation between the
"power variable" and the entire community power structure is barely
sketched'.[66] There have been suggestions that types of leadership
structure could be related to degrees of 'urbanism'. Bonjean and Olsen,
for example, argue that the greater the influx of population and the
greater the community poverty, the less visible was the leadership
structure.[67] However, more contributions have been made from this
debate to the *study* of community power and to problems of research
procedures and methodology than to our substantive knowledge.

[65] Harry Scoble, *Admin. Science Quarterly*, IX, 1964, p. 315.
[66] William Spinrad, 'Power in Local Communities', *Social Problems*, 12,
p. 335.
[67] Bonjean and Olsen, *op. cit.*

There can be noted that, as in community studies in general, there is a marked tendency for individual investigators of individual community power structures to generalize their findings to *all* communities willy-nilly. So convinced are the proponents of their own righteousness and of the ideological and methodological iniquities of their opponents, that hardly ever does it seem to be contemplated that perhaps communities differ. Walton has, though, demonstrated that it is more than a co-incidence that certain methods lead to certain findings. He shows that in thirty-three studies 'the disciplinary background of the investigation tends to determine the image of the power structure that results from the investigation'.[68] There clearly are, as has been seen, difficulties and problems with both main methods of studying community power, so what can be made of the substantive findings? One possibility that must be contemplated by bewildered students is to say a plague on both your houses and reject them both. However, if there are difficulties in accepting the findings of both schools as equally valid and clearly there must be, there does remain a chance of helping future researchers. From the studies that have been carried out it is not possible to make a single descriptive statement, nor even a very general one, that applies to community leadership in general in the United States (unless that statement includes something about variability). The solution that has been suggested by Bonjean and Olsen in a useful article published in 1965 is that it is possible to construct ideal types of community power structure against which findings can be measured.[69]

They suggest that if Hunter's findings are exaggerated, an ideal type that could be taken as one polar extreme and used as a hypothetical yardstick and rough measure that would enable comparison would be the one they call the 'covert power elite' and its characteristics are:

1. Leaders do not hold public offices, or offices in associations.
2. Leaders are not recognized by the community at large as key decision-makers.
3. Leaders are active in a wide range of decision areas.
4. Leaders work together as a group, rather than independently or in opposition.

The opposite polar extreme they call 'legitimate pluralism' and as in many ideal types it has the opposite characteristics:

1. Leaders do hold public offices or offices in associations.

[68] John Walton, 'Discipline, Method and Community Power: A Note on the Sociology of Knowledge', *American Sociological Review*, 31, 1966, p. 684.
[69] Bonjean and Olsen, *op. cit.*

2. Leaders are recognized by the community at large as key decision-makers.

3. Leaders are concerned only with those decisions related to official areas.

4. Group structure not present.

Bonjean and Olsen go on to argue that these four characteristics which they call *legitimacy, visibility, scope of influence* and *cohesiveness*, are the most important in identifying the two ideal type leadership structures and therefore any structure falling between the two.

Once leaders have been identified (this, as has been seen above, is no simple task) by a comparable technique in several communities, the proportion who hold or have held public or associational offices could be calculated. This, Bonjean and Olsen argue, would be one measure of the leadership structure or otherwise of what Green calls structural and prescribed leadership. The use of the percentage partially gets over the problem that in different communities vastly different numbers of leaders have been identified (from five in Springdale to 415 in New Haven). Bonjean and Olsen recognize that what they call legitimacy tells us nothing about visibility unless all leaders *are* public or associational officers. If all community leaders held political or associational offices the leadership structure may be clearly visible. The reverse is not necessarily so. Leaders who do not hold positions of authority may or may not be covert. To measure visibility they fall back on the reputational approach. 'Visibility may be roughly measured if the nominations and rankings of a panel of judges (or better, the leaders themselves) are compared with the nominations and rankings of the general public or some other segment of the community.'[70] They feel that this technique may well reveal three types of leaders: *visible* (those recognized by both the judges and the general public), *concealed* (those recognized by the judges and not the general public) and *symbolic* (those recognized by the general public but not by the judges).

The third dimension in their ideal type, scope of influence, is more problematic for they recognize that in one community there may well be leaders who both participate in a wide range of issues as well as sets of leaders active in different areas. Each leader would be given a percentage score based on the number of decision areas in which he participated (note this assumes that a list of decisions can be produced and does not face the problem identified by Bachrach and Baratz discussed above). Again, decisions vary in number between communities. Given legitimate or non-legitimate, visible or concealed and general

[70] *Ibid.*, p. 293.

or issue leaders, they may or may not interact as members of a group – or perhaps several groups. Bonjean and Olsen claim that one measure of cohesiveness, the fourth dimension of their ideal type, would be the degree to which leaders nominate one another. Sociometric tests could also be applied to these groups.

Bonjean and Olsen sum up their case by saying that 'legitimacy, visibility, scope of influence and cohesiveness appear to be the most significant dimensions of community leadership structures in that (i) they have been the major sources of disagreement and criticism, (ii) a review of leadership studies indicates that variation may, in fact, be found along all four dimensions, and (iii) they are useful in the identification of different types or models of leadership structures.'[71] The significant point is that for two principle reasons no one has attempted to apply Bonjean and Olsen's comparative measures. First, despite there being two well-defined schools, they do not in fact collect comparable data even within schools and that data collected by the 'other' school is considered invalid. The second is that to do one community study is arduous enough, to do several probably prohibitive and therefore it is unlikely that another study could be done by a single investigation to, in fact, 'measure' the communities studied at least against each other. There seems no alternative to community power analysis but to collect comparable data with agreed techniques. It is difficult otherwise to see how this field can advance.[72]

Conflict

Despite this lack of comparability, James Coleman has made a notable attempt to pull together what was known about *Community Conflict*.[73] He shows that some generalizations can be made from diverse case studies and his discussion of the courses of community controversies, particularly his findings on their *similarity*, despite their cause, content or locale, is obviously of central relevance to the discussion of community power. 'Decision-making' plays an important part in the pluralists' approach to community power and Coleman's perceptive analysis, though not within the conventional community power framework, adds a new dimension to the debate. It would seem that community conflicts and issues have common dynamics not directly related to community leaders or to the community power structure.

[71] *Ibid.*, p. 295.
[72] There are in fact several groups working towards this end, notably that of Terry N. Clark in the States and the British Sociological Association in Britain.
[73] James Coleman, *Community Conflict*, Glencoe, Ill., Free Press (London, Collier-MacMillan, 1957).

Coleman begins by making the point that, though taking the literature as a whole there are a large number of conflicts that have been discussed, in any one community there will be very few. Communities, by their very nature, find it difficult to learn from each other. His conclusion is that, though there are few conflicts in a community, the 'outcome' (what this means will be discussed below) of one dispute 'loads the dice' in favour of a similar outcome the next time. A characteristic of communities as social systems, he claims, is that established patterns for resolving community conflicts continue. His aim was to diffuse knowledge about conflict resolution in communities because 'in our changing society' (in contrast to 'stable traditional societies') 'communities continually face problems unique in their own history and for which no precedents exist in the experience of community leaders'.[74] It is not until each individual problem with its unique elements are 'brought together, examined, compared and their common elements abstracted' that the full value of these case studies can be realized. He made his values quite explicit when he wrote in his introduction that 'for those concerned with the success of democratic processes of civil rights and civil liberties, or majority control of a community, it is important that community problems are met in one way rather than another'.[75] Coleman feels that if the administrators (of a community) 'had some realistic record and assessment of the experience of other communities rather than the pretty picture they received in school about what community life should be like' they might be more successful and their communities continue and prosper. 'It is to such an end that [his] monograph is directed.'[76]

Coleman succeeds in laying bare, necessarily with some considerable degree of abstraction, the processes underlying community controversy. In fact, he builds a model of community controversy. It will be seen when it is elaborated below that it is of such generality that it might be thought to be of little value in helping the hard-pressed community leaders who, being as involved as they are, will be unlikely to see the wood for the trees. The methodological interest for the sociologist of the community is that Coleman manages to provide some insights into the processes that move a controversy from start to finish and analyse the factors that modify this process. And he can do this from uneven and scattered accounts of diverse incidents in various communities. He comments that community disagreements, far from being an indicator of the decline of community, may well be a measure of the strength of community life. This point is echoed in William Gamson's paper on 'Rancorous Conflict in Community Politics' when, after analysing

[74] *Ibid.*, p. 1. [75] *Ibid.*, p. 1.
[76] *Ibid.*, p. 2.

eighteen New England communities, he notes in conclusion that 'Many of the conventional communities are rather dull and stagnant, while some of the most rancorous ones are among the most vital. Some of the conventional towns not only have an absence of rancorous conflict but a general absence of change; the rancorous towns have the strains that accompany change but some of them also have the advantage of stimulation and growth. The absence of rancorous conflict is no necessary sign of an "ideal" community.'[77]

Coleman found that there was a relationship between the degree of involvement of the members of a community and the frequency of controversy. This parallelled his findings in the International Typographic Union reported in that major modern sociological classic, *Union Democracy*.[78] If participation is high, and by common agreement high participation is good for democracy, then rates of controversy will be high. There is though, an interest ('for those concerned with the success of democratic processes . . . ') in keeping these controversies within bounds. An examination of the case studies brings Coleman to the conclusion that the *type of event* will determine whether a crisis will unite, defeat or cause controversy. The second factor that shapes the nature of the crisis is the kind of community in which it happens. Unfortunately Coleman does not elaborate this point nor provide a classification of communities.

Three criteria become evident from the data he assembles, in the development of controversy out of an event. Firstly, it 'must touch important aspects of the community members' lives' – though in a footnote which, to be charitable, may be a masterpiece of understatement he says 'the event, of course, need not be important to all persons in the community; some controversies are carried on only by a minority of the community'.[79] Secondly, they must affect different people differently and finally, the event must be one on which the community members feel action can be taken – not one which leaves the community helpless. He then enumerates thirteen examples in some detail. It should be noted that Coleman concentrates, as is inevitable as he only has secondary sources, not all of them sociological, on the 'manifest' aspects of community conflicts. He takes conflicts to be about what they seem to be about; however, conflicts that manifest themselves, say about fluoridation in a community, may reflect more latent conflicts about basic values and orientations in the community.

[77] William Gamson, Rancorous Conflict in Community Politics', *American Sociological Review*, 31, 1966.
[78] S. M. Lipset, M. Trow and James Coleman, *Union Democracy*, Glencoe, Free Press, 1956 (London, Collier-Macmillan, 1956).
[79] Coleman, *op. cit.*, p. 4.

He sums up his evidence by saying that the 'numerous case studies make evident that it is neither the kind of problem facing a community nor the communities characteristics which alone determines the pattern of conflict, but rather a conjunction of the two'.[80] He wishes to distinguish between disputes that arise *internally* and those which are a consequence of some *external* incident and feels perhaps as a consequence of the processes of urbanization, industrialization and bureaucratization described by Stein – Warren's 'great change,' that 'like it or not, the community is less often the locus of important social decisions than it once was'.[81] Empirically it is, of course, as Coleman realizes, always difficult to distingusih clearly between externally and internally caused events. The source of the event is, then, the first cause of difference among the incidents which set off community disputes and the second is the 'area of life' they effect.

Coleman 'roughly distinguishes' three 'areas of life': firstly, *economic*, secondly, *power or authority* (but he makes explicit that very few in a community are involved in this) 'only those who have something at stake feel their pulses quicken as events lead to a dispute'[82] and thirdly, *cultural values or beliefs*. There is a fourth *basis for response* to an incident and this derives from attitudes to particular *persons* or *groups* in the community: 'If he's for it I'm against it.' His argument so far is summed up in the diagram. He sums it up like this: 'an incident, event or problem requiring solution faces a community and meets differing responses among the members as it touches upon areas of life which act as a *basis of response* to the event. The basis of response, primarily economic interests, power and values, provide the initial dynamics for the controversy. They drive a nucleus of adherents to carry forward the dispute, to expand and intensify it until perhaps the whole community is involved.'[83] Coleman apparently does not question these pluralist assumptions. Hunter probably would have argued that the 'nucleus of adherents' would settle among themselves.

However, Coleman continues by examining the 'conditions of controversy' and after having reviewed the data on differences in economic structure of communities in conflict, concludes that 'towns with different economic structures differ widely in the kinds of economic controversy they generate . . . and it can hardly be said that one kind of controversy is specific to a particular kind of community'.[84] He also recognizes that the basis for response changes over time, the 'old-time' religion is less important, and so on. It is not possible in the light of the data to say much about the precise initiation of the controversy.

[80] *Ibid.*, p. 4.   [81] *Ibid.*, p. 5; see pp. 38-40 and 50-51 above.
[82] *Ibid.*, p. 5.   [83] *Ibid.*, p. 6.
[84] *Ibid.*, p. 7.

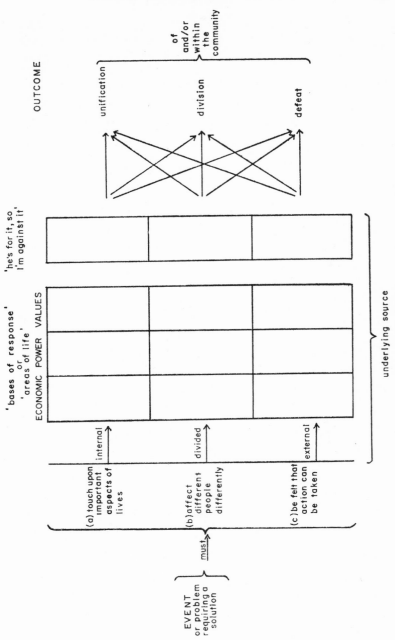

The Argument of James Coleman's *Community Conflict*

Coleman's most significant contribution was his discovery that the important thing 'about the development and growth of community controversies is the similarity they exhibit despite diverse underlying sources and different kinds of precipitating events. Once the controversy has begun, they resemble each other remarkably.'[85] The issues which had provided the initial basis of response in a controversy undergo great transformations as the controversy develops: a) from the specific to the general. This is especially the case where there are deep cleavages of values and interests which just require a spark to set them off. b) New and different issues arise. Once the community's stability is upset, suppressed topics can come to the surface. c) There is frequently a shift from mere disagreement to pure antagonism, to the personalizing of issues.

The process and progress of the controversy leads to changes in the social organization of the community. There will be a polarization of social relations: 'associations flourish *within* each group but *wither between* persons on opposing sides'.[86] In his oft-quoted phrase there will be a 'stripping for action' a getting rid of social encumbrances which impede the action necessary to win the conflict. There will also be the formation of partisan organizations and the emergence of new, often extremist partisan leaders to 'wage war more efficiently'. Bernadette Devlin and the Reverend Ian Paisley in Northern Ireland are two such examples. This will be associated with the mobilization of existing community organizations on one side or the other. And in the end, as the pace hots up and the issue becomes personal and personalized, word of mouth communications replace the more formal media. Northern Ireland, at the time of writing, again provides an all too relevant example.[87]

Coleman stresses that the pattern of community disputes are often the same, but there seems to be four variations in the social organization of the community which are most crucial for the course of the controversy. There are variations in *identification* with the community: where there is high identification the controversy is inhibited from deteriorating into an unrestrained fight, for those who do not identify with the community are 'quickest to overstep the bounds of legitimate methods and carry the dispute into disruptive channels'.[88] Secondly there are variations in the *density* of communities, especially in their organizations and associations. In a highly organized town the pressures

[85] *Ibid.*, p. 9.
[86] *Ibid.*, p. 11.
[87] See for example, F. W. Boal, 'Territoriality on the Shankill-Falls Divide, Belfast', *Irish Geography*, 1969.
[88] Coleman, *op. cit.*, p. 21.

to take sides are very great. Thirdly, there are variations in the *distribution* of participation among the inhabitants of the community. In a highly stratified community a large proportion of the population is likely to remain effectively out of the conflict. And finally there are variations in the *interlocking* of organizational memberships which may or may not create cross-pressures that strengthen or weaken controversy. Coleman also compares communities by their formal authority structure, economic structure and the role played in them by the mass-media.

His singular contribution has been the discovery that 'over and over again, as one case study after another was examined, the same patterns appeared; the same kinds of feelings were generated between the participants; the same kinds of partisan activity occurred'.[89] Coleman's answer to the question, why should this be? is that 'apparently the autonomous nature of conflicts creates them. Once set off, controversies develop quite independently of the incident. Early stages generate later ones; conflicts which began quite differently end up alike; the community divided into opposing factions, angry and adamant, arguing about old quarrels which have nothing to do with the original issue.'[90]

Coleman's analysis is original and extremely perceptive and adds a new dimension to the understanding of community, particularly when treated as an independent variable. He finds that the community has little predictive or causal power regarding the nature of conflicts. In particular three points should be noted. Coleman nowhere defines community but appears to take it as being synonymous with 'political unit'. This being so, it is surprising that there is so little emphasis in his analysis on the formal as opposed to the informal political structure. Thirdly, his analysis under-emphasizes both stratification in general as a base for political mobilization in the community and class and ethnic differences in particular. However, because systematic inter-community comparisons are so rare, they must be welcomed. Cross community analysis would seem to hold the greatest promise for the future and is certainly more profitable than the all too common assertion that 'all America is in Jonesville' or that 'Banbury is a microcosm of Britain'.

[89] *Ibid.*, p. 25.
[90] *Ibid.*, p. 25.

8

Conclusions

THERE have accumulated since the Lynds' study of Middletown literally hundreds of studies of small towns. They are, at one and the same time, some of the most appealing and infuriating products of modern sociology. They are appealing because they present in an easily accessible and readable way descriptions and analyses of the very stuff of sociology, the social organization of human beings; and infuriating because they are so idiosyncratic and diverse as to steadfastly resist most generalizations. As has been seen, while community studies provide an almost inexhaustible quarry for collectors of social facts to buttress their theories, nevertheless they do not readily facilitate the construction of what might be called a 'theory of community'. It has also been seen that the pursuit of the latter has been thought by some to be mistaken, as it is argued that the community is not an object of study in its own right; it is not a thing, let alone a social thing, the proper study of sociologists. Rather, community study has been seen as a method of sociological investigation.

This is why this book differs from the others in this series, none of which have the appendage 'studies' to their title. We should not know quite what to expect from a book called 'Family Studies' or 'Industrial Studies'. Most introductory texts are either about a social institution which is agreed to be a legitimate object of study for the sociologist, like the family, or about an area of study of which it is well established that there should and can be a 'sociology' like industry and education. Whether or not there is something 'out there' that can be called 'community' is a matter, as has been seen, of some dispute, whereas no sociologist disputes the existence of the family.

The title of this book, *Community Studies*, catches the tensions and strains of the field, particularly the conflict which has been one of its central themes. The conflict is between community studies as studies of communities seen as objects and community study as a method, as a way of getting at social facts. This book has, then, been more concerned than the others in this series with what might be called the sociology of sociology – how it was that certain sociologists went about their work in the way they did. It has also been more concerned than is usual in introductory texts with methodology and the collection of data. The book has been an attempt to break-down the conventional barriers of undergraduate teaching that distinguish between both something called 'theory', something called 'method' and something else called 'social structure' or 'social institutions'. This book has been an introduction to an area of sociology and it explores some of the kinds of things sociology is about and what some sociologists do. We would argue that theory, method and substance should be more closely related in sociology, especially in its teaching.

Despite the fact that 'community' has been one of sociology's core ideas, it is by no means certain what will be found in a book which includes the word in its title. Nicholas Haine's *Community and Privacy* or Robert Nisbet's *The Quest for Community* are very different in style and content to books like Ronald Frankenberg's *Communities in Britain* or Roland Warren's *The Community in America*. Both are different again from the essays in Vidich, Bensman and Stein's *Reflections on Community Studies*. The first tends to be 'utopian' and to make statements about the good life. There is, of course, nothing wrong with this. At best this aspect of community spills over into political and moral philosophy, but at worst into naïve value judgements pervaded by a curious posture of nostalgia. This approach was earlier labelled as the study of community as normative prescription. The second approach can be called that of community study as empirical description. The distinction between these two should not be thought of as that between theory and substance, for to quite marked degrees the first has not informed the second and when it has, the results have often been disastrous. Slipping from empirical description into normative prescription has been all too frequent and is well illustrated in Maurice Stein's *The Eclipse of Community*.

This second approach has not always, as has been shown, necessarily been towards atheoretical or just 'abstracted empiricism', to use the pejorative term. Community studies as empirical description are frequently informed by theoretical notions drawn from the mainstream of sociology, from the Marxian and Durkheimian inheritance of conflict and cohesion through anthropological and Mertonian and Parsonian functionalism to Goffmanesque interactionism. Indeed, even Cicourel and Garfinkel's southern Californian ethnomethodology is beginning to make its impact. This second approach is, however, distinguished by its firm empirical reference, usually in small towns and villages, by having scientific aims and by tending to treat communities as objects of study in their own right.

The essays in *Reflections on Community Studies* seem to be more united by a stance and a style of research, by their methods than their objects of study. However, the distinction between this third approach, as method, and the second, outlined above, at first sight seems unhelpful. Of course, it will be said, if there is empirical description there must be a method. The distinction, though, is between those studies which treat communities as objects, that is to say, those that tend to go in for classifying communities, as different sorts of communities (and then often slip over into the first approach and hint at what is a good or bad community), and those empirical studies of a sociological problem in a locality, that, to put it rather crudely use the community as a laboratory to get at social facts in the raw and are primarily interested in saying something about this problem rather than about the locality. It may be discovered that there are local variations that effect these problems and certainly it will always be perilous to ignore the particular local configuration of social institutions that has resulted from the unique history of the community. These are, however, not the prime consideration of studies which have used the community study as a method.

The task that faces the sociologist of the community is to generalize, whilst avoiding normative prescription, from the basis of empirical descriptions based on a myriad of theoretical positions which vary enormously in their explicitness. The studies themselves are too often incomplete descriptions of the locality because the 'problem' or the 'theory' dictated that only certain areas were investigated. This is an enormously difficult and challenging task. This book has concentrated on community studies in the second and third usage of the term. There has not been a detailed discussion of community as normative prescription or as ideology. Most of the discussion of theory has been in relation to those theories used in empirical description, e.g. of ecology, communities as organizations and the structural-functional approach of British social anthropology.

One final word on the avoidance of normative prescription in community studies. The authors of this book are as keen as any on the good life. We also have some pretty clear ideas as to what it consists of. But we felt it would be unreasonable, not to say dangerous, if we were to foist our normative prescriptions on unsuspecting readers, especially if they were masquerading as sociology.

FURTHER READING

We are not going to provide a separate bibliography, as that can be gleaned from our footnotes. There are, however, several sources that, separately or together would provide a reasonable starting place for the student of community .

1. Robert J. Havighurst and Anton J. Jansen: 'Community Research: A Trend Report and Bibliography', *Current Sociology*, Vol. V,X No. 2, 1967. Besides an introductory article there is an annotated bibliography of 410 titles.

There are three excellent readers:

2. Roland L. Warren, *Perspectives in the American Community*, Chicago Rand McNally, 1966 (London, Rand McNally, 1967).

3. David W. Minar and Scott Greer, *The Concept of Community: Readings with Interpretations*, Chicago, Aldine, 1969

4. Robert Mills French, *The Community: A Comparative Perspective*, Itasca, Ill., Peacock, 1969.

There are also four interpretative texts that should be treated with more care:

5. Maurice Stein, *The Eclipse of Community*, New York, Harper Torch book, 1964. (originally published 1960).

6. Roland L. Warren, *The Community in America*, Chicago, Rand McNally, 1963.

7. Josephine Klein, *Samples from English Cultures*, London, Routledge and Kegan Paul, 1965.

8. Ronald Frankenberg, *Communities in Britain*, Harmondsworth, Penguin Books, 1966.

Klein and Frankenberg both have excellent bibliographies.

There is also the descriptive sociology of sociology and quasi-auto-biography and self-analysis of the essays in:

9. A. J. Vidich, J. Bensman and M. Stein (eds), *Reflections on Community Studies*, New York (and London), Wiley, 1964.

We have prepared a reader to accompany this text:

10. Colin Bell and Howard Newby, *The Sociology of the Local Community: a book of readings*, London, Frank Cass, 1972.

None of these ten works, nor this eleventh, are a substitute for the original community studies which should be read in conjunction with both this book and those listed above.

SUBJECT INDEX

Aberdeen, 220
Aberystwyth, 137
Adi-Dravidas, 210–17
Alcala de la Sierra, 171–5
Amoral familism, 150–61
Andalusia, 171–5
Anderen, 147–50
Anomie, 23, 44
Anthropological techniques, 54–81
    passim, 252, 253
  in Middletown, 85–87
  in Chicago, 93–94
  in Yankee City, 101–5, 196–7
  in Southern Ireland, 131–2
  in Gosforth, 142–6
  in Ashton, 167
  in Alcala de la Sierra, 171–5
  in Banbury, 181
  see also field worker
Ashton, 166–71, 175, 179, 180
Ashworthy, 64, 162–4, 166
Atlanta, 223–9, 232–3

Banbury, 15, 58, 67, 76, 171, 175, 177,
    178–85, 186–7, 188, 196, 201,
    202, 203, 249
Bethnal Green, 19, 184
Bigtown, *see* Toronto
Birmingham, 34, 94, 204–6, 220
Boston (Mass.), 59, 64, 94, 199
Brahmins, 201–17
Bristol, 227–9
Bureaucratization, 24–25, 38–40, 51–
    52, 110, 165, 175–85 *passim*, 246

Cairo, 62
Calcutta, 62, 213
Caste, 112–16, 188–9, 195, 208–17
Change, social, 21–25, 38–40, 42–48,
    50–53, 64, 75–79, 171
  in Middletown, 87–91
  in Yankee City, 109–10
  in Springdale, 116–21
  in Llanfihangel, 137, 139–40
  in Gosforth, 145–6
  in Anderen, 150
  in Southern Italy, 159–61
  in Ashworthy, 162–4
  in Westrigg, 164–6

in Glossop, 175–8
in Banbury, 178–84
in Swansea, 184–5
see also bureaucratization, indus-
    trialization, urbanization
Cheviots, 164
Chicago, 14, 34, 39, 91–101, 113, 191,
    221
Chicago school, 14, 39, 55, 91–101,
    112, 197, 204
Cibola, 232
City, *see* urbanism
Class, 186–217
  defined, 188, 219
  in Middletown, 84
  in Yankee City, 14, 104–11, 112,
    189–204
  in Deep South, 111–16
  in Springdale, 118–19
  in Crestwood Heights, 122–4
  in Levittown, 128
  in Llanfihangel, 138–9
  in Gosforth, 142–5
  in Anderen, 149
  in Southern Italy, 150–61
  in Ashworthy, 162
  in Westrigg, 165–6
  in Ashton, 168–9
  in Alcala de la Sierra, 173
  in Glossop, 175–8
  in Banbury, 175–185
  in Jonesville, 189–204
  in New Haven, 231ff
Coal mining, 166–71
Colchester, 220
Collina, 157–61
Communism, 153
Community
  and community studies, 13, 48–53,
    250–2
  and locality, 18–19, 24–32, 44, 48–
    53, 60–62, 201–3
  see also local social systems
  and network, 48–53, 138, 142–5,
    170–1, 197, 207
  and propinquity, 18–19, 34, 125ff
  and theories of community, 21–53,
    250
  and the theoretical inheritance, 21–
    27

255

AUTHOR INDEX